THE
MARILYN HARRIS
COOKING SCHOOL COOKBOOK

THE
MARILYN HARRIS
COOKING SCHOOL COOKBOOK

By Marilyn Harris

Foreword by
Shirley O. Corriher

PELICAN PUBLISHING COMPANY
Gretna 2001

*The word "Pelican" and the depiction of a pelican are trademarks
of Pelican Publishing Company, Inc., and are registered in the
U.S. Patent and Trademark Office.*

Library of Congress Cataloging-in-Publication Data

Harris, Marilyn (Marilyn Marion)
    The Marilyn Harris cooking school cookbook / by Marilyn
Harris ; foreword by Shirley O. Corriher.
        p. cm.
    ISBN 1-56554-076-X (alk. paper)
    1. Cookery, International. I. Title.

TX725.A1 H286 2001
641.59—dc21

00-067129

Printed in the United States of America
Published by Pelican Publishing Company, Inc.
1000 Burmaster Street, Gretna, Louisiana 70053

Contents

Foreword 7

Welcome to My Cooking School 9

Acknowledgments 11

Matching Food with Wine: A General
  Reference Guide. 13

Appetizers for Easy Entertaining 17

Stocks, Soups, and Stews 41

Salads and Their Dressings 69

Pasta and Risotto 99

Elegant but Easy Seafood. 127

Cooking Chicken and Turkey 145

Mainly Meats. 167

Great Grilling 181

Versatile Vegetables 211

Sweets 233

Index 254

Foreword

If you want to make dishes that taste wonderful—not just delicious, but absolutely wonderful—here is *The Marilyn Harris Cooking School Cookbook.* Marilyn's bottom line is taste, and she tells you the little things—the touches that take food from good to memorable. For example, the orange zest in the beef stew creates a dish that makes your mouth water when you think about it. Or just the right amount of salt (the same amount as in sea water) in the water to cook shrimp means you will never eat shrimp as good as Marilyn's.

I have been fortunate enough to have had many opportunities to eat and prepare Marilyn's food and to see her "in action." She is one of the most knowledgeable people in food today, and a top-school executive manager. I have watched her put on events for hundreds of the country's top medical doctors and nutritionists, a few college presidents, and even a former head of the Department of Health, Education, and Welfare, with the ease of having a few friends over for dinner. Everything Marilyn does is first class and this book is no exception.

This is much more than a cookbook—it's full of stories that will make you laugh out loud, priceless heirloom recipes, plus tips and tricks that will make you say, "Wow! I always wondered how to do that." Because of a story she tells, you will painlessly absorb culinary training that you will never forget.

Here is a book that lets you take personal classes from one of our great food experts. Managing major events for hundreds is just one of Marilyn's many talents. Her food experiences include teaching throughout the country, writing a number of cookbooks, consulting for restaurants and food companies, and developing products for a large corporation.

She has experienced foods and cultures all over the world during many overseas stays with her professor husband. On an eat-our-way-through-Italy trip, Marilyn impressed me and other food writers time and time again with her knowledge of, or a story about, a dish or an ingredient.

In addition, Marilyn is a longtime radio talk-show celebrity. Everyone within a hundred miles of Cincinnati knows that Marilyn's three-hour food show is the most fun in town, and what you learn is amazing. The night watchman at a shopping center told me, "Over the radio, mind you, Marilyn taught my wife to cook. I love that lady! She changed my life."

If you want both innovative and classic recipes, you will love this book. Marilyn's heritage, a lineage of outstanding Southern cooks, has been expanded by a multitude of listeners and participants from her talk show. Through the years, Marilyn has chatted with literally thousands of cooks. She has shared and received recipes, kitchen know-how, tips to make cooking easier, as well as food culture and lore. What an incredible wealth of cooking knowledge! And all of this can be experienced right here in *The Marilyn Harris Cooking School Cookbook.*

SHIRLEY O. CORRIHER
Author of *CookWise*

Welcome to My Cooking School

That is what this book is: lessons presented with recipes written as simply and clearly as I know how. I've tried to organize them based on the same concept and goals I've always used when teaching my cooking classes: not just to educate, but to entertain too, because cooking should be fun. I hope you will find in my book some recipes to your liking that inspire you to go into your own kitchen to make them. If you enjoy the making as well as the eating, this cooking teacher will be pleased. Of course there is that other essential element of satisfaction for those of us who cook and that is basking in the glow of compliments we receive from our dear families and friends as they consume our carefully prepared food. That is the real payback for washing all of those dirty dishes.

There are a few simple rules in my school. I have always set them forth for my students, including those who listen to me "teach" on the radio. The first is: flavor is the bottom line. Always bear in mind that what you are creating is food that should be savored and enjoyed. That's why I take time in each and every class to tell those cooks in the audience how important it is to enhance and refine the flavors of your food, whether sweet or savory, fancy or plain.

Finally, a phrase so well known to my loyal students: it's not the atom bomb you're making. In my many years of teaching and talking to thousands of cooks on the radio, nobody has reported blowing up his or her kitchen. Remember it's only dinner. The worst that's likely to happen is you'll have to throw the mess out and make reservations. So relax, have fun, and enjoy.

Maybe the information that follows will be just the lesson you need to get off to a good start, giving you beginners the confidence you need and you experienced cooks a fresh reason to try a new recipe.

Happy cooking.

Acknowledgments

Without the loving encouragement (not to mention hours of typing, correcting, and gentle nagging) of my best of all husbands, E.P., this book would still be a dream. So many other wonderful friends have encouraged me and supported my efforts in the creation of this book. Here are some of their names:

Gene and Francine Archbold, Giuseppe Bovo, May Bsisu, Rita and Rob Burnett, Sandy and Bob Cohan, Shirley and Arch Corriher, Jean-Robert de Caval and Annette Pfund, Julia della Croce, Nathalie Dupree, Alice Fixx, Mary, Paul and Steve Fricke, Sara and Hardy Friedrichsmeyer, Mary Fruehwald, Girl's Night Out Bunch, Renate and Jerry Glenn, Violet Graham and Rosamunde, Jo Hassall and Chris Hassall, Dave Henry and Tori Houlihan, Yen and Ron Hsieh, Martha and Rege Jensen, Sean Kagy, Deb Lackey, my sisters and brothers, Jan Neltner, Charlotte and Bob Otto, Lisa and Will Papa, Dave Patania, Peg Pauly, Richard Perry, Nancy Pigg, Glenn and Liz Rinsky, Kitty Sachs, Lana Santavicca, Monica and Cheyenne Schierbaum, Matthew Shapiro, Loren Sheffield, Sharon Shipley, Carol and Rex Stockwell, Brett Stover, Amy Tobin, Mary and Keith Triebwasser, Marj Valvano, Faye Volkman, Connie and Russell Wiles, all my friends at 55KRC, and lastly—but only alphabetically—Cindy Young.

Diane Bowman designed the dust jacket; Jay Bachemin took the photos. Many thanks to both of them.

This book is dedicated to all of my cooking students.

ABBREVIATIONS

Standard

tsp.	=	teaspoon
tbsp.	=	tablespoon
oz.	=	ounce
qt.	=	quart
lb.	=	pound

Metric

ml.	=	milliliter
l.	=	liter
g.	=	gram
kg.	=	kilogram
mg.	=	milligram

STANDARD-METRIC APPROXIMATIONS

$\frac{1}{8}$ teaspoon	=	.6 milliliter		
$\frac{1}{4}$ teaspoon	=	1.2 milliliters		
$\frac{1}{2}$ teaspoon	=	2.5 milliliters		
1 teaspoon	=	5 milliliters		
1 tablespoon	=	15 milliliters		
4 tablespoons	=	$\frac{1}{4}$ cup	=	60 milliliters
8 tablespoons	=	$\frac{1}{2}$ cup	=	118 milliliters
16 tablespoons	=	1 cup	=	236 milliliters
2 cups	=	473 milliliters		
$2\frac{1}{2}$ cups	=	563 milliliters		
4 cups	=	946 milliliters		
1 quart	=	4 cups	=	.94 liter

SOLID MEASUREMENTS

$\frac{1}{2}$ ounce	=	15 grams		
1 ounce	=	25 grams		
4 ounces	=	110 grams		
16 ounces	=	1 pound	=	454 grams

Matching Food with Wine: A General Reference Guide

The following are simply suggestions for choosing a wine to serve with your food. (I suggest taking your menu to the wine professionals at a good wine shop. They can make more exact recommendations.) Just remember that wine, like food, should be pleasing to your own palate, so drink what tastes best to you and fits your budget. One principle: wine should never overpower the food and food should never overpower the wine.

Mild fish dishes (e.g., trout or sole with a light sauce)
Sauvignon Blanc, Riesling, Chenin Blanc, Pinot Grigio, or Pinot Blanc

Hearty or spicy fish dishes (e.g., grilled tuna or peppered salmon)
Chardonnay, Beaujolais/Gamay, Red Zinfandel, Pinot Noir

Simple shellfish and seafood (e.g., lobster, shrimp, and oysters with mild sauces)
Chardonnay, White (French) Burgundy, Sauvignon Blanc

Hearty shellfish and seafood (with spicy or robust sauces)
Côte de Rhone, Zinfandel, Gewurztraminer, Riesling

Light chicken dishes (e.g., chicken breasts with light seasoning)
Chardonnay, Pinot Noir, Chenin Blanc, Beaujolais/Gamay

Hearty chicken dishes (e.g., dark meat or any chicken with a robust sauce)
Shiraz, Chianti/San Giovese, light Rhone, Red Zinfandel

Turkey (traditional—roasted)
Pinot Noir, Beaujolais, Chardonnay, American or German Riesling

Duck (sautéed breast or whole roasted) and game birds (pheasant, quail, etc.)
Cabernet Sauvignon or Franc, Merlot, Red Zinfandel, Shiraz, Rhone

Light pork dishes (e.g., simple grilled chops or roasted loin mildly seasoned)
Pinot Noir, Chianti

Hearty pork dishes (e.g., barbecue, smoked, or highly seasoned)
Red Zinfandel, Rhone, Australian Shiraz, Merlot

Simple beef dishes (e.g., steak, grilled and mildly seasoned, or plain roast beef)
Cabernet Sauvignon or Franc, Merlot, Bordeaux, Italian Reds

Hearty beef dishes (e.g., with complex sauces, spicy marinades)
"Big Reds," robust Cabernet Sauvignon or Franc, Meritage, Barolo, Shiraz, big Rhones

Burgers and meatloaf (e.g., with all of the trimmings or a spicy glaze)
Merlot, Red Zinfandel, Pinot Noir

Simple lamb dishes (e.g., chops or rack with mild seasonings)
Cabernet Sauvignon or Franc, Merlot, Chianti/San Giovese, Rhone

Hearty lamb dishes (e.g., roasted or grilled with robust sauces and seasonings)
"Big Reds" such as Cabernet Sauvignon or Red Zinfandel

Mild vegetable main dishes (creamy casseroles, mild seasonings)
Pinot Noir, Chardonnay, Riesling

Hearty vegetable main dishes (spicy bean casseroles, eggplant with cheese)
Beaujolais, Chianti/San Giovese, Pinot Noir

Mild pasta and risotto (with cream sauces, mild seasonings)
Chardonnay, Chenin Blanc, Pinot Grigio

Hearty pasta and risotto (with tomato, meat, or spicy seasonings)
Chianti/San Giovese, Shiraz, Pinot Noir

(With thanks to Russ and Connie Wiles)

THE
MARILYN HARRIS
COOKING SCHOOL COOKBOOK

Appetizers for Easy Entertaining

Almond-Stuffed
Spiced Olives

Spicy Mixed Nuts

Homemade Herb Cheese

Bay Harbor Whitefish
Bread Spread

Easy Caviar Spread

Oven-Roasted Caponata

May's Hummus

Herbed Pita Triangles

Green Olive Spread

Cured Salmon (Gravlax)
with Dill Sauce

Herbed Tartar Sauce

Smoked Salmon Roulade
with Onion Cream, Lentil
Salad, and Dill and Lemon
Dressing

Brie Wafers

Baked Cheese Dip

Skewered Raspberry
Chicken

Pork Satay
with Spicy Peanut Butter
Sauce

Hot Beef Dip
with Party Rye

Shrimp and Brie
Quesadillas
with Avocado-Corn Salsa

Apple-Cheddar
Quesadillas

Hot Lobster Puffs

In each of the twenty-plus years I've taught cooking I've offered at least one new class with a party theme. One year when we were in Berlin on sabbatical, I even managed to teach a holiday party class in German. My classes with titles such as "Easy Appetizers," "Make-Ahead Hors d'oeuvres," "Holiday Party Buffet," or "How to Give a Cocktail Party" never fail to be fully subscribed. Don't we all love a party and good party food?

My first rule for the host and hostess is to have as much fun as your guests. In fact, many of us who love to cook and to entertain our friends will tell you it is often more fun to be the one giving the party. I know that is easy to say and I will be first to admit that planning and hosting a successful party requires a lot of effort. Here are some of my time-tested tips that will help you to have as much fun as your guests at your next party.

- Plan ahead. Make lists of everything you need and make a time plan for everything from shopping to cooking ahead.

- Choose a menu with a variety of recipes that can be prepared at different times and one with a good balance of hot and cold items.

- Select dishes that don't have to be kept either freezing cold or piping hot, especially if the food is served buffet style.

- Begin the food preparation several days before the party and plan on making one or two recipes a day, leaving only a couple of fresh items for the actual day of the party.

- Do all of the cleaning at least two days ahead. Set the table, arrange flowers, etc., the day before. That leaves you free to do the fun part, finishing and garnishing the food, as well as some private time for getting yourself ready.

- Be realistic. It's not the time to try new, complicated recipes. Feel comfortable with any new recipes and rely on some that you know you do well.

- Keep it simple. You do want your food to be attractive as well

17

as tasty, but you don't have to buy out a watercress farm or make forty perfect tomato roses.

- Calculate as closely as possible how much food you need for your number of guests. Nobody wants to run short, but most of us are guilty of making far too much. That not only means expending more time and energy on the preparation, but lots of pesky leftovers to face afterwards.

- If you are entertaining more than six or eight people, make it a rule to get some help. It may just mean enlisting the services of a friend or employing neighborhood teenagers. For a large party you may want to hire a professional from an agency that specializes in catering.

- Today's parties tend to rely less on mixed drinks, eliminating the need for a bartender. Guests can be invited to help themselves to opened bottles of wine or nonalcoholic beverages or from the punchbowl.

- Finally: relax! Remember your goal to have as much fun as your guests. They will enjoy it more if they know you are.

To make a tomato rose: start with a medium to large firm tomato. With a sharp knife—not serrated—using a sawing motion, cut a round off the bottom, leaving it attached. Continue to slice off a continuous strip of peel. Peel two-thirds of the tomato; detach peeling and set aside. Peel the remainder. Roll the bottom strip of peeling around the base, forming a circle with a hollow center. Roll the second strip of peeling into a tight coil and place in the center. Voila!

Figure on 75 servings from a case of wine or champagne.

For passed canapés at a cocktail party, plan 3 to 5 per person per hour.

Wine temperatures:
Serve champagne at refrigerator temperature (38 to 40 degrees).
Serve white wine at or just above refrigerator temperature.
Serve light red wine at a cool 50 to 55 degrees; robust reds at 60 to 65 degrees.

Almond-Stuffed Spiced Olives

This is an easy way to dress up plain pitted green olives from the grocery-store shelf. Buy the very large ones so the almonds fit inside.

12-oz. jar large pitted green olives
8 oz. whole blanched almonds
2 tbsp. extravirgin olive oil
1 or 2 large cloves garlic, peeled
2 or 3 small strips lemon peel
½ to 1 tsp. crushed red chile peppers

- Drain olives, reserving brine. Stuff each olive with one of the almonds and place in the empty jar. Pour the olive oil over the olives.

- Add the garlic, lemon peel, and red pepper flakes. Pour in as much of the brine as needed to fill the jar. Seal and refrigerate at least 24 hours.

- Will keep a month in the refrigerator. Olives become spicier the longer they marinate.

- Serves 10-12 as an appetizer.

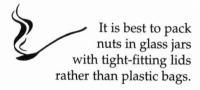

Almonds, rich in calcium, offer more fiber than any other nut or seed. So have a few more.

Spicy Mixed Nuts

During the holidays, I like to have a bowl of these wonderful spicy treats on hand for guests who drop by and I always have several bowls of them for large parties. A tin of them makes a nice hostess gift too.

2 large egg whites
2 tsp. salt
¾ cup sugar
1 tbsp. Worcestershire sauce
2 tbsp. Hungarian sweet paprika
1 tsp. cayenne pepper
8 oz. whole blanched almonds
8 oz. pecan halves
8 oz. walnut halves
6 tbsp. unsalted butter, melted and cooled

It is best to pack nuts in glass jars with tight-fitting lids rather than plastic bags.

- Preheat oven to 325 degrees.
- Beat egg whites with salt in electric mixer until very foamy. Gradually beat in the sugar and beat until soft peaks form. Fold in the Worcestershire sauce, paprika, and cayenne pepper. Stir in nuts and butter, coating the nuts well.
- Spread into a single layer on a greased baking sheet. Bake in the middle of the preheated oven. Stir every 10 minutes. Bake until crisp and golden, 30 to 35 minutes. Remove nuts while hot and spread on a sheet of foil until cool. Break into clusters or into individual nuts.
- Makes 1½ lb.

Homemade Herb Cheese

There are a number of good commercial herb cheeses available. The best ones come from France. This easy homemade one is a far less expensive, very tasty substitute. Multiply the recipe for a large party. It will keep in the refrigerator for a couple of weeks.

> **1 8-oz. pkg. cream cheese, softened**
> **1 stick sweet butter, softened**
> **¼ cup chopped parsley**
> **1 large clove garlic, finely chopped**
> **1 tsp. dried dill (1 tbsp. fresh)**
> **1 tsp. mixed dried herbs (marjoram, oregano, chervil, etc.)**
> **¼ tsp. salt, or to taste**
> **½ tsp. coarsely ground black pepper**

To make toast rounds: stack 3 slices of thinly sliced bread. Cut out the center with a biscuit cutter. Place in a single layer on a baking sheet and put in a preheated 350-degree oven until lightly browned on the edge and crisp.

- Blend together in the food processor until creamy. Put into crock or decorative bowl and chill.
- Serve with toast triangles.*
- Makes about 1½ cups.

*Toast triangles: cut the crust from sandwich bread. Cut each slice in half on the diagonal. Cut each half into two smaller triangles, to make 4 from each slice.

Bay Harbor Whitefish Bread Spread

My friend Connie Wiles and I mixed up this savory spread for the first time in her lovely summer home overlooking Lake Michigan. Smoked whitefish is a local specialty in that part of Michigan and always available. If you don't have access to smoked whitefish this also tastes great with smoked trout. Here's a leftover tip for after the party: put a large spoonful in an omelet for breakfast or lunch.

Cheese dips and spreads using cream cheeses and other firm cheeses are easy to blend together in the food processor. Sour cream and yogurt should not be mixed in the food processor. The quick mixing action of the processor will liquefy both and make the mixtures too thin. The other ingredients may be blended together in the processor, but use a rubber spatula to fold in the sour cream or yogurt last.

1½ lb. whole smoked whitefish*
8 oz. cream cheese, softened
¼ cup fresh dill, stems removed
2 tbsp. mayonnaise
1 or 2 tsp. horseradish, to taste
2 tbsp. sour cream or yogurt
2 tbsp. fresh lemon juice
2 tbsp. capers, drained and rinsed

- Pull the fish from the bone. Tear into pieces and place half of it into the food processor bowl. Set remainder aside.

- Cut the cream cheese into 8 cubes and add to the food processor along with the dill, mayonnaise, and horseradish. Process until mixture is smooth. Remove to a side dish.

- Fold in the sour cream, lemon juice, and capers. Shred the rest of the fish coarsely and fold into the mixture. Taste and correct the seasonings. Cover and chill for several hours or overnight.

- Spread onto thinly sliced French bread or little cocktail toasts.

- Makes 2 cups.

*If you buy fillets of either whitefish or trout you need only 1 lb.

Easy Caviar Spread

Just a bit of precious caviar can perk up a party table. This tasty spread allows you to include a touch of luxury without making a major investment. You don't have to use the good stuff in this spread, but a bit of beluga or sevruga will go far in adding elegance as well as taste. A less expensive alternative is salmon caviar, but you will need twice as much because the eggs are larger and it doesn't cover as well as the smaller caviar eggs.

> **6 hard-cooked eggs**
> **2 sticks butter, softened**
> **½ tsp. salt**
> **Hot pepper sauce, to taste**
> **½ cup chopped sweet salad onion**
> **1 cup sour cream**
> **4 oz. caviar**
> **Chopped flat-leaf parsley**

- In food processor with steel blade, chop eggs and add butter. Blend together, season, and spread in a small serving bowl. Cover with plastic wrap and chill for at least 30 minutes.

- Fold the onion into the sour cream and spread over the egg mixture. Top with caviar and cover the dish with plastic wrap.

- At serving time, garnish with chopped parsley. Spread onto toast points or cocktail toasts.

- Serves 12.

When a recipe calls for "sweet onion" or "salad onion," use one of the following varieties, available at different seasons of the year—Texas Sweet Onions, Vidalia Onions, Walla Walla Onions, Maui Onions, or O-So-Sweet Onions. Red Spanish Onions are also mild enough for salads or other recipes that call for raw onion. They are generally available year round. Because sweet onions are mild in flavor, they should be used only uncooked or cooked for a short period of time and served as a vegetable, such as grilled onion slices or baked onions.

Though flat-leaf or Italian parsley is always preferable to use for flavoring, curly parsley is the best choice for a garnish because it is a coarser texture and stays fresh and pretty longer.

Oven-Roasted Caponata

Another favorite of mine is this delicious, attractive, and versatile appetizer. All of my cookbooks have some version of caponata, including one I prepare on the outdoor grill. This oven-roasted one is so versatile because it knows no season. All of these vegetables are generally available year round. When I can find eggplant with tender skin, I prefer to roast and serve it with the skin on. If the skin seems to be thick and tough, it is best to peel it. This keeps for a week to 10 days in the refrigerator. Always make it at least a day ahead.

If a recipe calls for a fresh herb that is not available, use one-third as much of the dried herb. Just be sure the dried herbs still have some flavor. The shelf life of dried herbs is no longer than one year. To refresh and enhance the flavor of the dried herb add a few sprigs of fresh parsley (always readily available) and chop the parsley with the dried herbs either with a knife or in the food processor.

2 medium to large red bell peppers
1 small eggplant
1 large red Spanish onion
4 or 5 fresh Roma tomatoes*
Extravirgin olive oil
Coarse sea salt
3 tbsp. red wine vinegar
1 tbsp. brown sugar
¼ tsp. hot pepper sauce, or to taste
½ cup pitted kalamata or Greek black olives
2 tbsp. chopped parsley
1 tbsp. chopped fresh basil (1 tsp. dried)

- Preheat the oven to 500 degrees. Wash and dry the peppers. Place on top oven rack with a sheet of heavy-duty foil on bottom rack to catch any drippings. Roast for 12 to 15 minutes, or until skin turns dark and puffs.

- Remove with a long-handled fork to re-closable-top plastic bag. Leave oven on. Close bag and allow the peppers to sweat in the bag as they cool.

- When the peppers are cool, peel them, twist out the stems, and cut peppers in half lengthwise. Remove seeds and strip out membranes. Cut crosswise into small strips. Set aside.

- Wash, trim, and cut the eggplant into 1" cubes. Place in a large, shallow roasting pan large enough to accommodate all of the vegetables when arranged in a single layer.

- Peel the onion, leaving the root end intact. Slice lengthwise into 1" slices. Add to pan with eggplant.

- Cut the tomatoes in half, lengthwise, and place skin side down in the roasting pan. Drizzle a light coating of the olive oil over the vegetables, tossing with your fingertips to lightly coat. Sprinkle with coarse sea salt.

• Place in the preheated oven. Roast 10 to 12 minutes. Stir or shake the pan halfway through the cooking time.

• Remove from the oven, take the peeling off tomatoes, and coarsely chop tomatoes. Turn off oven.

• Coarsely chop the onions, discarding the root end.

• Stir together the vinegar, sugar and hot pepper sauce in Pyrex measuring cup and heat in the microwave to dissolve the sugar. Toss with the vegetables.

• Toss in the pepper strips, olives, basil, and parsley. Cover and chill until ready to serve.

• Serve on toasted pita triangles or Melba toast.

• Makes about 4 cups.

Note: leftover roasted caponata is good stuffed into some fresh pita bread for a cold lunch or snack.

*When Roma tomatoes are hard and lacking in flavor, coarsely chop some whole canned imported plum tomatoes (be sure to use "plum" tomatoes and the imported ones always seem to have the most flavor) and toss with the eggplant and onion during the last 5 minutes of roasting time. Roasting time is extended by 2 or 3 minutes because vegetables will cool when tomatoes are added.

May's Hummus

This traditional Lebanese dish is served as an appetizer or a side dish with grilled lamb, beef, or chicken. The recipe comes from my friend May Bsisu (see her Web site, www.maycooks.com, for many more excellent Middle Eastern recipes). It is a great dip to serve with toasted pita-bread triangles and makes a tasty spread for sandwiches and wraps.

> **1 cup dried and split chickpeas**
> **3 cups water**
> **½ tsp. baking soda**
> **3 cloves garlic, peeled**
> **½ tsp. salt**
> **¼ cup tahini (sesame paste)**
> **½ cup fresh lemon juice**
> **Cold water**
> **2 tbsp. chopped parsley**
> **Olive oil**

- Soak the chickpeas overnight in the 3 cups of water with the baking soda added. (Or for a time-saving recipe, use 1 15-oz. can chickpeas, drained and rinsed.)

- Place garlic and salt in food processor and pulse three times. Add drained chickpeas, tahini, and lemon juice. Pulse until mixture is creamy. Add just enough cold water to lighten the color.

- Season to taste, adding more salt and lemon juice if needed. Pour into serving dish, garnish with chopped parsley, and drizzle with olive oil.

- Serve with Herbed Pita Triangles (see below).

- Serves 6.

Herbed Pita Triangles

These savory bread triangles are good to have around as a snack by themselves or to serve with some cheese to accompany a glass of wine. If they are not crisp enough after the initial baking time, turn off the oven and allow them to sit in the warm oven until they are dried and crisp. They will keep for several days in a tightly sealed canister.

1 pkg. white or whole-wheat pita bread
1/2 cup extravirgin olive oil
1 tsp. dried thyme leaves
1 tsp. dried dill
1 clove garlic, peeled and crushed
1/2 tsp. sea salt
Dash cayenne pepper, to taste

- Wrap the pita bread in foil and heat in a 400-degree oven for 8 to 10 minutes or until slightly warm so it separates easily. Remove and cut each round into quarters. Separate the quarters and place, inside up, on a baking sheet.

- Heat the olive oil with the herbs and garlic. Allow to bubble a couple of minutes. Remove from heat and let sit for at least 30 minutes for the flavors to infuse. Season with salt and pepper.

- Using a soft-bristle pastry brush, lightly brush each triangle with the oil mixture. Place in a single layer on baking sheet. Bake in a preheated 375-degree oven for 8 to 10 minutes or until crisp and edges are golden brown.

- Cool and store in a tightly sealed container.

- Makes 32 triangles.

Green Olive Spread

This delicious olive spread is a bit different from the typical "tapenade" made with black olives. Buy the best-quality imported olives for this. I like the very flavorful ones from France. The fresh jalapeño adds a fresh flavor and just enough spice. Be conservative when spreading this onto the bread. It is rich and flavorful and you don't need very much.

To pit olives, place an olive or two on a cutting board. Lay the widest end of a chef's knife over the olives. Hold knife firmly with one hand and sharply rap the side of the blade with the heel of the other hand. The olive(s) will split open and you can pop the pit(s) right out.

> **2 cups whole green olives in brine**
> **1 small to medium fresh jalapeño pepper**
> **1¼ cups pine nuts**
> **2 tsp. fresh thyme leaves**
> **1 tsp. fresh lemon juice**
> **¼ cup extravirgin olive oil**

- Pit the olives and place in the food processor with chopping blade.
- Cut the chile pepper into thin strips, discarding stem and seeds. Add to the processor bowl.
- Add the remaining ingredients and process into a coarse paste. If mixture is too dry, drizzle in a bit more olive oil for a creamy texture.
- Remove to a covered container and chill until ready to serve. Let warm up slightly before spreading a small amount onto Herbed Pita Triangles (see above) or toast rounds.
- Makes about 2 cups.

Cured Salmon (Gravlax)
with Dill Sauce

I first ate gravlax, or salmon cured simply with seasoned salt and sugar, in Denmark and thought it was one of the best things I had ever tasted. Since then I have tried many preparations of this dish. The method doesn't vary much, but this is the seasoning mixture I like best. Some basic rules for making gravlax: be sure to use very fresh salmon. Some chefs I have interviewed say they always freeze the fish for a few days, thaw it in the refrigerator, and then proceed with the recipe. If you have very fresh, farm-raised salmon, this is not necessary. With a bit of advance planning, this can be an easy but elegant party dish. As an hors d'oeuvre I prefer serving it with the Dill Sauce and some thinly sliced rye bread. For a first course at the table, arrange very thin slices on a small plate and garnish with lemon and fresh dill. French bread and butter can be served with it if desired. It is important to note that the amount of curing ingredients should correspond to the weight of the salmon. If your salmon fillet is larger (or smaller) adjust the other ingredients accordingly. Finally, you will notice I don't give a dried dill equivalent for the recipe since it should be made only with fresh dill.

> 6 tbsp. chopped fresh dill
> 6 tbsp. coarse sea salt
> 6 tbsp. sugar
> ½ tsp. coarsely ground black pepper
> 1 tsp. crushed coriander seed
> 1 tbsp. vodka
> 2 lb. salmon fillet
> Extra chopped dill, for garnish

- Mix together the seasonings with the vodka.
- Place the salmon, skin side down, in a glass or ceramic dish. Coat the skinless top entirely with the seasoning mixture. Cover with plastic wrap and place another pan or board on top. Weigh with a weight.* Place in refrigerator.
- After 24 hours, turn and baste. After 24 more hours, remove weight. Keep salmon in brine for another 2 days. Remove, brush off the seasonings, and dry salmon.
- Using a sharp, thin-bladed knife, slice the salmon very thinly on the diagonal. Sprinkle with freshly chopped dill and serve with the Dill Sauce and/or wedges of lemon.

- Serves 12-14 as an appetizer.

*For the proper texture, use enough weight to press down very firmly on the fish—I use one or two foil-wrapped bricks.

Dill Sauce

½ **cup Dijon mustard**
2 tbsp. olive oil
1 tbsp. apple cider or white wine vinegar
1 tbsp. sugar
½ **tsp. salt**
½ **tsp. freshly ground black pepper**
2 tbsp. chopped fresh dill (2 tsp. dried)

- Whisk together until smooth. Cover and chill until ready to serve.
- Makes about ¾ cup.

Herbed Tartar Sauce

I serve this sauce with smoked salmon and other smoked fish. It is good with sliced cold meats too. It is lighter and more flavorful than commercial tartar sauce. To reduce calories and fat even further, use nonfat plain yogurt instead of sour cream. Make this at least an hour ahead so flavors have time to blend in the refrigerator. It is best when used within a day or two.

1 cup mayonnaise
½ **cup reduced-fat sour cream (or nonfat plain yogurt)**
½ **tsp. sugar**
2 tbsp. finely chopped sweet salad onion
1 tbsp. chopped fresh dill (1 tsp. dried)
2 tbsp. chopped Italian parsley
2 tbsp. drained capers
½ **tsp. hot pepper sauce**
1 tbsp. fresh lemon juice

- Gently stir together the mayonnaise and sour cream with a whisk or fork until blended.

- Stir in the remaining ingredients. Cover and chill for at least an hour. Serve with boiled shrimp, smoked fish, or cold, sliced, rare roast beef.
- Makes about 2 cups.

Smoked Salmon Roulade with Onion Cream, Lentil Salad, and Dill and Lemon Dressing

Jean-Robert de Caval, five-star chef de cuisine of La Maisonette in Cincinnati, has an incredible sense of flavor and presentation that makes his food very special. I am pleased to call him a good friend and always pleased to eat anything he makes. Besides presiding over the kitchen of the country's most honored restaurant (La Maisonette holds the record for Mobil five-star awards in this country), Jean-Robert finds time to teach cooking classes and to cook for many charitable events. We are so happy he shared his recipe for one of my favorite dishes. Don't be intimidated by the number of ingredients or steps in this recipe. You can do it all ahead of time. It is quickly assembled and well worth the effort to serve such an elegant and tasty appetizer for your next fancy dinner party.

2 medium onions
⅓ cup clarified butter
1 carrot
1 rib celery
2 lemons
2 medium red bell peppers
1 cup extravirgin olive oil
Salt and pepper
½ cup crème fraiche
2 tbsp. each chopped fresh chives, flat-leaf parsley, and fresh tarragon
2 tbsp. chopped fresh dill
2 tbsp. red wine vinegar
1 tsp. Dijon mustard
12 oz. thinly sliced smoked salmon
1 cup cooked green lentils

Lightly cooked
bell peppers (or
tomatoes) puréed,
blended with olive oil, and
seasoned make a flavorful and
decorative sauce called a
vegetable "coulis."

- Cut the onions into small dice. Sauté in the clarified butter until very tender. Drain off the excess butter, cover onions, and chill.

- Cut carrot and celery into very fine dice. Cover and chill.

- Peel lemons, dice the segments, cover, and chill.

- Bring a small pot of water to a boil. Cut the bell peppers into strips and blanch for 1 minute. Place in the food processor or blender with $1/4$ cup of the oil and purée to make a bell-pepper coulis. Season to taste with salt and pepper. Cover and chill.

- Make the onion cream: stir the cooked onion into the crème fraiche and add chopped chives, parsley, and tarragon. Season to taste with salt and pepper. Chill until it is a firm consistency.

- Make the dill dressing: whisk the dill into $1/4$ cup of the olive oil. Stir in the diced lemon pulp and season to taste with salt and pepper.

- Whisk the remaining $1/2$ cup olive oil with the vinegar, mustard, and salt and pepper to taste.

- Spread a slice of salmon with some of the chilled onion cream and roll up into a spiral.

- Toss the lentils with the diced carrot, celery, and the vinaigrette. Taste and correct the seasonings.

- To serve: spoon $1/4$ cup of the lentil salad in the center of a small plate and top with a smoked salmon roll (with the spiral facing up). Drizzle over $1/4$ of the dill dressing. Drizzle over $1/4$ of the bell-pepper coulis.

- Repeat to make 4 servings. Serve chilled.

- Serves 4.

Brie Wafers

My friend Mary Triebwasser brought this recipe to Cincinnati when she moved from California. Mary enjoys good food and likes to take cooking classes and exchange ideas and recipes. She says these wafers are a perennial favorite among her guests. Make up several rolls of dough and store them in the freezer, where they are ready to be sliced and baked on relatively short notice. "They are great with champagne," reports Mary, and indeed they are.

> **1 lb. Brie cheese**
> **4 oz. unsalted butter**
> **1 cup all-purpose flour**
> **½ tsp. cayenne pepper**
> **1 tsp. seasoned salt**
> **½ cup (approximately) sesame seeds**

- Trim the white rind from the cheese and cut cheese into cubes. Cut the butter into 4 pieces. Place the butter and cheese in the food processor bowl and let stand until they have softened to room temperature.
- Add the flour, cayenne pepper, and seasoned salt to the processor bowl. Process until mixture is well blended and holds together in a ball. Divide the mixture in half and place one portion on waxed paper.
- Form the mixture into a long round roll and wrap the waxed paper around the roll. Follow the same procedure for the other half. Refrigerate for at least 12 hours.
- Slice the chilled rolls into thin wafers about ¼" thick. Sprinkle with the sesame seeds. Place on a cookie sheet and bake in a preheated 400-degree oven for about 8 minutes or until lightly browned. Remove and cool on a rack.
- Store in a tightly covered container.
- Makes about 60 wafers.

Note: to store in the freezer, place the waxed-paper-wrapped rolls into a freezer bag, force out the air, and seal tightly. They may be frozen as long as 6 months.

Baked Cheese Dip

A fun dish on a chilly day, this hot cheese dip can be informal enough for a Super Bowl party or can go on the cocktail buffet where it should be kept warm while served. This can be stirred together, placed in its baking dish, then chilled for several hours before it goes into the oven. Just be sure the baking dish is one that can go from the refrigerator to the oven. Otherwise, allow it to sit out on the counter for an hour before baking it. Use natural cheeses for this dish. I recommend Jarlsberg or Emmenthaler for the Swiss cheese. If you don't want to open a bottle of white wine just for 2 tbsp., use dry vermouth.

8 oz. Gruyere cheese, shredded
8 oz. Swiss cheese, shredded
1½ cups mayonnaise
2 tbsp. dry white wine
1 cup finely chopped onion
1 tsp. dried thyme leaves
1 tsp. hot pepper sauce

- Stir together ingredients in mixing bowl. Put into a 1½-qt. oven-proof serving dish and bake in a preheated 350-degree oven for 25 to 30 minutes or until bubbly and hot.
- Serve hot with slices of a crusty French baguette or toasted pita triangles.
- Serves 10-12 as an appetizer.

Creamy cheese with a high fat content—cream cheese, Brie, Camembert, etc.—and full-fat hard cheeses—Gruyere, havarti, etc.—freeze well. Wrap them tightly in plastic wrap and then put them into a freezer bag. Press out the air and seal well. Low-fat cheeses—cottage, ricotta, feta, etc.—are not recommended for freezing. There is no need to freeze the aged grating cheeses such as Parmigiano-Reggiano. Tightly wrapped in a couple of layers of plastic wrap, they will keep for months in the refrigerator cheese drawer.

Skewered Raspberry Chicken

Sharon Shipley, of Mon Cheri Catering and Cooking School in Sunnyvale, California, and I met several years ago on a cooking tour in France. That started a long friendship and lots of food talk and exchanging recipes. This is Sharon's California version of the classic Southeast Asian kebabs, "satay." Sharon likes to serve them right off the grill at her outdoor parties.

6 skinless, boneless chicken breast halves, pounded flat
Raspberry Vinegar Marinade (see below)

- Cut the chicken breasts, crosswise, into strips. Cut the strips into bite-sized pieces. Place in a heavy-duty plastic bag with a resealable top. Pour the marinade in. Close the bag and turn several times to coat all of the chicken with the marinade.
- Marinate in the refrigerator for 2 to 4 hours.
- Soak small bamboo skewers in cold water while the chicken is marinating.
- Thread two or three pieces of chicken onto each skewer. Grill the skewered chicken on an open grill over a medium-hot fire for about 3 to 5 minutes, turning once.
- Makes 16 to 20 appetizers.

Raspberry Vinegar Marinade

³/₄ **cup red raspberry vinegar**
¹/₂ **cup dry white wine**
¹/₄ **cup olive oil**
2 shallots, finely chopped
6 green onions, chopped
2 tbsp. chopped fresh basil (2 tsp. dried)
2 tsp. fresh lemon juice
Freshly ground pepper, to taste

- Combine all of the ingredients in a bowl and whisk to emulsify.
- Makes 1³/₄ cups.

For quick and easy cooking, boneless chicken breasts should be divided in half and trimmed of all fat, cartilage, and tendons. Rinse under cool running water and pat dry with paper towels. Place between 2 sheets of plastic wrap and pound with a veal pounder (or some other heavy smooth object) to flatten. The chicken breast should be the same thickness throughout. For some recipes it may be appropriate to pound them thin, but for grilling they should not be too thin.

Pork Satay
with Spicy Peanut Butter Sauce

This is my own version of this classic Asian appetizer. Grill these indoors or out, or pop them under a hot broiler and broil just an inch or two from the heat source. Make the flavorful sauce ahead and warm it before serving. You will find unsweetened coconut milk with the Thai foods in the Asian food section of the grocery store or in any Asian specialty store.

> **1 pork tenderloin (about 1 lb.), trimmed**
> **Tangy Marinade (see below)**
> **Spicy Peanut Butter Sauce (see below)**
> **Small bamboo skewers soaked in water for**
> **1 hour**

- Slice the tenderloin, across the grain, into ½" slices. Cut the slices into fourths. Place in a shallow glass dish or a heavy-duty plastic bag with a resealable top. Make the Tangy Marinade and pour over the pork. Cover or seal and chill for at least 3 hours or overnight.

- Meanwhile make the Spicy Peanut Butter Sauce. (May be made ahead and reheated in the microwave.)

- Thread two or three pieces of pork onto small bamboo skewers that have been soaked in cold water. Cover and chill until ready to cook. At serving time, grill the skewers over a hot preheated grill for 6 to 8 minutes, turning once.

- Serve hot as an appetizer with the Spicy Peanut Butter Sauce as a dipping sauce.

- Serves 6-8.

Tangy Marinade

> **2 tbsp. peanut oil**
> **2 cloves garlic, finely chopped**
> **¼ cup fresh lime juice**
> **½ cup soy sauce**
> **2 tbsp. dark brown sugar**
> **¼ tsp. cayenne pepper**

- Whisk together all ingredients or process in blender or food processor.

Spicy Peanut Butter Sauce

2 tbsp. hot chile sesame oil
½ cup creamy peanut butter
¾ cup coconut milk
¼ cup lime juice
2 tbsp. soy sauce
2 tbsp. dark brown sugar
1 tsp. finely chopped gingerroot
½ cup finely chopped green onions (including
    some of the green tops)
½ cup chicken stock

• Place all of the ingredients in a small heavy saucepan. Stirring over medium heat, bring to a boil. Reduce to simmer and cook, stirring, for 10 minutes. Serve hot.

Hot Beef Dip with Party Rye

A quickly assembled and hearty treat that's perfect for a winter party, this tasty concoction uses everyday ingredients. Buy the leanest ground beef for this dish. I often buy a lean beefsteak such as top round and grind it finely with the steel blade in the food processor. Save the leftovers to toast on an English muffin for lunch or supper.

2 tbsp. extravirgin olive oil
1 lb. very lean ground beef
1 cup finely chopped onion
1 clove garlic, finely chopped
1 tsp. curry powder
8 oz. cream cheese
¼ cup dry red wine
½ cup canned beef consommé
1 tbsp. fresh lemon juice
1 tbsp. Worcestershire sauce
1 tsp. salt, to taste
½ tsp. hot pepper sauce, or to taste
¼ cup chopped parsley
Party rye bread

• Heat the oil in a heavy skillet over medium heat and add the beef, onion, and garlic. Cook, stirring, until onion is tender and

the red is gone from the beef. Stir in the curry powder and cook a minute or two longer, stirring.
- Cut the cream cheese into cubes and stir in over low heat until melted.
- Add remaining ingredients except bread and cook for 3 to 4 minutes.
- Serve hot with party rye bread.
- Serves 12-16.

Shrimp and Brie Quesadillas with Avocado-Corn Salsa

Quesadillas are grilled cheese sandwiches Mexican style. They are wonderfully quick and easy to make for a small group. Assemble them as far ahead as several hours, cover tightly in plastic wrap, and chill. Toast them in a skillet just before serving or keep them in a warm oven up to an hour. For a large party create a "quesadilla station" with a designated cook (professional or volunteer) making and serving them right out of the skillet.

The following two recipes are ones that I invented for a class I taught called "The Versatile Tortilla." You can easily create your own combinations based on what appeals to you or simply rely on what's in the refrigerator. Strips of chicken, beef, or pork combined with just about any kind of cheese make good impromptu food for a casual gathering or for a quick Sunday-night family supper. Simple cheese quesadillas made from whatever cheese you have on hand make a tasty snack. Add extra flavor to ones filled with mild cheeses like Jack or mozzarella by browning them in spicy chile oil and topping with a salsa garnish. (See index for Infused Chile Oil or buy one of the several brands available in the grocery store or specialty stores.)

The Brie for this recipe should be ripe, but still firm and not runny. The rind should be thick, velvety, and snow white.

> 1 lb. Brie, chilled
> 1 lb. medium raw shrimp
> 2 tbsp. butter or extravirgin olive oil
> 1 large red Spanish onion, peeled, halved, and thinly sliced
> 6 extralarge flour tortillas (burrito size)
> Extravirgin olive oil, for frying
> Avocado-Corn Salsa (see below)

- Trim the white rind from the cheese. Cut cheese into ¼" slices and set aside.
- Peel and devein the shrimp. Slice in half, lengthwise. Cover and chill until ready to cook.
- Heat the butter or oil in a heavy skillet over medium heat. Sauté the onion slices, stirring, for 3 minutes.
- Add the shrimp and cook until done through—2-3 minutes.
- Place a few cheese slices on half of a tortilla, leaving a ½" margin on the edge. Spoon some of the shrimp mixture on top. Fold tortilla in half. Repeat to make all of the quesadillas.
- Pour just enough of the olive oil in a large, heavy skillet to lightly coat the bottom of the skillet. Heat over medium heat until hot. Place one or two of the filled tortillas in the skillet.
- Cook until quesadilla is golden on the bottom side; turn and brown on second side.
- Remove to a cutting board and cut each with a pizza cutter or sharp knife into 4 triangles.
- Repeat with other quesadillas. Serve hot with the Avocado-Corn Salsa to spoon on the top.
- Makes 24 appetizers.

Avocado-Corn Salsa

2 tbsp. extravirgin olive oil
1 cup corn kernels (fresh or frozen)
1 cup chopped onion
2 large jalapeño peppers, seeded and finely
    chopped
1 cup chopped tomatoes
½ cup chopped cilantro
2 large ripe avocados, peeled and diced
1 tsp. salt, or to taste
2 tbsp. fresh lime juice

- Heat the oil in a large, heavy skillet over medium-high heat. Sauté the corn and onions, stirring often, for 5 minutes.
- Stir in the jalapeño peppers and cook, stirring, for a minute longer. Remove from heat and cool completely.
- Toss together all of the ingredients. Cover and chill for at least 30 minutes (not longer than 3 hours). Serve chilled.

Note: for a spicier salsa add another jalapeño pepper.

A "tortilla" is a round, thin, unleavened pancake, made either of flour or corn-meal. When a corn tortilla is fried crisp and flat it becomes a "tostada." When folded into a U shape, it is a taco shell. Flour tortillas are used for burritos and quesadillas. Corn tortillas are used for enchiladas.

Apple-Cheddar Quesadillas

Perfect for a cold winter's night and great for holiday entertaining, these quesadillas are best with an aged, sharp natural cheddar cheese. I like to use one of the firm, flavorful varieties of all-purpose apples such as Braeburn or Fuji. Granny Smith is also good, but must be very thinly sliced. The raspberry salsa-sour cream topping is optional, but certainly makes for a tasty treat. Raspberry salsa is available at specialty food stores.

Dense cheeses such as cheddar, Gouda, or Provolone are much easier to shred when they are well chilled. If they have been sitting out for a while, chill them quickly in the freezer before shredding. When using the shredding disc in the food processor, cut the cheese into cubes that easily fit into the food processor and use little or no pressure when processing them through the shredding disc.

3 tbsp. unsalted butter
1 large red Spanish onion, halved and thinly sliced
2 all-purpose apples, cored, halved, and thinly sliced
$\frac{1}{4}$ tsp. cayenne pepper, or to taste
Pinch salt
6 extralarge flour tortillas
1 lb. sharp cheddar cheese, shredded
Extra butter, for frying
Sour cream
Raspberry salsa

- Heat the butter in a large heavy skillet. Add the onion and apple slices and sauté over medium-high heat, stirring often, for about 5 minutes or until apples are "crisp tender." Season with cayenne pepper and salt. Remove from heat.

- Place a tortilla on a plate. Sprinkle cheese on half of it, leaving a $\frac{1}{2}$" margin on the edge. Spoon some of the apple-onion mixture on top. Fold in half. Repeat to make all of the quesadillas.

- Put just enough butter in a large, heavy skillet to lightly coat the bottom. Heat until hot. Place one or two of the filled tortillas in the skillet.

- Cook over medium heat until quesadilla is golden on the bottom side; turn and brown on second side.

- Remove to a cutting board and cut each with a pizza cutter or sharp knife into 4 or 6 triangles.

- Repeat with remaining quesadillas. Serve hot topped with a dollop of sour cream (reduced fat may be used) and a small spoonful of raspberry salsa.

- Makes 24-36 appetizers.

Note: for a heartier quesadilla, crumble, cook, and drain 1 lb. spicy bulk sausage. Stir into the onion-apple mixture. Omit the cayenne pepper.

Hot Lobster Puffs

For this recipe I usually buy frozen lobster tails and broil or microwave them. I have also purchased a 12- or 16-oz. can of frozen lobster meat, which is also OK for making these appetizers. Of course you can also substitute shrimp or crabmeat. You may cut the bread rounds from firm white bread several days before the party and freeze them. Thaw on baking sheets, brush lightly with melted butter, and toast for a few minutes in a 375-degree oven, turning once.

> 2 cups cooked lobster
> ½ cup mayonnaise
> ¾ cup finely chopped celery
> ¼ cup finely chopped parsley
> 2 tbsp. fresh lemon juice
> Salt, to taste
> ¼ tsp. hot pepper sauce
> 4 egg whites, room temperature
> ½ tsp. cream of tartar
> 1 cup finely shredded Swiss cheese (4 oz.)
> 24 bread rounds, lightly buttered and toasted

- Chop lobster very finely in food processor and remove to a bowl. Stir in the mayonnaise, celery, parsley, lemon juice, salt, and hot pepper sauce.

- With electric mixer, beat egg whites with cream of tartar until stiff, but still shiny.

- Fold into the lobster mixture and fold in cheese.

- Spoon into a large pastry bag fitted with a plain #7 or 8 tip. Pipe onto bread rounds.

- Just before serving time, bake in a preheated 450-degree oven for 8-10 minutes or until puffed and golden. Serve hot.

- Makes 24 puffs.

Stocks, Soups, and Stews

Beef Stock

Chicken Stock

Fish Stock

Aromatic White Wine
Stock

California Consommé

Summer Beet Soup

Spicy Chilled Tomato Soup

Frankfurt Herb Soup

Cream of Leek Soup
with Tomatoes

Red and Yellow Pepper
Soup

Southwest Chile-Tomato
Soup

Easy Cajun Chicken
Gumbo

Baked Bean Soup

Zesty White Bean Soup

Lentil Soup

Black Bean Chili
(with Jalapeño Cornbread)

Quick Chili
with Pinto Beans

Carbonades of Pork
with Spaetzle

Fish Stew
with Herbed Rice

Goulash Soup

Kentucky Burgoo

Bordelaise Beef Stew

I doubt there's anybody anywhere who appreciates a good bowl of soup more than I. Hardly a week goes by at our house when I don't make a pot of some kind of soup—we call it my "soup of the week." Soup is a great convenience food for feeding busy people because you can make it ahead. Most soups keep nicely in the refrigerator for several days. Many freeze well and there is no food that is easier to reheat. Often they improve in flavor the second time around.

I've taught many classes on this chapter's topic. Taken mostly from those classes, this chapter ranges from hearty and healthy everyday fare to some elegant recipes to make for your next dinner party.

Making a good pot of soup is not the most difficult culinary task, but there are some rules to follow and tricks to know to make your soups the best they can be. It is often the little details that make the difference in how your recipes turn out, so I have peppered this chapter with a number of my teaching tips. I hope they will serve as helpful guidelines when you are trying these recipes as well as any of your own.

Beef Stock

Stock is the basis for so many soups. My beef-stock recipe ideally contains veal as well as beef. The veal knuckles do add a lot of flavor, but if you can't locate them in your area just increase the number of beef bones. Making a successful beef stock with great flavor and good color begins with browning the bones. Use your heaviest pot and take your time to thoroughly brown them to a deep golden brown. The vegetables should be caramelized too. It is not necessary to have homemade stock to make a good soup, but a flavorful fresh stock can almost always turn a good soup into a great one.

¼ **cup vegetable oil**
2 lb. beef shank, with bone
2 lb. veal knuckles
2 to 3 lb. veal and beef bones (with marrow)
3 carrots, washed, trimmed, and cut up
2 large onions, cut up
4 ribs celery, washed and cut up
1 bouquet garni composed of:
   Fresh thyme
   Parsley and 3 bay leaves
1 tsp. peppercorns
6 qt. water
Salt, to taste

- In a large heavy stockpot, heat the oil and add the bones. Cook over medium-high heat, turning occasionally until the bones are well browned.

- Add the vegetables and cook, stirring often, until they are well browned. (Do not allow to burn.)

- Add the bouquet garni, peppercorns, and water. Cook over low heat, uncovered, for 6 to 8 hours. Cool and strain. (For a clear broth, strain through cheesecloth or a white paper towel.)

- Salt to taste.

- Skim off the fat before using stock or cover and chill for several hours or overnight, then remove the solidified fat.

- Makes about 1 gallon.

Never cover a stockpot. Cooking the stock in an open pot gives it a better flavor. It also allows some of the liquid to evaporate as it cooks, giving a more concentrated flavor to the finished stock.

The easiest way to remove the fat from a stock is to chill it first. Then the fat comes to the surface and can be quickly and easily skimmed off.

Chicken Stock

Chicken stock is easier and quicker to make than beef or veal stock. In this "white" chicken stock there is no browning of the chicken. It is simply tossed into the stockpot with the aromatic ingredients. If you want a fuller-bodied, brown chicken stock, start with browning the chicken pieces well in some vegetable oil. You may brown the vegetables as well. As in all stocks it is important to keep the pot at a constant, steady simmer and to cook the stock uncovered. After the stock is strained you may want to return it to the pot and reduce it further to intensify the flavors (see tip), adding the salt last. Though you never want your stock too salty, do be sure to add enough salt to bring out the other flavors.

> **1 3-lb. chicken, cut up (or 3 to 4 lb. bony chicken pieces)**
> **4 qt. water**
> **2 carrots, cut up**
> **3 ribs celery, cut up**
> **2 onions, cut up**
> **Salt, to taste**
> **6 sprigs parsley**
> **3 sprigs thyme**
> **½ tsp. peppercorns**
> **2 bay leaves**
> **½ cup white wine**

- In a large pot, combine all ingredients and bring to a boil. Simmer, uncovered, for 45 minutes to 1 hour.

- Skim and strain.

- Makes about 3 qt.

For a more concentrated chicken or beef stock, return the strained stock to a washed-out pot and continue to cook over medium high to reduce the stock. For a more flavorful soup base, reduce by about one-third. For stock-based sauces, reduce by about one-half. Don't salt the stock at all until the reduction is complete.

When skimming hot stock or soup, add an ice cube or two. The ice will force the fat to the top.

Fish Stock

Fish stock is an important component of many fish stew and chowder recipes. Reduced, it makes the flavorful basis for many sauces for fish and shellfish dishes. You need to know a good fish merchant in order to obtain good fish bones. Fish heads may be used too. Just be sure they are very fresh. The bones and heads, along with trimmings from any firm, white, mild-flavored fish (examples: halibut, flounder, sea bass), make the best stock. Those from oily fish aren't good for stock. If you are buying a lovely whole fresh fish that you intend to fillet, use the bones and trimmings to cook up some fish stock. Store it in the freezer to flavor a future gumbo, chowder, or stew.

2 lb. fish bones, trimmings, and pieces of fish
2 cups dry white wine
6 cups water
3 ribs celery, coarsely chopped
1 large yellow onion, peeled and coarsely chopped
3 sprigs parsley
2 sprigs fresh thyme (1 tsp. dried)
1 tsp. black peppercorns
1 tbsp. fresh lemon juice
Salt, to taste

- Combine all ingredients, except the lemon juice and salt, in a large nonreactive pot. Bring to a boil. Reduce to simmer and cook, uncovered, for 30 minutes.
- Cool slightly and strain. Season with lemon juice and salt. Chill, covered, until ready to use.
- Makes 6-7 cups.

Beef and chicken stock can be stored 3 to 5 days in the refrigerator. Fish stock is best used within 1 to 3 days. Make extra stock and pour the cooled stock into glass canning jars or plastic freezer containers and store in the freezer for as long as 6 months. Remove from the freezer at least 24 hours before using and thaw in the refrigerator.

When freezing liquids such as stock be sure to leave a couple of inches head space at the top of the container to allow for expansion when the liquid freezes.

Aromatic White Wine Stock

Though not a true stock, this flavorful mixture would best be described in French terms as a "courtbouillon." I learned to make it several years ago in France. It is very handy for adding zip to a simple sauce. It is great mixed with mayonnaise for a salad dressing or to use as a poaching liquid for poultry or fish. Return the strained and cooled stock to its original wine bottle and cap it with a tight-fitting cork. It keeps for 3 to 4 weeks in the refrigerator. The better the wine you use, the better your stock will taste. I recommend a good California Sauvignon Blanc.

>   1 bottle good dry white wine
>   2 cups water
>   3 carrots, peeled and coarsely chopped
>   1 onion, peeled and stuck with 1 whole clove
>   1 bouquet garni
>   3 shallots, peeled and sliced
>   2 garlic cloves, peeled and sliced
>   2 ribs celery, including leaves, coarsely chopped
>   Pulp of 1 lemon
>   1 tsp. white peppercorns
>   Salt, to taste

- Place all ingredients, except salt, in a large nonreactive pot. Bring to a boil and cook, uncovered, over high heat for about 30 minutes.
- Cool, strain, and season with salt to taste. Refrigerate.
- Makes enough to refill the wine bottle (⅘ liter).

California Consommé

This easy recipe that makes a most attractive soup comes from my good friend Mary Triebwasser. It's an ideal light starter for a fancy lunch or dinner and great for the busy cook. If you have some homemade chicken stock on hand it will be great in this soup. It works, too, with a good-quality canned broth.

>   8 cups chicken broth
>   2 avocados, peeled and thinly sliced
>   2 lemons, thinly sliced
>   8 tbsp. sherry
>   ½ cup chopped fresh parsley

- Heat chicken broth to near boiling in a medium-sized saucepan.
- Place the thin slices of avocado (about ¼ of an avocado per person) and 2 to 3 lemon slices in the bottom of each soup bowl. Ladle the hot chicken broth over the avocados and lemons.
- Add 1 tbsp. of sherry to each serving and sprinkle parsley on the top.
- Serves 6-8.

Summer Beet Soup

I adore good cold soups. In the hot summer months I love having a large batch of ice-cold soup stashed in the refrigerator. It makes a perfect light lunch or snack and it's convenient to have on hand as a starter when guests come for dinner. This one is a favorite because it doesn't require turning on the range on a hot day. Quickly assembled in your food processor, this tangy soup will keep for several days. If you have a French-fry disc as an attachment to the food processor, use it to quickly julienne the beets and cucumbers. As with all uncooked soups, be sure to use a sweet salad onion so the onion flavor won't be too dominant.

To peel and seed cucumbers, trim the ends. Peel lengthwise with a swivel peeler. Cut in half lengthwise. Hold over sink or a bowl and scrape down the entire length with a teaspoon to remove all of the seeds.

16-oz. jar pickled whole beets, drained
2 cucumbers, peeled and seeded
2 cups sour cream
7 cups chicken stock, chilled
½ cup finely chopped sweet onion
3 tbsp. fresh lemon juice
¼ cup chopped fresh dill
Dash salt, or to taste
Sour cream and small sprigs of dill, for garnish

- Cut the beets and cucumbers into a small julienne (approximately 1" x ¼"). Set aside.
- In the food processor or blender, blend together the sour cream and 1 cup of the chilled chicken stock. Pour into a large bowl and whisk in the remaining stock. Stir in the beets, cucumbers, and onion.
- Stir in the lemon juice and chopped dill. Cover and chill until very cold.
- Taste to correct seasoning. Serve topped with more sour cream and a sprig of dill.
- Serves 8-10.

Spicy Chilled Tomato Soup

Always a fan of the traditional Spanish cold tomato soup, gazpacho, I am notorious for inventing my own versions of it. It was certainly the inspiration for this flavorful cold soup with its own unique flavors. Peeling and seeding the tomatoes is a necessary step for the success of this soup. Use regular domestic cucumbers (versus the European seedless variety) for the best cucumber flavor, but be sure to peel and seed them. Plan to make this soup 24 hours before you serve it so the flavors blend. Serve it well chilled.

8 large ripe tomatoes
1 cup tiny grape tomatoes
2 medium cucumbers
1 large sweet salad onion
3 large jalapeño peppers
2 cups canned tomato juice
3 tbsp. red wine vinegar
3 tbsp. extravirgin olive oil
2 tsp. salt, or to taste
1 tsp. red hot pepper sauce, or to taste
½ cup chopped cilantro
2 ripe avocados
Sour cream
Extra chopped cilantro, for garnish

- Peel, halve, and seed the large tomatoes (see tip). Put 2 of them in the food processor and chop, pulsing on and off, to a fine chop. Remove and set aside. Add the remaining large tomatoes and purée to a fine-textured purée. Pour into a large bowl.

- Halve the grape tomatoes. Place in a small bowl and sprinkle with salt. Reserve.

- Peel and seed cucumbers. Chop finely in the food processor and add to the puréed tomatoes. Peel and finely chop the onion and add to the mixture.

- Mince the jalapeños. Add to puréed tomatoes.

- Pour in the tomato juice. Stir in the vinegar, oil, salt, hot pepper sauce, and cilantro. Stir in the chopped tomatoes and the small tomatoes. Cover and chill until very cold.

- Just before serving peel and cube the avocados. Gently stir into

To peel and seed a tomato, pierce the tomato with a long-handled fork and lower it into a pot of rapidly boiling water. Ripe tomatoes should remain only 30 seconds. (Firmer ones may take a few seconds longer.) Remove and cool slightly. Remove peeling with fingertips. Cut tomato in half, crosswise. Hold the tomato over the sink, cut side out, in the palm of your hand. Squeeze lightly and flip out the seeds and pulp with your fingertip. To reserve the juice, seed a tomato into a sieve placed over a bowl.

the soup. Taste and correct the seasoning. (It may need more salt at this point and you may want to make it spicier with more hot pepper sauce.)
- To serve, top each bowl with a dollop of sour cream and sprinkle with some of the extra chopped cilantro.
- Serves 8.

Frankfurt Herb Soup

Here is an indication of the German influence in my life and my cooking. This recipe came as a result of one of the many culinary adventures we've had with our close friends Klaus and Barbara Jeziorkowski, who live in the Frankfurt area. I liked this soup so much I came home and made my own version of it. I always use homemade chicken stock. A good starter for a dinner party, it is rather rich, so a small cup or bowl is all you need for a serving.

  4 tbsp. unsalted butter
  ½ cup chopped green onions
  4 tbsp. flour
  6 cups chicken stock, hot
  1 tbsp. fresh tarragon
  1 tsp. chopped dill
  4 tbsp. chopped flat-leaf parsley
  1 tbsp. chopped fresh chervil
  ½ tsp. salt, or to taste
  ¼ tsp. freshly ground white pepper, or to taste
  1 cup shredded Gruyere cheese (4 oz.)
  1 cup heavy cream
  Extra chopped parsley, for garnish

- Melt the butter in a heavy pot. Stir in the green onions and flour. Cook over medium heat, stirring, for 2 minutes.
- Whisk in the chicken stock and add the herbs. Cook, partially covered, for 20 minutes. Season with salt and pepper.
- Gradually whisk in the cheese, whisking as it melts. Stir until cheese is melted. Whisk in cream and reheat; do not boil.
- Top with more chopped parsley to serve.
- Serves 8-10.

Unsalted butter is usually preferred by good chefs and pastry chefs of the world because it is more likely to have a fresher and sweeter butter flavor. Since salt acts as a preservative (and is, in fact, our oldest preservative) the butter that is salted can be kept in cold storage much longer. It doesn't oxidize, but it does lose much of its fresh dairy character. The unsalted version will go rancid much sooner so has to be frozen or sold sooner while it is still fresh.

When a recipe calls for chopped green onions, use the white part along with the tender green top. The tough, stringy parts of the green tops should be discarded. They can also be used as flavor in the stockpot.

Cream of Leek Soup
with Tomatoes

The addition of tomato to this mild and creamy mixture creates a soup with a different flavor twist. The leek is certainly one of my favorite soup ingredients. An elegant member of the onion family, delivering flavor with a special soft touch, it is an excellent addition to all sorts of soups, from mixed vegetable to a classic creamy "potage" like this one. You may substitute fat-free "half and half" for the heavy cream in this recipe. It doesn't have the same velvety texture, but it is still a tasty (and healthier) treat.

> 3 tbsp. butter
> 4 large leeks, white and light green parts only,
>   washed and thinly sliced
> 3 tbsp. all-purpose flour
> 3½ cups chicken stock
> 2 medium sprigs thyme
> 1 bay leaf
> 1 cup heavy cream
> 1 large ripe tomato, peeled, seeded, and diced
> Dash freshly grated nutmeg
> 1 tsp. salt, or to taste
> ¼ tsp. hot pepper sauce
> 1 tbsp. finely chopped fresh parsley

- In a large heavy pan, melt the butter over medium heat and stir in the leeks. Cook over low heat, stirring often, for about 10 minutes, or until leeks are softened but not browned.

- Stir in the flour and cook, stirring constantly for at least 2 minutes. Stir in the stock, scraping the bottom of the pan to incorporate all of the leek mixture.

- Tie the thyme and bay leaf together to make a bouquet garni; add it and bring to a boil over medium-high heat, stirring constantly. Reduce heat to low and, stirring often, simmer uncovered about 15 minutes, or until leeks are tender. Discard bouquet garni.

- Purée the soup in a blender or food processor until smooth. Stir in the cream and reheat. Do not boil.

- Stir in the tomato and heat a minute or two—do not boil.

- Stir in nutmeg, salt, hot pepper sauce, and parsley. Serve hot.

- Serves 6.

A handy gadget for puréeing soup is an "immersion blender." Instead of ladling the soup into a blender or food processor and then back into the pot, this portable appliance can be placed right in the soup pot to quickly purée the soup. Not a large investment, immersion blenders are available at kitchen specialty shops.

To make cream soups ahead, finish the soup with the exception of the cream. Cool and chill. At serving time, reheat the soup to serving temperature and then add the cream.

Boiling a cream soup after the cream is added will cause it to curdle and separate. After the cold cream is added, heat gently just until soup reaches serving temperature, but don't allow the soup to return to a boil.

It is best to use only whole nutmeg and grate it with a nutmeg grater (or in a nutmeg mill), as it is needed. Like most spices, the fresh nutmeg flavor fades rather quickly after it is ground so a jar of ground nutmeg has a much shorter shelf life than the whole nutmeg.

Red and Yellow Pepper Soup

This colorful soup teaches a good lesson that may be applied to almost any creamed vegetable soup: It uses potatoes as the starch to thicken the soup. This soup also features some of the stars of the produce department for the past few years, colorful bell peppers. Not only are red and yellow bell peppers some of the most attractive vegetables around, they are very flavorful and nutritious too. Not too long ago, they were quite expensive and not always easy to find. Fortunately that has changed and these lovely sweet bells are usually available year round. Be sure to read the roasting directions in the Oven-Roasted Caponata recipe. It is the roasting process that brings out the natural sweetness and concentrates the delicious flavor of these peppers.

The secret to a good cream soup is making it just the proper thickness. Too much starch makes a thick heavy soup that is unacceptable. A good cream soup should be just thick enough to coat a spoon.

2 tbsp. extravirgin olive oil
1/2 cup chopped carrot
1/4 cup chopped celery
1 cup chopped onion
3 large red bell peppers, roasted, peeled, seeded, and cut into strips
3 large yellow bell peppers, roasted, peeled, seeded, and cut into strips
1 tsp. salt, or to taste
1/4 tsp. cayenne pepper
1 1/2 cups peeled and diced potatoes
6 cups chicken stock
Sour cream
Chopped Italian parsley

- In a large pot, heat the olive oil over medium heat. Add the carrot, celery, and onion. Cook, stirring, for 8 to 10 minutes or until the vegetables are just tender.
- Add the peppers and cook for 2 to 3 more minutes. Season with salt and pepper.
- Add potatoes and chicken stock and cook for 20 minutes—or until potatoes are tender. Purée. Taste and correct seasonings.
- Serve hot with a dollop of sour cream (or crème fraiche) on top. Sprinkle with chopped parsley.
- Serves 8.

Southwest Chile-Tomato Soup

This is a simple soup to prepare, filled with great flavor. Your choice of peppers will determine how spicy the soup will be. Anaheim chiles are mild, but very flavorful when roasted. For a zesty, piquant flavor use the poblano chiles. For easy last-minute preparation, roast and prepare the peppers as long as a couple of days ahead. To preserve them, drizzle a bit of olive oil over them and store in a covered dish in the refrigerator. (Roasted peppers freeze well, too.) The green Tabasco sauce adds flavor without adding a lot of spiciness. If you want it spicier, use Jack cheese with chile peppers in it. When tomatoes are out of season, substitute a 28-oz. can of chopped plum tomatoes with their juice.

3 Anaheim or poblano chile peppers
4 large ripe tomatoes
1 tbsp. butter
2 tbsp. extravirgin olive oil
1 cup finely chopped onion
3 tbsp. flour
4 cups chicken stock, hot
2 cups light cream
Salt, to taste
2 tsp. green Tabasco sauce
1 cup shredded Jack cheese
3 tbsp. chopped cilantro

- Roast, peel, and finely chop the peppers.

- Peel, seed, and coarsely chop the tomatoes. Reserve juice.

- Melt the butter with the oil in a large heavy pot. Add the onion and tomatoes and sauté over medium-high heat, stirring, for 5 minutes.

- Add the flour and cook over medium heat, stirring, for 2 minutes without browning. Whisk in the chicken stock along with the reserved tomato juice. Bring to a boil, reduce to low heat, and simmer for 10 minutes.

- Stir in the peppers and cream. Season with salt to taste and the Tabasco sauce. Heat until hot, but do not allow to boil.

- Stir in the cheese and sprinkle over the cilantro. Serve immediately.

- Serves 6-8.

To season soups, stews, and other longer-cooking dishes, add the hearty herbs (dried or fresh) such as thyme, oregano, sage, rosemary, savory, or marjoram early in the cooking process. Spices such as pepper, chili powder, ginger, cloves, cinnamon, cardamom, coriander, cumin, and allspice are also added in the beginning. The delicate herbs such as dill, parsley, cilantro, chervil, and tarragon should be added at the end of the cooking time.

Instead of stirring in the cream for a cream soup, whip some heavy cream seasoned with a bit of salt and spoon a large dollop over the top of a hot bowl of soup. Sour cream may also be spooned on top of the finished soup in lieu of making a classic cream soup.

Any leftover cooked meats or poultry can be diced and added to soup in the last 5 or 10 minutes of cooking. It's a good way to use leftovers and create a more substantial soup.

Easy Cajun Chicken Gumbo

I've had many a discussion with cooking students and radio listeners about how to make a "roux." It is usually not the "roux blanc" or light roux that is never browned and used as a base for many soups and sauces that starts the discussion. The consternation centers on how to make the dark-brown (some Cajun chefs describe it as "mahogany") roux necessary to begin a gumbo and other soups and stews that originated in that region of Louisiana. The problem is how to brown it enough without going too far and scorching it. When a cooking teacher from there told me she makes a perfect brown roux in the microwave oven I had to try it for myself. It works! Just be careful. Be sure to use a measuring cup that is heatproof such as Pyrex and remember that the mixture is very hot and will burn you if it splatters. Canned broth may be used for this recipe.

> ⅔ **cup vegetable oil**
> ⅔ **cup flour**
> ½ **cup each finely chopped onions, green onions, celery, and green bell pepper**
> **1 tsp. finely chopped garlic**
> **1 lb. spicy sausage, cut into bite-sized pieces (or 2 cups cubed ham)**
> **1 lb. sliced frozen okra**
> **2 large onions, chopped**
> **6 cups chicken stock**
> **1 tbsp. brown sugar**
> **1 cup tomato sauce**
> **1 tsp. Cajun Seasoning (see below)**
> **3 cups bite-sized pieces cooked skinless chicken**
> **2 cups cooked long-grain white rice**

- Mix together the oil and flour in a 1-qt. glass measuring cup. Microwave, uncovered, on high for 6 minutes. Carefully stir in the finely chopped vegetables and garlic. Cook another 45 to 60 seconds on high or until color is "mahogany." Carefully stir to mix well.

- Place the microwaved mixture in a large heavy pot. Stir in the sausage. Add the okra, onions, chicken stock, brown sugar, tomato sauce, and seasonings.

- Over high heat, bring the mixture to a boil, stirring. Reduce heat to low, cover, and simmer for 30 minutes. Stir in the chicken and continue to cook for 15 minutes.

- Remove from heat. Taste and correct the seasonings. Serve ladled over a large spoonful of fluffy long-grain white rice.
- Serves 8-10.

Cajun Seasoning

1 cup coarse sea salt
3 tbsp. coarsely ground black pepper
2 tbsp. garlic powder
1 tbsp. onion powder
¼ cup dried parsley flakes
1 tbsp. cayenne pepper
2 tbsp. chopped mild chile pepper
2 tbsp. dark brown sugar

- Stir together to blend well. Store in a tightly sealed glass jar.

Baked Bean Soup

I wouldn't dream of writing a cookbook without including a recipe from my good buddy Gene Archbold. Gene shares the honor (with my good husband) of convincing me to write my first book. Though he caused me so much hassle and hard work, I know he meant well. Gene is a fine amateur chef in his own right and really should be writing his own book. This is one of his favorite soup recipes that he acquired and adapted in turn from a good friend of his, Chris McQueen. Though there are no baked beans in this recipe, the flavor is inspired by the traditional baked-bean dish.

2 lb. navy beans
2 tbsp. brown sugar
1 tbsp. Worcestershire sauce
1 tbsp. hoisin sauce
2 cups beef broth
2 tbsp. spicy brown mustard
Water
3 tbsp. butter or vegetable oil
2 large yellow onions, chopped

If you want to add a leftover ham bone to any bean soup add it in the early stages before you start simmering the soup.

To soak dried beans quickly, rinse and drain them. Place in a large, heavy pot. Add enough water to cover by 2". Cover and bring to a rolling boil. Remove from heat and allow to sit for 1 hour. Drain and rinse again. The beans are ready to cook.

The proper amount of salt needed to season a soup depends largely on the salt level in the stock. If a salty stock is used, always wait until the soup is finished to decide if extra salt is needed. Though enough salt to enhance other flavors is imperative, too much can spoil the soup.

1 green pepper, chopped
1 clove garlic, finely chopped
16 oz. tomato sauce
2 tbsp. red wine vinegar
1 cup dry red wine
Salt and pepper, to taste

- Soak the beans overnight in cold water.
- Pour off the water and rinse the beans. Place the beans in a large, heavy pot. Add the sugar, Worcestershire, hoisin, broth, and mustard. Add enough water to cover the beans by about 2".
- Melt the butter in a skillet and sauté the onions, green pepper, and garlic over high heat, stirring, for 5 minutes. Add to the pot. Bring to a boil over high heat.
- Reduce heat to low and simmer for 1½ to 2 hours or until beans are tender. Add the tomato sauce, vinegar, and wine and simmer 30 minutes longer. Season to taste with salt and pepper. Serve hot.
- Serves 10-12.

Zesty White Bean Soup

It's no secret that the common bean has gained a new respect from chefs and cooks. I guess the number-one reason has to be our unprecedented interest in eating healthy. That includes a growing number of the population who eat a vegetarian diet exclusively, which depends on all sorts of legumes as necessary staples. Others of us simply appreciate the fact that beans are a great source of fiber and contain essential vitamins and minerals, not to mention the fact that they are versatile, inexpensive, and taste great. This all-vegetable soup, made with the old-fashioned, simple white bean, is seasoned with Southwestern flavors. Note that removing a cup or so of the cooked mixture to purée and returning to the soup is what makes it especially creamy. You can do this with almost any bean soup. Serving this bean soup over rice is optional, but it does make a delicious as well as nutritious main dish.

1 lb. dried white beans
¼ cup extravirgin olive oil
1½ cups chopped onion
4 cloves garlic, finely chopped
2 large jalapeño peppers, finely chopped
1 red bell pepper, chopped
½ cup chopped carrots
8 cups water
1 tsp. oregano leaves
2 large bay leaves
3 large tomatoes, peeled, seeded, and chopped*
2 tsp. salt, or to taste
½ tsp. sugar
3 tbsp. chopped cilantro
2 tbsp. lemon or lime juice
Hot pepper sauce, to taste
2 cups cooked rice

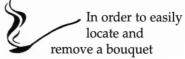 In order to easily locate and remove a bouquet garni or bay leaves from a pot of soup or stew, tie a long piece of kitchen string around the herbs and tie the other end to the pot handle. A tug on the string removes the herbs. Snip with shears to remove from the pot and discard.

- Rinse and drain the beans. Place in a pot and cover with 2″ water. Bring to a rolling boil.

- Turn off the heat and allow to sit for 1 hour. Drain and rinse well.

- Heat the oil over medium-high heat in a large heavy pot. Sauté the onion, garlic, and peppers in the oil, stirring, for 5 minutes. Pour in the beans.

- Add the carrots, water, oregano, and bay leaves. Over high heat, bring to a boil. Reduce to low and simmer, partially covered, for 1½ hours or until the beans are tender but not falling apart.

- Stir in the tomatoes, salt, and sugar. Simmer on low for 30 minutes more. Remove the bay leaves.

- Scoop out 1 cup of the beans with a bit of the liquid. Purée in the food processor or blender. Return to the pot.

- Stir in the cilantro and lemon juice. Bring to a boil on high heat and cook 2 minutes more. Taste and correct the seasonings. Add some hot pepper sauce if more spice is desired. Serve over a spoonful of cooked rice.

- Serves 10-12.

*When tomatoes are out of season, substitute 2 cups of diced canned plum tomatoes.

Lentil Soup

Lentils are a legume and closely related to other dried beans, but they are much smaller and more delicate than other beans so they don't have to be soaked. Just rinse them well, look them over for any unwanted debris or silt—this is called "picking over"—and they are ready to cook. Their cooking time is also shorter than most dried beans. I usually make this recipe with the common little brown lentils, but there are many more exotic and colorful varieties you can choose, still using all of the other ingredients in this recipe.

1 lb. dried lentils
3 tbsp. extravirgin olive oil
1 tsp. Hungarian sweet paprika
¼ tsp. cayenne pepper
2 cloves garlic, finely chopped
1 large yellow onion, chopped
½ cup chopped celery
1 cup chopped carrots
½ tsp. dried thyme leaves
3 cups beef stock
5 cups water
28-oz. can plum tomatoes, chopped (with juice)
1½ tsp. salt, or to taste
½ tsp. freshly ground black pepper
¼ cup chopped fresh flat-leaf parsley
1 tbsp. fresh lemon juice

• Wash the lentils under cold running water and drain. Put them in a 4-qt. saucepan.

• Heat the olive oil in a large skillet on medium high. Add the paprika, cayenne pepper, garlic, and onions. Cook, stirring, for 5 minutes. Add to the lentils.

• Add the celery, carrots, thyme, stock, and water. Bring to a boil, stirring to mix well. Cover, reduce to low heat, and simmer for 1 hour or until the lentils are tender.

• Add the tomatoes, salt, and pepper and cook, uncovered, 20 minutes longer.

• Stir in the parsley and lemon juice. Taste and correct the seasoning.

• Serves 10-12.

Black Bean Chili
(with Jalapeño Cornbread)

You don't have to be a vegetarian to appreciate this vegetable chili featuring flavorful black beans. High in fiber and filled with great flavor, this is a good soup to make ahead on the weekend for reheating on a busy day. Another convenient approach is to cook just the beans ahead. It is also possible to substitute canned black beans that are well drained and rinsed, but it tastes much better with dried ones. I like it with all of the garnishes I have listed together in a bowl of soup, but it can also be served with any one or more. Topping it with just green onions or cilantro makes for a lighter dish.

4 cups dried black beans, washed and drained
Water
½ cup extravirgin olive oil
½ tsp. cayenne pepper, or to taste
1 tbsp. Hungarian sweet paprika
1 tbsp. cumin
2 large yellow onions, chopped
3 large cloves garlic, finely chopped
4 medium to large jalapeño peppers, seeded and
**   chopped**
28-oz. can plum tomatoes, chopped (with juice)
1 tbsp. oregano
½ tsp. thyme
1½ tsp. salt, or to taste
½ lb. mild cheddar cheese, shredded
1 cup sour cream
½ cup chopped green onions
¼ cup chopped cilantro

- Place the beans in a large pot. Cover with several inches of water. Cover and bring to a boil over high heat. Remove from heat and allow to sit for 1 hour.

- Drain and return to the rinsed-out pot. Cover with fresh water again. Bring to a boil.

- Cover, reduce to low heat, and simmer for about 2 hours, or until tender but not falling apart. Drain, reserving 1 cup of the cooking liquid.

When soups or other dishes call for paprika, cayenne pepper, cumin, or chili powder, stir the spices for a minute or two in the hot oil or shortening before adding the fresh ingredients. Toasting the spices in the hot oil improves their flavor and makes the dish taste better.

When cooking dried beans, add any ingredients that contain acid, such as vinegar, lemon juice, or tomatoes, only after the beans are tender. The beans will not get tender if there is acid present.

- Heat the oil in a heavy pot over medium heat. Stir in the cayenne pepper, paprika, and cumin. Cook, stirring, for 2 minutes.

- Add the onions and sauté, stirring, for 5 minutes. Stir in the garlic and peppers; cook for 2 more minutes. Stir in the tomatoes and herbs. Bring to a boil and cook, stirring occasionally, for 15 minutes.

- Add the beans and the bean liquid. Cook, covered, for 10 minutes longer. Season with salt.

- To serve, place a large spoonful of cheese in bottom of bowl. Ladle over some chili and top with a spoonful of sour cream, a generous sprinkle of green onions, and some chopped cilantro (if desired).

- Serves 10-12.

Jalapeño Cornbread

A favorite accompaniment for many of the soups in this chapter, this zippy cornbread is especially tasty alongside a bowl of bean soup. I like to make it with fresh corn, but frozen kernels taste fine too. Serve it piping hot with or without butter.

$\frac{1}{4}$ **cup vegetable oil**
1 cup yellow cornmeal
$\frac{2}{3}$ **cup all-purpose flour**
1$\frac{1}{2}$ tsp. baking powder
$\frac{1}{2}$ **tsp. baking soda**
$\frac{1}{2}$ **tsp. salt**
1 tbsp. sugar
$\frac{3}{4}$ **cup buttermilk (or sour cream)**
2 eggs
1 cup shredded cheddar cheese
1 cup whole-kernel corn
1 to 2 tbsp. chopped canned jalapeño peppers

- Preheat oven to 400 degrees.
- Pour half of the oil into a 9" square baking pan.
- Stir together all the dry ingredients. Set aside.

- Whisk together the buttermilk, eggs, and remaining oil. Fold in the dry ingredients, cheese, corn, and jalapeños. Do not over-mix.

- Heat the oiled pan in the preheated oven for just a few minutes until hot but not smoking. Pour the cornbread batter into the hot pan and return immediately to the center rack of the oven. Bake for 30 to 35 minutes or until golden brown and baked through.

- Serves 6-8.

Quick Chili with Pinto Beans

A great recipe for a busy day when there are hungry folks to feed, this is proof that good chili doesn't have to cook for hours. Though many of my favorite Southwest chili recipes call for dried beans that have to be soaked and cooked and chunks of beef that require hours of cooking before they are tender, this quick recipe has such good flavor and is so easy. The secret is in the choice of ingredients. It is important to use good-quality, lean, and very fresh ground beef. I usually buy top round steak and quickly chop it with the steel blade in the food processor. It is important to use pinto beans (not kidney beans) and to find a good-quality canned brand. My favorite brand is packed in glass jars. The beans must be drained and thoroughly rinsed. For a hearty main dish, serve this over freshly baked cornbread and sprinkle with some shredded mild cheddar cheese and a sprinkling of chopped cilantro. Pass the hot sauce for those fans of spicy food.

> 2 lb. extralean ground beef
> 3 tbsp. olive or vegetable oil
> ¼ cup good chili powder
> 1 tbsp. cumin
> 1 cup chopped onion
> 2 large cloves garlic, finely chopped
> 1 tsp. dried oregano leaves
> 1 tsp. salt, or to taste
> 28-oz. can plum tomatoes, coarsely chopped
>   (with juice)
> 2 cups water
> 3 cups canned pinto beans, drained and rinsed
> Hot pepper sauce, to taste

- In a heavy pot, brown the meat over medium heat, stirring, until all red is gone. Skim off any visible extra fat.
- Heat the oil in a skillet over medium heat. Add the chili powder and cumin. Cook, stirring, for 3 minutes.
- Add the onion and garlic and cook, stirring, for 3 minutes more. Pour into the beef.
- Add the oregano, salt, tomatoes, and water. Simmer over low heat, uncovered, for 10 minutes.
- Add the beans, bring to a boil on high, reduce to low, and simmer 10 minutes longer. Season to taste with hot sauce. Taste and correct the salt, if necessary.
- Serves 8.

Carbonades of Pork with Spaetzle

It has been a number of years since I brought this recipe back from one of our sojourns in Germany. Carbonades, or meat cooked in beer, actually originated in Belgium, but the German chef who gave me the recipe made it more international by adding the little dumplings called "spaetzle" that are native to the Black Forest region of Germany and the German-speaking part of Switzerland. This is a good one to keep in mind for cold-weather casual dining. Make this ahead with everything in it but the fresh parsley. It tastes better the second day. Add the parsley just before serving. The spaetzle can also be made ahead and quickly sautéed in a nonstick skillet in a bit of butter.

2½ lb. boneless pork loin
Salt and pepper
6 tbsp. unsalted butter
2 tbsp. olive oil
4 medium onions, chopped
1 bay leaf
½ tsp. dried thyme leaves
2 cups beer
1 cup chicken stock
½ lb. medium to large mushrooms, quartered
¼ cup currant jelly
½ cup chopped parsley
2 tbsp. cornstarch
2 tbsp. water

- Trim fat from pork and cut into $\frac{1}{2}$" pieces. Season with salt and pepper.
- Heat 4 tbsp. of the butter and all the oil in a heavy pan. Sauté pork over high heat until lightly browned.
- Remove from skillet, add onions, and sauté until softened.
- Return pork and add bay leaf, thyme, beer, and chicken stock. Bring to a boil, reduce to low, and cook, partially covered, for 1 hour, stirring occasionally.
- Meanwhile, over high heat, sauté mushrooms in remaining butter for 3-4 minutes. Add to mixture along with currant jelly and parsley. Cook over medium heat for 10 minutes.
- Whisk cornstarch and water together and stir in. Cook 2 minutes more. Serve with spaetzle.
- Serves 6-8.

Spaetzle
3 cups flour
1 tsp. salt
4 large eggs
1 cup milk
6 tbsp. unsalted butter, melted

- Put flour and salt in food processor with steel blade and mix. Add eggs, milk, and 4 tbsp. of the butter. Process until well blended.
- Spoon into a spaetzle maker that is placed over a large pot of boiling salted water. Gradually press the dough into the water. Cook for 1 minute. The dumplings will come to the surface when they are done.
- Drain and toss with remaining butter. Serve immediately.
- Serves 6-8.

Note: if you don't have a spaetzle maker you may use a colander with large holes. Simply place the colander over a large saucepan filled about $\frac{3}{4}$ full with boiling salted water. Use a large spoon or ladle to force the dough through the holes and into the water.

Cover and chill leftover spaetzle for another meal. To serve: melt some butter in a skillet and toss them in the hot butter until hot through and lightly browned. Season with pepper and sprinkle with some chopped parsley.

Fish Stew with Herbed Rice

I first made this recipe in a special class for Lenten foods. This fish stew actually fits in any time of the year and it is elegant enough to set before your favorite guests. It is good for the cook too, because it goes together quickly.

2 cups chopped onions
⅓ cup extravirgin olive oil
1½ lb. snapper, halibut, cod, or any firm, fresh
    fish, cut into chunks
3 large cloves garlic, finely chopped
1 cup Aromatic White Wine Stock (see index)
6 medium tomatoes, peeled, seeded, and diced
    (reserve juice) (or a 28-oz. can plum tomatoes,
    chopped)
3 tbsp. chopped fresh basil
Salt and freshly ground black pepper, to taste
Chopped parsley

- Over high heat sauté onions in oil for 4 to 5 minutes, stirring.

- Stir in fish and garlic, tossing fish around pan until cooked on all sides, about 3 minutes. Add wine stock and cook on medium for 1 or 2 minutes.

- Add tomatoes, basil, salt, and freshly ground black pepper. Cook for 5 minutes. Season to taste.

- Ladle the stew over the rice in a shallow bowl. Garnish with chopped parsley.

Herbed Rice

1¾ cups water
½ tsp. salt
1 cup Basmati rice
2 tbsp. chopped fresh basil
2 tsp. chopped fresh dill (1 tsp. dried)
2 tbsp. chopped Italian parsley
Dash black pepper

- In a small heavy pot with a tight-fitting lid, boil the water on high with the salt. Stir in the rice. Cover and turn heat to low.

- Simmer, covered, for 15 minutes. Remove from the heat and allow to rest, covered, for 10 minutes. Toss in the herbs and pepper.

- Serves 6.

Goulash Soup

I learned to make this hearty beef dish when I lived in Berlin. It ranks in my personal top-ten list of soups. It is, in fact, so hearty I have placed it here with my "stew" recipes. It is also one of my "soup of the week" soups. Cook it on a weekend afternoon when there is time to keep an eye on it and look forward to reheating a hot and hearty bowl during the week. I like to serve this complete supper in a bowl with a big slice of hot cornbread or a slice of toasted hearty whole-wheat bread with some melted Gruyere or sharp cheddar cheese on top.

2 lb. lean boneless beef chuck, cut into ½" cubes
Salt and pepper, to taste
2 tbsp. unsalted butter
2 tbsp. vegetable oil
2 tbsp. Hungarian sweet paprika
4 large yellow onions, peeled and coarsely
   chopped
1 clove garlic, finely chopped
1 tsp. dried thyme leaves, crumbled
4 cups water
2 cups beef broth (I use Campbell's canned Beef
   Consommé)
3 tbsp. tomato paste

- Season the beef with salt and pepper. Heat the butter and oil together in a heavy Dutch oven. Over high heat, brown the beef in 2 or 3 batches, turning until brown on all sides. Remove browned beef with a slotted spoon to a side dish.

- Add the paprika, onions, and garlic to the pot, reduce to medium, and cook, stirring often, for 6 to 8 minutes or until tender. Add the thyme and cook for 2 minutes, stirring. Return the beef to the pot and stir to coat with the seasoning.

- Pour in the water and broth. Stir in the tomato paste. Raise heat to high and bring to a boil. Cover, reduce to low heat, and simmer for 1½ hours or until beef is very tender. Taste and adjust the salt and pepper.

- Serves 6-8.

Kentucky Burgoo

My "Cooking with Marilyn" radio show has a lot of listeners in Kentucky, so we often discuss specialties from that lovely "Bluegrass State." This is a traditional favorite that always comes up at Derby time. This recipe is a diplomatic consensus of recipes called in by my listeners.

2 lb. lean beef with bone (chuck)
1 lb. veal (round or shoulder)
1 medium stewing chicken, cut up
Salt and pepper, to taste
4 qt. water
1 stick butter
2 cups chopped onions
1 large clove garlic, finely chopped
2 large green peppers, chopped
2 cups diced raw potatoes
3 carrots, chopped
2 ribs celery, chopped
2 cups frozen lima beans
2 cups sliced okra (fresh or frozen)
28-oz. can plum tomatoes, chopped (with juice)
8-oz. can tomato sauce
1 small dried red chile pepper
2 cups fresh corn kernels (or frozen)
1 cup chopped parsley

- In a large, heavy pot with a tight-fitting lid, boil the beef, veal, and chicken with salt and pepper to taste in the water over high heat. Cover, reduce to low, and cook until very tender (1 to 1½ hours). Remove from the heat and cool.

- Remove meat and chicken and take the meat from the bones. Cut or shred into bite-sized pieces. Strain the stock and reserve.

- Rinse the pot, return to the heat, and melt the butter. Over high heat, sauté the onions, garlic, and green peppers in the butter, stirring, for 5 minutes. Add the meat and stock. Add potatoes, carrots, and celery. Reduce to medium and cook about 15 minutes. Add lima beans and cook for 2 hours, simmering slowly.

- The mixture should be very thick. If too thick, add a small amount of water from time to time to prevent sticking.

- Stir in the okra, tomatoes, tomato sauce, and red chile pepper.

Add a couple more cups of water here, if needed. Let simmer on low heat another hour. Add corn and cook 30 minutes.

- Remove the chile pepper. Stir in the parsley. Season with salt and pepper to taste.
- Serve Kentucky style with cornbread and your favorite salad.
- Serves 12-15 (generous servings).

Note: for best results, serve with genuine Kentucky bourbon.

Bordelaise Beef Stew

One of my students called this dish "beef stew with personality." The "personality" is actually flavor and this recipe does make a tasty pot of stew. The method of flouring the beef cubes and browning them very well gets this stew off to a good flavorful start. It is important to brown the beef in fairly small batches so that the pieces don't touch when they are browning. That assures a nice brown crust on each cube and seals the vital juices inside. The other special flavor components are the caramelized onions and the wine. It is important to use a good-quality red wine, even though it is only a stew. Remember it is the flavor that remains and good wines do taste better. You don't have to use a vintage French Bordeaux, but a good-quality California Cabernet Sauvignon is recommended. Homemade beef stock (see index) will make the best stew. If not available, use a canned beef consommé.

3 lb. cubed lean beef
Salt and freshly ground pepper
All-purpose flour
2 tbsp. butter
2 tbsp. vegetable oil
2 large yellow onions, halved and thinly sliced
3 cloves garlic, finely chopped
1 cup dry red wine
2 cups beef stock
2 tbsp. tomato paste
1 bouquet garni composed of:
    2 sprigs thyme
    2 sprigs parsley and a large bay leaf
1 tbsp. orange zest
1 tsp. fresh lemon juice
$\frac{1}{2}$ cup chopped flat-leaf parsley

Store leftover Parmigiano-Reggiano rinds, tightly wrapped in plastic wrap, in the cheese drawer in the refrigerator. Cut them into small cubes and add to a hearty vegetable or minestrone soup. The dried rinds are completely edible and will soften and become chewy as the soup cooks.

Cooking Terms:
Boil: to cook in water or other liquid that is cooking rapidly—at 212 degrees (sea level and normal pressure).

Purée: to turn into a smooth pulp by mashing, straining, or processing in blender or food processor.

Reduce: to cook by simmering or boiling until quantity decreases, to concentrate flavor.

Sauté: to cook quickly over high heat in a small amount of fat.

Simmer: to cook in water or other liquid that is bubbling gently—at 185 to 200 degrees (low heat).

Stew: to cook in water or other liquid that is served as part of the dish.

Sweat: to cook in a small amount of fat over low heat in a pot.

- Season the beef generously with salt and pepper. Dredge in flour, shaking off the excess.
- Heat the butter and oil in a large heavy pot. Brown the beef in small batches over high to medium-high heat, turning to brown to a deep golden brown on all sides. Remove browned beef to a side dish with a slotted spoon.
- Add the onions and garlic to the pan and sauté, stirring, for 5 minutes.
- Return the beef and pour in the wine. Stir, scraping the bottom of the pan. Cook for 2 minutes.
- Add the stock, tomato paste, and bouquet garni. Cover and bring to a boil. Reduce to low and simmer for 1½ hours or until the meat is fork tender.
- Stir in the orange zest and lemon juice. Cook 10 minutes more, uncovered. Add the parsley.
- Taste and correct the seasonings. Serve with crusty French bread.
- Serves 6-8.

Salads and Their Dressings

Tomato, Avocado, and Onion Salad

Roasted Vegetable Salad

Mushroom, Fennel and Parmesan Salad
with Balsamic Vinaigrette

Corn Salad

My Best Green Bean Salad

Winter Salad

Berry Green Salad

Refrigerator Crock Slaw

Belgian Endive
with Sliced Crisp Apples, Toasted Walnuts, and Bleu Cheese with Walnut Oil Vinaigrette

Luscious Lentil Salad

Black Bean and Corn Salad
with Peppers

Potato Salad Deluxe

Summer Couscous

Piquant Egg Salad

Tomatoes Stuffed
with Southern Shrimp Salad

Curried Chicken-Fruit Salad

Marilyn's Chicken Salad

Steak and Potato Salad

Grilled Pork Tenderloin Salad
with Mango and Avocado

Digging into a perfectly made salad is one of my favorite culinary delights. I especially enjoy ones that have interesting contrasts in flavor and texture. A great salad should look pretty too and there is such a lovely variety of colorful salad ingredients that have marvelous eye appeal when presented together on a plate. It doesn't matter whether it is a simple tossed salad or an artistically composed one—the same rules apply for making it a dish you are proud to put on your table.

On the other hand, I have my "salad pet peeves" that my cooking students have heard so often. Number one is torn iceberg lettuce versus lovely crisp shreds. All you need to do is take a washed, dried, and chilled head of iceberg, cut it into quarters, and shred it into ¼ to ½" shreds to see how much prettier it looks than those ugly torn pieces we see in salad bars. Toss with some dressing, take a bite, and you will discover how much better it tastes.

A "pet peeve" that is a close second is a whole cherry tomato plopped atop a salad. How are you supposed to eat it? It is difficult at best to cut with a table knife and you shouldn't have to struggle with a salad to eat it. That whole tomato is also unseasoned because it has to be cut in order to be properly salted, which is so important for bringing out the sweet flavor. A whole tomato also absorbs none of the dressing that is supposed to flavor the entire salad.

Greens that are wet and limp are another obvious "don't" when it comes to salad making. That is why I remind you in this chapter to wash those salad greens as soon as you bring them into your kitchen. Then get them as dry as possible before storing them in the crisper drawer of your refrigerator. My students know that I recommend a salad spinner for every well-equipped kitchen.

In the case of salad dressing, I believe that "less is more" is a prudent rule to follow. Sure, the dressing is an important flavor component of any salad, but it can quickly overpower the other

69

ingredients. That is why a salad drowning in its dressing also ranks high on my peeve list. As you look through this chapter I hope you will pay special attention to my tips. They point out those little rules I emphasize in my classes so your salads will never make my peeve list.

The recipes in this chapter were taken from a large list of favorite salads that I've shared with my students as well as ones borrowed from friends. My "Salads That Make a Meal" classes have been my most popular summer offerings for many years. I always have fun coming up with new recipes each year, and that is one of the reasons why my salad files are so full. I hope you will find my lineup of homemade salad dressings helpful and that you will use them to design your own salads. They are all quickly made and a good fresh dressing can mean the difference between just a salad and a sensational one.

Duck Pastrami
with Frisée Salad and
Huckleberry Vinaigrette

Garlic-Herb Croutons

Classic Vinaigrette

Italian Vinaigrette

Shallot and Herb Dressing

Celery Seed Dressing

Mango-Ginger Cream
Dressing

Tangy French Dressing

Bleu Cheese Dressing

Green Goddess Dressing

Guacamole Dressing

Tomatoes taste better if they are kept at room temperature rather than stored in the refrigerator.

"Virgin" olive oil means the first pressing of the olives. They are cold pressed to maintain their fresh flavor and color. "Extravirgin" olive oil is the highest grade and has a rich flavor and bright gold-green color.

Tomato, Avocado, and Onion Salad

This is a side salad to be savored in the summer when vine-ripened tomatoes are in abundance and at their juicy best. Lightly salting them before the salad is assembled brings out their sweet flavor. Choose avocados that are ripe but not too soft and without dark spots. The Haas variety is the creamiest and has the best flavor.

4 large ripe tomatoes, cored
Fine sea salt
2 ripe avocados
Juice of 1 lemon
1 medium sweet salad onion, halved and thinly
  sliced
3 tbsp. extravirgin olive oil
1 tbsp. balsamic or red wine vinegar
¼ tsp. sea salt
Freshly ground black pepper, to taste
2 tbsp. chopped cilantro

- Cut the tomatoes crosswise into ½" slices. Sprinkle lightly with salt and set aside.

- Cut the avocados in half lengthwise, remove the pits, and peel (see tip). Cut the avocado halves lengthwise into thin slices. Sprinkle with lemon juice to prevent discoloration.

- Arrange the tomatoes so they just overlap in the center of the plate. Place the avocado slices in a fan shape outside the tomatoes.

- Separate the onion slices and sprinkle the pieces over the tomato slices.

- Whisk together the oil, vinegar, salt, and pepper. Lightly drizzle over the vegetables. Sprinkle with the cilantro and serve immediately.

- Serves 6-8.

To pit and peel an avocado, cut the unpeeled avocado in half by running a sharp knife lengthwise around the avocado, cutting all the way to the pit. Twist the halves in opposite directions to separate. To remove the pit, give the pit a quick chop in the center with the wide end of a sharp chef's knife, planting the blade in the pit. Twist sharply and lift to extract the pit. (Carefully remove the pit from the knife blade.) To peel, slide a large oval-shaped serving spoon between the peel and the avocado, scooping the avocado half out of the peel. To slice or cube the peeled halves place flat side down, on a cutting board.

Roasted Vegetable Salad

"Never dilute flavor; always add or intensify flavor." I quote myself with a quote my students and radio listeners will recognize. Roasting vegetables is a good example. Boiling or even steaming adds moisture and doesn't intensify flavor. Roasting not only reduces the natural moisture and intensifies the flavor, but also caramelizes the natural sugars so the vegetables are filled with flavor. Roasted vegetables are delicious hot off the grill or out of the oven, but they also taste great at room temperature. For a flavor variation, top with crumbled fresh goat cheese instead of the Parmigiano-Reggiano.

1 fennel bulb
2 small heads radicchio
3 to 4 small zucchini
3 to 4 small summer squash
2 medium red onions
1/3 cup extravirgin olive oil
2 tsp. coarse sea salt
1/4 cup chopped flat-leaf parsley
1/4 cup finely shredded fresh basil
3 tbsp. balsamic vinegar
1/4 tsp. freshly ground black pepper
1 clove garlic, finely chopped
1 tsp. brown sugar
1 head Romaine lettuce, washed, dried, and
    crisped
6 oz. Parmigiano-Reggiano
Parsley sprigs, for garnish

- Trim and slice the fennel bulb into 1/4" lengthwise strips.

- Cut the radicchio into wedges.

- Slice the zucchini and summer squash in half crosswise and then slice lengthwise.

- Cut the onions in half lengthwise and into 1/4" slices.

- Toss the vegetables with 2 tbsp. of the oil and the sea salt. Spread into a single layer on a baking sheet and roast in a preheated 450-degree oven for 12 minutes. Stir once. Remove and cool.

- Sprinkle with the parsley and basil.

Before storing salad greens and fresh leafy herbs, submerge in a sink of cool water. Soak for a few minutes to allow the grit to wash off and go to the bottom. Lift out the greens and spin dry in a salad spinner or dry with soft white paper towels. Place in a plastic bag with 1 or 2 soft white paper towels. The towels will absorb excess moisture and help keep the greens fresh and crisp. Seal the bag and store in the refrigerator crisper drawer. Allow the greens to chill thoroughly before adding them to a salad.

- Whisk together the remaining oil with the vinegar, pepper, garlic, and sugar. Toss the vegetables with the dressing.
- Shred the Romaine and put on a platter. Top with the vegetable mixture.
- Cut the cheese into shards with a Parmesan knife. Top with shards of the cheese and garnish with parsley sprigs.
- Serves 6-8.

Mushroom, Fennel, and Parmesan Salad with Balsamic Vinaigrette

For several years now I have escorted a more or less constant group of students and friends on culinary adventures. (My husband refers to us on these jaunts as "Marilyn and the Gastronauts.") For the past few years our destination has been some interesting corner of Europe. A favorite was a trip to the Emilia Romagna region of Italy, where we ate more than our share of Parmigiano-Reggiano and where I first ate this salad.

The secret of this salad is to slice mushrooms and fennel as thinly as possible. The very thin setting on a mandolin (or a similar slicer) can be used to shave off paper-thin slices. If you have the very thin slicing disc (1 mm) as an extra accessory to your food processor it can be used. You can also use the same thin slicer or food processor blade to shave the cheese into thin slivers. Be sure to choose very fresh, snow-white, and firm mushrooms for this salad and use only the real cheese.

> **1 lb. medium white mushrooms**
> **2 medium to large fennel bulbs**
> **6 oz. Parmigiano-Reggiano**
> **¼ cup extravirgin olive oil**
> **¼ cup good balsamic vinegar**
> **Salt and freshly ground black pepper, to taste**

- Wash and dry the mushrooms. Slice crosswise into very thin slices.
- Wash and trim the fennel bulbs. Slice crosswise into very thin slices.
- Shave the cheese into slivers.

Balsamic vinegar, a dark, aged-in-wood vinegar made in Italy from grape juice, adds a rich flavor to many salad dressings and marinades. The authentic artisan "Aceto Balsamico" or "Tradizionale" is always made in Modena and aged at least 12 years. This vinegar is far too precious to use for dressings or marinades. It is literally served by the drop to add flavor to sauces or on top of a shard of Parmigiano-Reggiano as an appetizer. For salad dressings, look for imported commercial aceto balsamico that has been aged at least 6 years—but the longer the better. The good ones all come from Modena and investing a few dollars extra pays off in extra flavor in your food.

- Whisk together the oil and vinegar. Gently toss the vegetables and cheese with the dressing. Season to taste with salt and pepper. Serve immediately as an appetizer or side salad.
- Serves 8-10.

Mushrooms used in salads should be very fresh and firm and without blemishes. A sign of freshness is a cap that is tightly sealed on the bottom. If the cap is separated from the stem, revealing the brown "gills" on the underside of the mushroom, it is not fresh enough to use in a salad.

Never soak mushrooms in water. They can quickly become waterlogged. The correct method is to hold them, one or two at a time, under a steady stream of lukewarm water, using your fingertips to quickly and gently rub away any grit or dirt. Trim the end of the stem after washing to prevent excessive absorption of water. Place on soft paper towels or a dishtowel to dry before slicing.

Corn Salad

One of my favorite picnic salads, taken from a class menu on that subject, this crunchy corn salad should be made when you can buy the best summer corn from the market. It is very practical to make for outdoor dining because it doesn't have to be kept well chilled like so many salads. An alternative method is to roast the whole ears of corn on the grill, cool, then cut the kernels from the cobs.

6 ears corn
2 tbsp. extravirgin olive oil
2 tbsp. fresh lime juice
1 tsp. Dijon mustard
½ tsp. sugar
1 tsp. salt
¼ tsp. cayenne pepper
1 cup seeded and diced tomato
½ cup chopped green onions
2 tbsp. chopped cilantro
2 to 3 heads Bibb lettuce

- Cut corn from cobs. Place corn on a sheet pan and toss with 1 tbsp. oil. Roast in a preheated 425-degree oven for 20 minutes. Stir several times. Let cool.

Coarse-textured and crisp lettuces such as iceberg, Romaine, Belgian endive, and radicchio look prettier and taste best when shredded with a sharp knife. Tender, delicate leaf lettuces such as Bibb and Boston are always torn into bite-sized pieces for a tossed salad.

- In a large bowl, whisk together the remaining oil with the lime juice, mustard, sugar, salt, and pepper. Toss in the corn and remaining ingredients, except the lettuce. Pile onto Bibb lettuce leaves and serve.

- Serves 4 to 6.

My Best Green Bean Salad

The little French green bean haricot vert *is another favorite at my house and I love this salad made with those delicate little beans. I know they are not always available in this country. Some of my gardening friends grow them in their kitchen gardens. If you don't have such innovative gardening friends or a gourmet vegetable source, just choose the smallest and greenest beans you can find. With any decent green bean this is truly an outstanding salad. It is the perfect accompaniment for fish, chicken, or any type of chop or steak from the grill.*

> **3 cups water**
> **1 tbsp. salt**
> **2 lb. young tender green beans, washed and**
>   **ends trimmed**
> **1 pt. cherry tomatoes**
> **1 tsp. fine sea salt**
> **1 medium red Spanish onion, halved and very**
>   **thinly sliced**
> **1 cup pitted kalamata olives, cut in half**
> **2 tbsp. chopped fresh dill**
> **Crisp lettuce leaves**
> **Classic Vinaigrette Dressing (with balsamic**
>   **vinegar)**

- Bring water to a boil. Salt with 1 tbsp. salt. Add the green beans and cook 5 to 7 minutes or until "crisp tender." (Cooking time will depend on size of beans.)

- Drain and immediately refresh in ice water. Drain well and place in a large bowl. Chill until ready to complete the salad.

- Cut the tomatoes in half and toss with 1 tsp. salt.

- Cover the sliced onion with ice water and allow to sit for 30 minutes. Drain well and pat lightly with some soft paper towel to dry.

Soaking sliced onion in ice water not only makes it crisper, but gives it a milder, sweeter flavor. Drain well on towels before adding to a salad.

- Toss the beans, olives, and onion slices with the dill.
- Line a shallow bowl with the lettuce leaves. Chill.
- Just before serving time, toss the bean salad in the dressing. Pile the bean salad onto the lettuce leaves and arrange the tomatoes around the edge of the beans. Serve immediately.
- Serves 8.

Winter Salad

Matthew Shapiro, an actor with aspirations and a truly good friend, first showed an interest in helping me in the kitchen when he was barely tall enough to reach the countertop without standing on a stool. In his teen years he loved coming to my cooking classes and even assisted me a couple of times. Now that he is all grown up with lots of other interests and talents, he is also a creative amateur chef. Matthew says he created this salad one cold day when he needed to clean out the refrigerator vegetable bin.

> **2 cups finely shredded cabbage**
> **½ cup sliced celery**
> **1 cup shredded carrots**
> **¼ cup extravirgin olive oil**
> **2 tbsp. balsamic vinegar**
> **1 tbsp. soy sauce**
> **½ tsp. coarsely ground black pepper, or to taste**
> **½ cup grated Romano cheese**
> **1 cup finely shredded Swiss chard**
> **2 tbsp. chopped parsley**
> **¼ cup chopped walnuts (or toasted pine nuts)**
> **¼ cup sliced pitted kalamata or green olives**

- Toss together the cabbage, celery, and carrots.
- Combine the oil, vinegar, soy sauce, pepper, and cheese and toss into the salad. Chill, covered, for 30 minutes.
- Toss with the shredded chard and parsley. Top with the nuts and olives.
- Serves 6.

Berry Green Salad

This is another winning recipe from my friend and student Mary Triebwasser. One secret of this salad's success is to make sure the spinach is as dry as possible.

Don't wash strawberries until you are ready to use them. Rinse them quickly under a steady stream of water. Remove caps and stems after they are so cleaned.

1 lb. fresh spinach
1 pt. strawberries

- Stem and wash the spinach. Dry thoroughly and chill.
- Wash the strawberries. Remove caps and stems and cut berries in half (quarters if they are very large). Place in a bowl. Chill until ready to toss with the dressing.
- Serves 4-6.

Dressing

¼ **cup sugar**
2 tbsp. poppy seeds
1½ tsp. finely chopped onion
¼ **tsp. Worcestershire sauce**
¼ **tsp. paprika**
1 cup salad oil
¼ **cup cider vinegar**

- Put first 5 ingredients into the food processor. With motor running, add oil and vinegar slowly. Blend until well blended.
- Toss with spinach and strawberries and serve.

Refrigerator Crock Slaw

Nancy Pigg and I became great pals while working together at the Cooks'Wares Cooking School, where she serves as director and I often teach cooking classes. Nancy has also taught classes for years on using the food processor and has lots of great recipes that are so easily made using that magic kitchen machine. This is one that will come in handy. Definitely a make-ahead recipe: "the longer it sits the better it gets," says Nancy.

1 medium head cabbage, washed and trimmed
2 carrots, peeled
1 green pepper, cored
1 red pepper, cored
1 medium sweet salad onion
2 tsp. celery seed
1 tbsp. salt
Water to cover
½ cup cider vinegar
½ cup red or white wine vinegar
1 cup raspberry vinegar
1½ cups sugar

- With 1-mm disc in food processor, slice cabbage.

- With 3" x 3" square julienne disc, process carrots.

- With 2- or 3-mm disc, slice remaining vegetables into long strips.

- Add celery seed and soak in salted water for 2 hours.

- Drain well.

- Mix vinegars and sugar and pour over vegetables. Place in a covered container and refrigerate.

- Serves 8.

THE MARILYN HARRIS COOKING SCHOOL COOKBOOK

Belgian Endive with Sliced Crisp Apples, Toasted Walnuts, and Bleu Cheese with Walnut Oil Vinaigrette

This salad that will add color and texture to your meal. It is an excellent choice for a fall or winter meal, tasting great alongside ham or roasted pork or chicken.

2 large crisp red apples
Juice of 1 lemon
Green salad leaves (leaf or Bibb lettuce), washed and crisped
Walnut Oil Vinaigrette
5 or 6 heads Belgian endive, washed, trimmed, and chilled
1 cup walnut halves, toasted 7-8 minutes at 350 degrees and cooled
6 oz. good bleu cheese, crumbled
Watercress sprigs

- Core and slice the apples into thin slices. Acidulate with lemon juice.

- Line salad plates with the lettuce leaves. Make the vinaigrette according to the following recipe. Slice the endive into ¼" rounds and toss with just enough dressing to coat.

- Mound a large spoonful on the lettuce leaves. Surround with apple slices. Top with walnuts and bleu cheese. Garnish with watercress sprigs and serve immediately.

- Serves 6.

Walnut Oil Vinaigrette

½ **cup walnut oil**
¼ **cup sherry vinegar or raspberry vinegar**
½ **tsp. salt**
¼ **tsp. cayenne pepper**
1 **tsp. brown sugar**

- Whisk together.

Toss apples or pears with equal parts of lemon or lime juice and water so that they don't turn brown in a salad. If a dressing containing citrus is used, toss a bit of it on the fruit as soon as it is peeled. Toss later with the remainder of the salad ingredients.

Store Belgian endive away from light so it stays white. Too much light and the tips will start to turn green.

Store walnut oil and all other cold-pressed nut oils in the refrigerator. Use within 2 to 3 months.

Luscious Lentil Salad

This vegetarian salad is versatile enough to fit into most any menu and practical because it can remain unrefrigerated for some time and still taste good. Make this salad with ordinary brown lentils or dress it up further by choosing one of the more exotic and colorful varieties.

3 cups cooked and drained lentils
½ cup chopped sweet salad onion
1 medium cucumber, peeled, seeded, and sliced
½ cup chopped cilantro (or parsley)
1 cup shredded carrots
1 cup diced red bell pepper
Salt, to taste
Italian Vinaigrette (see index)

- Toss together. Chill for 2 hours before serving.
- Serves 8-10.

For the crispest cucumbers, thinly slice peeled and seeded cucumbers and submerge them in ice water. Allow to sit in the refrigerator for at least 30 minutes. Drain well and quickly pat with some soft white paper towels before adding to a salad.

Black Bean and Corn Salad with Peppers

Black beans have a light texture as well as good flavor and interesting color, all of which makes them ideal to be eaten at room temperature or chilled. Combined with corn kernels and seasoned with chiles, this black bean salad has become a class favorite. Cook the beans and make this at least a day ahead. Add more flavor by grilling the corn on the grill. Canned black beans may be substituted. Use 2 16-oz. cans, drained and rinsed.

1 lb. dried black beans
4 tsp. salt
6 ears fresh corn
Olive or vegetable oil
3 mild green chile peppers
1 red bell pepper
2 large fresh jalapeño peppers, finely chopped
1 pt. cherry tomatoes
1 head leaf lettuce

Canned mild green chiles (chopped or whole) or canned roasted red peppers can be substituted for roasted fresh peppers when fresh ones are not available.

6 green onions, thinly sliced
½ cup extravirgin olive oil
3 tbsp. red wine vinegar
1 clove garlic, finely chopped
1 tbsp. Dijon mustard
1 tsp. freshly ground pepper
Parsley sprigs, for garnish

- Soak the beans: cover with 2 to 3" water in a saucepan covered with a lid. Boil on high for 5 minutes, remove from heat, and allow to sit, covered, for 1 hour. Drain and rinse.
- Return to rinsed-out pan and cover with 2 to 3" water. Add 2 tsp. of the salt and simmer on low, partially covered, for 40-45 minutes or until tender. Drain and set aside.
- Brush the corn with olive or vegetable oil. Place on a baking sheet and roast in a preheated 450-degree oven for 18 to 20 minutes. Remove, cool, and cut kernels from the cobs.
- Roast and peel the mild green chiles and red bell pepper. Cut into small strips.
- Cut the tomatoes in half. Sprinkle with 1 tsp. of the salt and lightly toss.
- Wash and dry the lettuce. Chill until ready to serve.
- Toss together the beans, corn, peppers, tomatoes, and green onions.
- Make the dressing: whisk together the olive oil, vinegar, garlic, mustard, remaining tsp. of salt, and pepper. Taste and correct the seasonings. Toss the dressing into the bean mixture.
- Line a platter (or individual plates) with the crisp lettuce leaves. Spoon the salad on top to serve. Garnish with parsley sprigs.
- Serves 8.

Cherry tomatoes must always be cut in half before adding them to a salad. For the best flavor, lightly salt them and allow to sit at room temperature until ready to go into the salad.

An interesting tossed green salad should have at least 3 different greens with different textures and colors (examples: torn Bibb lettuce leaves, shredded Romaine lettuce, and whole baby spinach leaves).

Potato Salad Deluxe

As much as I love a good potato salad, I hate the hassle of boiling, peeling, and cubing potatoes. Starting with raw sliced potatoes as in this recipe makes it quicker, easier, and tastier. I have shared it with many of my students, who have switched to this method, too.

> **2 lb. small red-skinned potatoes**
> **1 cup chicken stock (may use canned)**
> **½ cup cider vinegar**
> **2 large red bell peppers**
> **⅓ cup extravirgin olive oil**
> **2 tsp. fine sea salt**
> **1 tsp. freshly ground black pepper**
> **1 large red Spanish onion, thinly sliced (or sweet salad onion)**
> **⅓ cup chopped flat-leaf parsley**
> **⅓ cup fresh basil, cut into strips**
> **Whole basil leaves, for garnish**

- Slice the potatoes into ¼" slices. Place in a steamer and steam for 7 to 8 minutes or until just fork tender.

- Meanwhile, in a large bowl, stir together the chicken stock and vinegar. Pour in the hot steamed potatoes. Toss lightly and allow to cool. Drain.

- Roast the bell peppers. Cut the peeled and seeded peppers into small strips and toss with the oil, salt, and pepper. Lightly toss together the potatoes, pepper strips, onions, parsley, and chopped basil. Garnish with the whole basil leaves.

- Serves 8-10.

Summer Couscous

There is not a better dish to take to a picnic than this versatile salad. It goes with everything and you don't have to worry about keeping it perfectly chilled.

4 cups chicken broth
1 clove garlic, finely chopped
¼ cup plus 2 tbsp. extravirgin olive oil
¼ tsp. turmeric
¼ tsp. cinnamon
1 tsp. finely chopped gingerroot
2 cups couscous
½ cup dark raisins
½ cup golden raisins
2 small zucchini, shredded
1 cup shredded carrots
½ cup chopped sweet salad onion
2 large tomatoes, seeded and chopped
2 tbsp. fresh lemon juice
1 tsp. salt, or to taste
¼ tsp. freshly ground black pepper
¼ cup chopped flat-leaf parsley

- In a large pan bring the broth, garlic, ¼ cup oil, turmeric, cinnamon, and ginger to a boil. Gradually stir in the couscous. Boil another 1 to 2 minutes. Cover and remove from heat. Let stand 15 minutes.

- Transfer to a large bowl and toss in the raisins, zucchini, carrots, onion, and tomatoes.

- In a small bowl whisk together the remaining 2 tbsp. oil, lemon juice, salt, and pepper. Toss into the couscous mixture and top with chopped parsley. Chill until ready to serve.

- Serves 8-10.

Piquant Egg Salad

This is a good addition to a mixed salad buffet or a group of salads served on crisp lettuce leaves for a summer salad plate.

12 large hard-cooked eggs, peeled
⅔ cup mayonnaise
1 tsp. green-peppercorn Dijon mustard
2 tbsp. finely chopped fresh parsley
½ tsp. dried dill (1½ tsp. fresh)
¾ tsp. salt

• Chop eggs. Mix in remaining ingredients. Chill.
• Serves 8.

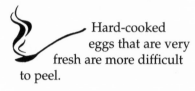

To hard-cook large eggs, place the eggs in a saucepan with a tight-fitting lid. Add cold water to cover by about 2". Cover and bring to a rolling boil. Reduce to low and simmer for 10 minutes. Refresh immediately in cold running water.

Hard-cooked eggs that are very fresh are more difficult to peel.

Tomatoes Stuffed with Southern Shrimp Salad

When I lived in New Orleans I learned to appreciate shrimp no matter how it was cooked, but a ladies' lunch in an elegant restaurant always called for a luscious shrimp salad. This is my favorite presentation. Of course, the real secret for making the perfect shrimp salad is great-tasting shrimp. See index for Boiled Shrimp, which gives directions for boiling shrimp that turn out tender and flavorful. Crabmeat or lobster may be substituted in this recipe.

8 large ripe but firm tomatoes
2 lb. peeled and deveined boiled shrimp
2 cups finely chopped celery
2 tbsp. finely chopped sweet salad onion
¼ cup chopped fresh parsley
2 tbsp. chopped fresh dill
1 cup mayonnaise
½ cup bottled chile sauce
½ tsp. hot pepper sauce
1 tbsp. fresh lemon juice
½ tsp. salt
Parsley sprigs and lemon slices, for garnish

- Turn the tomatoes stem side down. Using a small, sharp knife, make 5 deep wedge cuts, keeping the tomato intact. Carefully spread the wedges outward.
- Scoop out some of the center pulp. Turn the tomatoes upside down on a paper-towel-lined tray to drain.
- Make the shrimp salad by coarsely chopping the shrimp and tossing with the celery, onion, parsley, and dill.
- Stir together the mayonnaise, chile sauce, hot pepper sauce, and lemon juice. Add the salt. Toss the dressing into the shrimp mixture. Chill until ready to serve.
- Spoon the shrimp into the tomatoes. Place the tomatoes on a lettuce-lined salad plate. Garnish with parsley sprigs and lemon slices.
- Serves 8.

Curried Chicken-Fruit Salad

Feature this at a summer lunch or put it on the buffet for a casual dinner party. It is a pretty dish so packed full of wonderful flavors. Use this method of cooking chicken for all of your chicken salads. It is quick and easy and you have all moist and flavorful white meat for your elegant salad.

6 skinless, boneless chicken breast halves
2 cups chicken broth
1 cup white wine
2 tsp. curry powder
2 cloves garlic, peeled and crushed
1 tsp. salt
1 tsp. hot pepper sauce
1 cantaloupe, peeled and diced
1 cup red seedless grapes, halved
1 cup green seedless grapes, halved
1 cup diced celery
1 cup mayonnaise
$\frac{1}{2}$ cup sour cream
2 tbsp. fresh lemon juice
Leaves from 1 head leaf lettuce, washed, dried, and chilled
$\frac{1}{2}$ cup toasted slivered almonds
Mint sprigs, for garnish

- Wash, dry, and trim the chicken. Place between two sheets of plastic wrap and pound to flatten to a consistent thickness.
- In a large nonreactive skillet, combine the chicken broth, wine, 1 tsp. of the curry powder, garlic, salt, and hot pepper sauce. Bring to a boil over high heat. Add the chicken in a single layer. Cover with parchment and the skillet lid.
- Reduce to low and simmer for 12 to 15 minutes or until done through. Cool 5 minutes in the poaching liquid and remove. Cool the chicken and cut, across the grain, into small strips. Turn the stock to high and reduce by two-thirds. Strain and chill.
- Toss the fruit and celery with the chicken.
- To make the dressing, whisk together the mayonnaise, sour cream, 1/4 cup of the reserved liquid, the remaining curry powder, and lemon juice. Toss into the fruit-chicken mixture to mix well. Pile the chicken on a bed of crisp lettuce leaves and sprinkle with the almonds. Garnish with mint sprigs. Serve immediately.
- Serves 8.

Marilyn's Chicken Salad

Here is another chicken salad made with poached chicken breasts. I invented this one when asked to plan a menu for a charity lunch. I've since shared it with many students and friends. It is a rather hearty salad—certainly all you need for a meal.

> 8 skinless, boneless chicken breast halves
> 2 cups chicken stock
> 1/2 cup dry white wine
> 2 large cloves garlic, peeled and lightly crushed
> 1 bay leaf
> 1 tsp. salt
> 1/4 tsp. hot pepper sauce
> 2 cups small broccoli florets
> 1 cup mayonnaise
> 2 tbsp. chopped parsley
> 1 tbsp. chopped fresh basil (1 tsp. dried)
> 1/2 tsp. salt

¼ tsp. hot pepper sauce
1 tbsp. fresh lemon juice
2 red bell peppers, cut into small julienne strips
1 cup sliced black olives
Crisp lettuce leaves
1 cup halved cherry tomatoes (salted to taste)
Parsley sprigs

- Wash, dry, and trim chicken. Place between two sheets of plastic wrap and pound to a consistent thickness.

- In a large skillet over medium heat, heat together the stock, wine, garlic, bay leaf, 1 tsp. salt, and ¼ tsp. hot pepper sauce. Add the chicken breasts, cover with parchment, reduce to low, and simmer 10 minutes or just until cooked through. Remove chicken to a side dish, cover and cool. Cut into cubes and chill until ready to use. Strain the poaching liquid and return to pan. Reduce by two-thirds.

- In a saucepan boil 1 qt. water. Add 1 tbsp. salt and add the broccoli florets. Blanch for only 1 minute.

- Drain immediately and refresh with cold water. Drain well. Pat dry on paper towels and chill until ready to add to the salad.

- To make dressing, stir together the mayonnaise and parsley, basil, salt, hot pepper sauce, and lemon juice. Add 2 tbsp. of the reduced poaching liquid.

- Combine the chicken pieces, broccoli, bell pepper strips, and olives. Toss in the dressing. Pile onto lettuce leaves and garnish with the halved cherry tomatoes. Top with parsley sprigs.

- Serves 8.

Broccoli and cauliflower should never be served raw. Blanch for 30 seconds to 1 minute in lightly salted, rapidly boiling water. Plunge immediately into ice water. Drain well. The vegetables look prettier, taste better, and can stay fresh longer in the refrigerator.

Steak and Potato Salad

This hearty main-dish salad is simple to make. It uses the same recipe for both marinade and dressing. If you want a more elegant salad to serve to company, substitute tenderloin of beef instead of sirloin steak. The sirloin is best marinated overnight or all day, but the tenderloin can be cut into ½" slices and needs only a couple of hours to be infused with the marinade flavors.

4 to 5 cloves roasted garlic
¾ cup extravirgin olive oil
¼ cup red wine vinegar
1 tbsp. Dijon mustard
1 tsp. chopped fresh rosemary leaves
1 tbsp. fine sea salt
1 tsp. freshly ground black pepper
1 tsp. brown sugar
1½ lb. boneless sirloin or flank steak
2 lb. small red potatoes
Cold water
2 tbsp. salt
1 red bell pepper
1 yellow bell pepper
1 medium sweet salad onion
8 oz. medium to large white mushrooms
1 tbsp. fresh lemon juice
¼ cup chopped flat-leaf parsley
1 cup halved cherry tomatoes

- Mash the roasted garlic cloves and add to the oil. Add vinegar, mustard, rosemary, salt, pepper, and sugar and whisk until well blended. (Or blend in the blender or food processor.)

- Place the steak in a plastic bag and pour in ⅓ of the marinade. Seal the bag and refrigerate 8 to 24 hours.

- To assemble the salad: scrub the potatoes. Cover with cold water seasoned with salt and bring to a boil. Cook for about 20 minutes or until fork tender. Drain, cool, and cut into quarters. Toss with half of the remaining marinade/dressing.

- Cut the peppers into small strips and slice the onion into thin slices. Chill. Wash, dry, and thinly slice the mushrooms. Toss with the lemon juice to coat.

Garlic is fresh when the several layers of thin peeling are intact around the cloves—very tight, close together, and firm. It should be difficult to separate them. Loosely adjoined cloves indicate age. A purple tinge is good. Any visible green is bad.

For roasted garlic, cut the top off of a large, firm head of garlic to expose the tips of the cloves. Place, cut side up, on a small sheet of heavy-duty foil. Drizzle a bit of olive oil over the garlic and sprinkle the cut top with sea salt. Encase in the foil, crimping the top tightly. Place directly on the rack of a preheated 375-degree oven. Roast for 30 to 40 minutes (depending on size of garlic) or until softened. Cool and press out the roasted garlic cloves by pushing gently on the bottom. Wrap unused garlic in a clean piece of foil or plastic wrap and store in the refrigerator.

- Remove the steak from the marinade. Grill or broil to a medium doneness. Cut, across the grain, into small strips. (For flank steak cut across the grain on the diagonal.)
- Toss the potatoes, peppers, onion, mushrooms, and steak with the remaining dressing. Garnish with the parsley and tomato halves.
- Serves 6-8.

Grilled Pork Tenderloin Salad with Mango and Avocado

When time is short here's a fast and efficient way to marinate pork tenderloin. First, slice it thinly. In one short hour it is infused with flavor from the marinade and then it cooks in minutes. This is an elegant salad to serve your guests for a casual summer dinner party.

> 1½ to 2 lb. pork tenderloin
> ½ cup soy sauce
> ¼ cup water
> ¼ cup vegetable oil
> 2 tbsp. fresh lime juice
> 1 tsp. lime zest
> 3 tbsp. dark brown sugar
> 1 tbsp. finely chopped gingerroot
> 2 cloves garlic, finely chopped
> ¼ tsp. cayenne pepper
> 1 large head Romaine lettuce, washed, dried, and chilled
> 2 large avocados
> 2 mangos
> Tropical Dressing (see below)
> 6 scallions, finely chopped
> ½ cup slivered almonds, toasted

- Trim the pork. Slice into thin slices and place in a shallow dish or plastic bag. Mix together the soy sauce, water, oil, lime juice, lime zest, sugar, ginger, garlic, and cayenne and pour over the pork. Marinate 1 to 2 hours.
- Grill (or broil) over high heat for just 3 to 4 minutes on each side. Cool and cut into small strips. Cover and chill until ready to make the salad.

To toast slivered or sliced almonds spread them on a heavy sheet pan. Place in a preheated 350-degree oven for 6 to 8 minutes. Remove after 4 minutes and stir so the almonds on the edge don't get too brown.

Lukewarm water does the best job of washing grit from fresh vegetables and herbs. It is also more comfortable for your hands.

- Shred the Romaine and spread in a large shallow bowl or on a platter. Cut the avocados and mangos into slices. Arrange on the lettuce around the edges.
- Drizzle half of the dressing over the lettuce, avocados, and mangos. Toss the pork in the remaining dressing and place in the middle of the bowl. Sprinkle over the scallions and almonds and serve.
- Serves 6-8 as a main course.

Tropical Dressing

½ cup mayonnaise
¼ cup sour cream
2 tbsp. fresh lime juice
2 tbsp. fresh orange juice
3 tbsp. vegetable oil
2 tbsp. finely chopped sweet salad onion
¼ cup mango chutney, finely chopped
1 tbsp. finely chopped fresh jalapeño pepper
1 tsp. fine sea salt

- Whisk together.

Duck Pastrami with Frisée Salad and Huckleberry Vinaigrette

Sean Kagy, executive chef of the beautiful Palace Restaurant at the Cincinnatian Hotel in downtown Cincinnati, generously shared this recipe. It is one of many great dishes I've eaten prepared by this talented young chef. He made this for a luncheon for us when Julia Child was the honored guest.

3 tbsp. coriander seed
2 tbsp. cumin
2 tbsp. thyme
2 tbsp. cinnamon
2 tbsp. freshly grated nutmeg
2 tbsp. allspice
2 tbsp. black peppercorns
1 tbsp. kosher salt

1 tbsp. garlic powder
4 boneless duck breast halves, with skin on
Frisée Salad (see below)
Huckleberry Vinaigrette (see below)

- Allow 2 to 3 days to make the pastrami. Place the coriander, cumin, thyme, cinnamon, nutmeg, allspice, pepper, salt, and garlic powder in a blender and pulse until finely ground.
- Wash and pat the duck breasts dry, then roll them in the spices, making sure they are well covered. Place the duck breasts on a wire rack on a sheet tray and refrigerate for 2 to 3 days.
- Remove duck breasts from refrigerator and lightly cold smoke the duck breasts with apple wood chips for about 20 minutes until the internal temperature of the duck breasts is 115 degrees. Refrigerate until ready to serve.
- Toss the Frisée Salad lightly in most of the Huckleberry Vinaigrette and divide onto 4 plates.
- Slice the duck breast thinly and arrange in a fan shape around the salad. Drizzle with remaining vinaigrette.
- Serves 4.

Frisée Salad

1 head frisée
2 blood oranges

- Cut off the core of the frisée, rinse, drain, and set frisée aside.
- Cut the skin and white pith from the oranges. Using a knife with a small flexible blade, cut out the orange segments and toss them with the frisée.

Huckleberry Vinaigrette

1 tsp. Dijon mustard
¼ cup wine vinegar
½ cup huckleberries (fresh or frozen)
1 cup olive oil
Salt and freshly ground back pepper, to taste

- In a blender, purée the mustard, vinegar, and berries. While the blender is on low speed, slowly add the oil until emulsified. Season with salt and pepper to taste.

Note: raspberries may be substituted for the huckleberries.

Garlic-Herb Croutons

Make your own croutons. They add a good crunch to so many salads and soups. You can be practical and thrifty by using up all of that stale bread instead of pitching it out. Another benefit: they taste better than the ones you purchase in the supermarket.

>   **2 tbsp. butter**
>   **2 tbsp. extravirgin olive oil**
>   **1 tsp. dried thyme leaves**
>   **½ tsp. dried rosemary leaves**
>   **½ tsp. dried marjoram leaves**
>   **2 large cloves garlic, finely chopped**
>   **1 tsp. coarse sea salt**
>   **½ tsp. freshly ground black pepper**
>   **2 cups cubed French bread**

- Heat the butter and olive oil in a small heavy pan over medium heat. Crush the herb leaves to release the flavor and add. Add the garlic, salt, and pepper. Heat to bubbling—do not allow butter to brown. Allow to sit for 30 minutes.

- Pour the bread cubes into a mixing bowl. Pour over the oil mixture and toss with fingertips to coat evenly. Spread into a single layer on a baking sheet and place in a preheated 325-degree oven for 20 to 30 minutes or until golden and crisp. Stir a couple of times.

- Cool and store in a tightly covered container.

- Makes 2 cups.

Classic Vinaigrette

Any of my regular students would tell you that one of my favorite topics when atop my culinary soapbox is the ridiculousness of buying salad dressings in a bottle. For so many delicious dressings all you need is a bowl and a fork, some good oil, flavorful vinegar, and salt and pepper. After that you can be creative with the flavor by adding condiments, fresh herbs, etc., and create a dressing to your taste and one tailored to go on the salad you are making. To get you started I've got some of my own favorite dressings for you to try, along with a number of suggestions of how I like to use them.

You will find many interesting variations for this basic dressing. For example, use fruit vinegars such as raspberry or flavored oils such as basil or rosemary. There are some good citrus-flavored oils on the market to experiment with too. Make it with or without the garlic and toss it on all combinations of greens and veggies.

¾ **cup extravirgin olive oil**
3 to 4 tbsp. red or white wine vinegar
2 tsp. Dijon mustard
1 medium clove garlic, very finely minced
1 tsp. fine sea salt
½ **tsp. freshly ground black pepper**
1 tsp. sugar (optional)

- Whisk together.
- Makes about 1 cup.

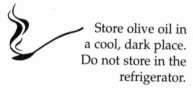

Store olive oil in a cool, dark place. Do not store in the refrigerator.

Italian Vinaigrette

¾ **cup extravirgin olive oil**
3 to 4 tbsp. balsamic vinegar
2 tsp. Dijon mustard
1 medium clove garlic, very finely minced
1 tsp. dried oregano
1 tsp. dried basil (1 tbsp. chopped fresh basil)
1 tsp. fine sea salt
½ **tsp. freshly ground black pepper**
1 tsp. sugar (optional)

- Whisk together. Let stand at least 1 hour, at room temperature, before using. This is delicious on potatoes for an instant potato salad, or drizzle it over cold poached chicken or salmon on a bed of shredded greens.
- Makes about 1 cup.

Shallot and Herb Dressing

2 medium shallots, peeled and finely chopped
$\frac{1}{2}$ cup dry white wine
$\frac{1}{4}$ cup white wine vinegar
1 cup mayonnaise
$\frac{1}{4}$ cup chopped fresh parsley
3 tbsp. chopped fresh tarragon
$\frac{1}{4}$ cup chopped fresh dill
$\frac{1}{4}$ tsp. hot pepper sauce
1 tsp. Dijon mustard

- In a small nonreactive saucepan, boil together the shallots, wine, and vinegar until the liquid is reduced to $\frac{1}{4}$ cup. Remove from heat and cool.

- Whisk the shallot mixture into the mayonnaise. Stir in the remaining ingredients. Cover and chill until ready to serve.

- Makes about $1\frac{1}{4}$ cups.

Celery Seed Dressing

This is a favorite for fresh fruit. It is also good on spinach salad: toss some crisp spinach leaves with toasted slivered almonds, thinly sliced sweet onion, and this dressing.

$\frac{3}{4}$ cup peanut oil
3 tbsp. fresh lime juice
$\frac{1}{3}$ cup sugar
1 tsp. Dijon mustard
$\frac{1}{2}$ tsp. salt
1 tsp. paprika
Dash cayenne pepper
2 tsp. celery seed

- Blend thoroughly in a blender or food processor.

- Makes about 1 cup.

The best way to peel fresh ginger-root is to simply scrape with an ordinary teaspoon. Scrape rapidly using a light touch so that only the thin brown peel is removed. It is quick and easy and leaves more usable gingerroot than peeling it with a knife.

Grapes must be cut in half, lengthwise, before putting them into a salad.

Mango-Ginger Cream Dressing

This is a great creamy dressing for fruit, especially good on melon. Use this dressing to make a chicken salad with grapes in it or use smoked turkey or pheasant instead of chicken.

1 cup mayonnaise
¼ cup sour cream or plain yogurt
2 tsp. finely chopped orange peel
1 tbsp. fresh orange juice
1 tsp. grated gingerroot
¼ cup finely chopped mango chutney (Major Grey's®)
¼ tsp. salt
¼ tsp. hot pepper sauce

• Stir together. Cover and chill.
• Makes about 1½ cups.

Tangy French Dressing

This very tasty red French dressing has New Orleans roots. Place 2 or 3 varieties of sliced tomatoes (red, yellow, etc.) on a bed of finely shredded iceberg and drizzle over this dressing. Use it to dress a grilled chicken salad. Fold in ½ cup of crumbled Roquefort or Gorgonzola and serve it over chilled sliced roast beef or turkey on a bed of greens. Crunchy Belgian endive cut into julienne strips and tossed with the bleu cheese version is a real treat too. Finally, use it on any chef salad, with or without the cheese.

¼ cup white wine or cider vinegar
3 tbsp. dark brown sugar
1 tsp. salt
¼ tsp. cayenne pepper
2 tsp. horseradish mustard
½ cup coarsely chopped scallions
¼ cup coarsely chopped flat-leaf parsley
½ cup chile sauce
¾ cup vegetable oil

- In a blender or food processor, blend together all ingredients until well mixed.
- Makes about 1½ cups.

Note: to make a Creamy French Dressing, omit ¼ cup of the oil and add ¼ cup mayonnaise.

Bleu Cheese Dressing

Vary the flavor of this indulgent dressing according to the type of bleu cheese you add. Roquefort, Gorgonzola, Maytag Bleu, and Stilton are all good choices. Lighten it a bit by using reduced-fat sour cream, but please not the fat-free kind. This is good tossed with crisp greens such as Romaine, frisée, or endive. It is also good on spinach with sliced hard-cooked eggs and bacon, or on any salad that calls for a classic bleu cheese dressing.

1 cup mayonnaise
2 cups sour cream
2 tbsp. fresh lemon juice
1 clove garlic, finely chopped
¼ tsp. hot pepper sauce
8 oz. Roquefort (or other bleu cheese), crumbled

- Stir together the mayonnaise, sour cream, lemon juice, garlic, and hot pepper sauce. Whisk in the cheese until mixture is smooth but some pieces of cheese remain. Cover and chill until ready to serve.
- Makes 3 cups.

Note: making a salad dressing containing sour cream or yogurt in the food processor or blender is usually not a good idea. Too much processing will cause the sour cream or yogurt to liquefy and the dressing will be too thin.

Store garlic and cooking onions in a cool, dry place away from bright sunlight. Never store in the refrigerator or in a plastic bag. The exception is the sweet salad onion varieties. They have a higher water content, making them crisper and sweeter. I like to store them in the refrigerator crisper drawer. Place them on paper towels to absorb excess moisture and don't allow them to touch.

To peel a clove of garlic, place it, flat side down, on a cutting board. Place the wide end of a chef's knife on top and firmly hit the knife with the heel of your hand. The hard rap on the garlic clove will break and loosen the skin, making it peel away easily.

Green Goddess Dressing

Try this tossed with some boiled shrimp and chopped celery on a bed of greens. Chicken and turkey go well with this. Use it for potato or pasta salad. If you don't like anchovies simply leave out the anchovy paste.

> 1 cup mayonnaise
> 1 cup sour cream
> ¼ cup finely chopped scallions
> ¼ cup finely chopped flat-leaf parsley
> 1 tsp. Dijon mustard
> 1 tsp. anchovy paste (optional)
> 2 tbsp. fresh lemon juice
> Salt and hot pepper sauce, to taste

- Stir together with a whisk until mixture is smooth. Cover and chill until ready to serve.
- Makes 2½ cups.

Guacamole Dressing

This is the perfect choice for any Mexican-style salad, such as the popular taco salad with chicken or ground beef. Pour it over chilled shrimp, crab, or lobster. Drizzle over fresh tomatoes on a bed of shredded crisp lettuce. Put it on a burger or a BLT.

> 2 avocados, peeled and sliced
> Small wedge sweet salad onion
> ⅔ cup mayonnaise
> Dash hot pepper sauce
> ½ tsp. salt
> 2 tbsp. fresh lime juice
> 1 medium tomato, peeled, seeded, and chopped
> ½ cup sour cream

- Place all ingredients except tomato and sour cream in food processor. Blend together; stir in tomato and sour cream. Chill. (Return the avocado pit to the dressing to prevent darkening.)
- Makes 2½-3 cups.

A tossed salad should always be tossed with its dressing (rather than pouring it over the top). Toss as close to serving time as possible.

Don't overdress your salads. Too much dressing will spoil the taste and texture of the other ingredients. Use just enough dressing in a tossed salad to lightly coat each leaf.

Pasta and Risotto

Homemade Pasta

Cheese Cannelloni
with Pink Sauce

Homemade Spinach-
Ricotta Ravioli
with Tomato Sauce

Fettuccine
with Porcini and
Prosciutto Sauce

Fettuccine
with Leeks, Carrots,
and Prosciutto

Fettuccine
with Spring Onions
and Asparagus

Pappardelle
with Elegant but
Easy Tomato Sauce

Rigatoni
with Roasted Vegetables

Rigatoni
with Roasted Garlic and
Toasted Walnut Sauce

Penne
with Veal Sauce

Spaghetti Puttanesca

Spaghetti
with Shrimp and
Green Olives

Spaghetti and Meatballs

Linguini in Herb Sauce

Grilled Eggplant Lasagna

Tomato-Basil Risotto

Three Mushroom Risotto

Risotto
with Roasted Radicchio
and Toasted Pine Nuts

I certainly don't claim to be one of the world's great experts on the topic of pasta or risotto, but I have been to Italy a number of times, where I ate more than my share of their fantastic food and then had great fun recreating those dishes back home in my kitchen. My favorite area of Italy is the region of Emilia Romagna, where you find the famous small cities of Parma and Reggio Emelia. I enjoyed my "culinary research" there as I ate my way through many fabulous meals and came back armed with much interesting and valuable information about their cuisines. I think that particular cuisine is so special is because of all of the fabulous food products that originate there: Italy's most famous cheese, Parmigiano-Reggiano; Parma ham or prosciutto, the famous dried ham cured to perfection; Balsamico or balsamic vinegar from the charming little city of Modena; and Italy's most revered mushroom, porcini, never cultivated but carefully harvested from the forest floor every autumn.

I've also had some fun and tasty times exploring in the equally famous culinary region of Tuscany. From elegant dinners in exquisite Florence restaurants to simple meals in trattorias in the countryside, I enjoyed every bite and every sip. Tuscany is, of course, famous for its olives, olive oil, and great wines, all natural resources that contribute to its culinary fame. I've had the opportunity to take some great cooking classes there as well as in Emilia Romagna. That's where I made my first homemade pasta. I have been making it ever since and passing along the recipes in my cooking classes.

These noodles called "pasta" are such a fabulous and versatile food, yet so simple. Pasta is only flour mixed with eggs or water. It's when you start reading menus and shopping in the delis and supermarkets that you begin to realize the scope of pastas available. It comes in so many different sizes, shapes, and colors. Then there are all the different ways it is prepared and served, with an infinite list of great sauces, some classic and others found only in one town or region. It is interesting to note that the kind of sauce determines how the pasta dish will taste and different sauces change character on different pasta shapes. It's all fun research. I look forward to going back and learning more. In the meantime, I hope you will enjoy some exploring of your own with a few of my favorite recipes that follow.

Of course in Italy pasta or risotto is always served by itself as a separate course. It is the second course in most meals, following a light appetizer course. If you plan your meal in this traditional fashion, serve just a modest portion for the pasta course. That should also apply to the subsequent course, which may comprise meat, poultry, or fish with some side vegetables. Both of these courses carry equal importance in an Italian meal, so concentrate your efforts on quality and good flavor as opposed to huge portions.

If you are serving American style and don't plan to have a multicourse Italian-style meal, you can simply serve any of the following dishes as the main course. Add a simple fresh salad and crusty bread to complete your meal.

The Pasta

The personality of a pasta dish may be determined by the sauce, but the soul of a pasta dish is in the pasta. A good Italian cook knows the proper sauce for each pasta and makes a great distinction between the factory-produced pasta and homemade. The biggest difference is usually that one is dried and the other is freshly made and usually cooked fresh. Of the two types of dried pasta, the most common is simply made of semolina flour and water. It is always produced in the pasta factory, where it is extruded into every shape, from thin tubes like spaghetti or spaghettini to thick rigatoni and more interesting designs such as farfalle or "bow ties." Shapes vary according to regions in Italy and some have different names in different areas. New shapes are still being invented. Because the semolina or hard winter-wheat flour is different in Italy and makes the best pasta in the world, I recommend buying only imported Italian pastas. There are a number of good brands available in specialty stores and supermarkets, but be sure to look for the "Made in Italy" label.

The second type of dried pasta is made from regular wheat flour and eggs and is simply a dried version of homemade pasta. It is available in the ribbon shapes like fettuccine, linguini, and lasagna, the same as the shapes made in the home pasta machine.

Cooking Dry Pasta

Semolina Factory Pasta: It is not difficult to cook a perfect pot of pasta. It is as simple as boiling plenty of water in a large pot.

The right amount of salt is important too. That is so the pasta will taste good. For a pound of pasta bring 6 to 8 quarts of water to a rolling boil. Add 3 tablespoons of salt and return to the rapid boil. Add the pasta slowly and put the lid on the pot just until it returns to a boil. Remove the lid, reduce the heat, but maintain a constant boil. Warning: never put oil in the water. It coats the pasta so that the sauce will not adhere as well.

Texture is so important. Avoid overcooking the pasta. This type of pasta should be cooked until "al dente" or "to the tooth," which means the pasta should be firm but cooked through without a hard line in the center. For commercial pasta, always check the package directions for the cooking time. If it gives a variable (e.g., 9 to 11 minutes), I always cook it the lesser amount of time. Set a timer so that you can remove the pasta pot from the heat as soon as it is done. To stop the cooking action, toss in a handful of ice cubes.

Dried Egg Pasta: The same rules apply as for the heartier semolina pasta. The biggest difference will be the cooking time. Since this is a more delicate pasta it takes much less time to cook. It requires more time than fresh since it has to be hydrated from its dry state, but only a fraction of the time needed for the semolina pasta.

The Sauce

Pasta "sauce" can be as simple as some flavorful olive oil tossed with hot pasta with just a bit of salt, pepper, and cheese for extra flavor. It can also be as complex as a rich, creamy, wild-mushroom sauce. The type of sauce can depend somewhat on where you are in Italy, but even more so on the type and shape of the pasta.

The sauce must match the pasta. Heartier broad ribbon pasta calls for a heartier, more complex sauce than delicate ribbons of homemade linguini, which should be sauced just enough to add flavor. The robust macaroni shapes of semolina pasta can partner with chunky flavorful sauces while a delicate filled ravoli calls for a subtle napping of an elegant velvety cream sauce.

Pasta, except for the filled shapes and stacked noodles, should be always tossed with its sauce for maximum flavor distribution throughout the dish. Use just enough sauce to coat the pasta. Too much sauce is not an advantage and will only take away from the quality of your pasta dish.

Risotto

There are some important tips to know in order to make proper Italian risotto.

Begin by making a flavorful stock. It should be kept simmering in a pot next to your risotto pot. Ladle the hot stock into the rice as needed. The simmering temperature of the stock is important to keep the risotto at a constant cooking temperature.

Use a heavy pan to cook the risotto. (I like to use a porcelain-clad cast-iron pot.)

Start by coating the raw rice thoroughly with the oil (or butter), but do not allow to brown. Then start adding the hot stock, just enough to barely cover the rice. Stir almost constantly to prevent sticking and to create a creamy mixture.

A well-cooked risotto must be slightly "al dente." The rice grains are cooked but still firm and never mushy.

Add the cheese at the very end of the cooking time. For an even creamier risotto, stir a tablespoon or two of butter or oil (depending on which one is in the dish) into the cheese before vigorously stirring it into the cooked rice.

Risotto must be served as soon as possible after it is finished. It cannot be held at a warm temperature because it loses its firm texture and becomes mushy.

A single serving of risotto is spooned into a bowl and served as a course by itself in lieu of the pasta course.

The Cheese

Parmigiano-Reggiano is the cheese the great chefs of Italy choose to flavor so many of their pasta and rice dishes and you will see from my recipes that I can't cook without it. It is in everything in this chapter except those dishes that contain fish and seafood, where tradition dictates no cheese at all. The main reason I so strictly specify Parmigiano-Reggiano is simple: there is no substitute. Please don't use just any "Parmesan cheese" because the food simply won't taste as good. Equally important is the unique texture of Parmigiano-Reggiano. Eat a sliver of it and notice how it melts on your tongue like an expensive piece of chocolate, in spite of the fact that it is relatively low in fat. That is how it melts into a creamy risotto and coats a plate of steaming pasta. Always buy it in a piece and shred or grate it as needed for a recipe. Keep your cheese securely wrapped in plastic wrap for storage in the meat/cheese refrigerator drawer and it will keep for months. It also makes a delicious and nutritious snack and is great to serve as an appetizer—try it with a few drops of a good balsamic vinegar on top. Serve it, too, in cold dishes like salads.

Homemade Pasta

I learned to make fresh pasta the way that Italian cooks have traditionally done it for centuries. That is to spoon the flour into a mound on a board and make a well in the center of the mound for the eggs. The eggs are gradually worked into the flour with the fingertips. When all of the eggs are incorporated the mixture is thoroughly kneaded until it is a smooth, satiny mass of pasta dough. Having done all of this I prefer the ease and speed of making fresh pasta dough in the handy food processor. This is the basic recipe I use.

2 to 2¼ cups all-purpose flour
3 large eggs
Pasta machine

- Place 2 cups of flour in the food processor. With the machine running, add the eggs, one at a time. Process just until the mixture is moist. It should not form a ball but stay in loose separate small pieces that are easily pressed together when you hold a small amount between your thumb and forefinger. If mixture is too sticky or tends to form one mass, add more flour until the proper texture is achieved.

- Remove and knead for a few minutes to press the pasta into a ball. Flatten the ball and wrap in plastic wrap, sealing well. Set aside and allow to rest for 30 minutes. Now you are ready to roll it through the pasta machine.

- The only pasta machine I recommend to my students is the simple hand-cranked one that you clamp onto your countertop. Start with about one-quarter of the dough made from this recipe. Flatten the dough into a rectangle and flatten one edge, making it easier to start in the roller.

- Pasta machines have dials that start with 1 and usually go up to 7 or 8. Always start with the lowest setting and simply roll the dough through by turning the handle. After one roll through, increase the dial to the next highest number and continue to roll until you have achieved the desired thickness, usually to a minimum of 6 on the dial, but higher for some of the delicate "ribbon" pastas. Not only will the dough become thinner and larger in diameter, but it is also being kneaded during this rolling process and giving the pasta good texture. If the pasta sheet becomes too long to handle comfortably, cut it in half and work with a shorter sheet.

- All hand-cranked pasta machines have at least 2 cutting attachments: narrow ribbons for making linguini and wider ribbons for making fettuccine. You can purchase extra attachments for making the widest ribbon, pappardelle (which I use often), and for ravioli.

Cheese Cannelloni with Pink Sauce

I brought this recipe back from an unforgettable trip to Bologna with some of my favorite cooking students. The secret to perfect cannelloni is blanching the squares of pasta, then refreshing them in cold water so they don't overcook. They should be firm but have a cooked flavor before you fill and roll them. Finish this dish in the oven where the pasta is coated with a layer of delicious Pink Sauce. Look for the freshest ricotta cheese you can find to make this. I prefer the fresh block-style ricotta sold in bulk in Italian delis and specialty grocery stores to the one packed in cartons in the supermarket dairy case. The sauce is the flavor secret in this dish. It is so simple, yet so tasty. The base is a classic béchamel with added flavor from infusing the milk with onion, herbs, and pepper. The tomato sauce adds a light touch and the contrast of the two makes the delicious final flavor. This is a perfect made-ahead dish. Start a traditional Italian-style meal with one or two of these or simply serve with a green salad and some crusty Italian bread to make a complete meal.

Homemade Pasta
Filling (see below)
Simple Tomato Sauce (see below)
Béchamel Sauce (see below)
Grated Parmigiano-Reggiano, to taste

- Roll the freshly made pasta into sheets at #6 thickness on the pasta machine. Cut into squares approximately 5" in diameter. Dry the pasta on the countertop for a few minutes before cooking.
- Boil rapidly for 1 to 2 minutes in a large pot of salted boiling water (as described in "Cooking Dry Pasta" at the beginning of this chapter). Then place immediately into cold water with the same amount of salt as in the cooking water. Remove pasta and place on a dishtowel to dry both sides before spooning the filling in the center of each square.

The basis for béchamel sauce is a "white" roux (pronounced "rue") of a mixture of flour and butter (sometimes oil) that must be cooked for a full 2 minutes without browning. Insufficient cooking time will result in a raw flour taste and will affect the sauce texture. Use a pan with a heavy bottom so you can cook the roux long enough without browning and changing the color and flavor of the sauce.

- Place a big tablespoon of filling on each rectangle of pasta and spread in a horizontal line. Roll and place, seam side down, in a greased baking dish. Stir the Simple Tomato Sauce into the Béchamel Sauce and heat for a minute or two to make the Pink Sauce. Cover cannelloni with the Pink Sauce and sprinkle with a bit more Parmigiano-Reggiano.
- Bake in a preheated 400-degree oven for 15 to 20 minutes or until hot through and sauce is bubbly. Serve hot.
- Serves 16 as an appetizer, 8 as a main course.

Filling

1 lb. fresh ricotta cheese
6 oz. grated Parmigiano-Reggiano (1½ cups)
2 large eggs, beaten
¼ cup chopped flat-leaf parsley
Salt, pepper, and freshly grated nutmeg, to taste

- Mix together. Cover and chill until ready to use.

Simple Tomato Sauce

28-oz. can plum tomatoes, finely chopped (with juice)
4 tbsp. butter (½ stick)
1 bouquet garni composed of:
  2 sprigs thyme
  2 sprigs parsley and 2 sprigs rosemary
1 large onion, peeled and quartered
2 tsp. sea salt
¼ tsp. cayenne pepper

- Place the chopped tomatoes in a nonreactive saucepan. Add the butter, bouquet garni, and onion. Bring to a boil and simmer, uncovered, for 30 minutes. Remove the bouquet garni and onion. Season with salt and pepper.

Béchamel Sauce

2 cups milk
1 small onion, cut into fourths
3 sprigs thyme
3 sprigs flat-leaf parsley
1 tsp. black peppercorns
½ stick butter
4 tbsp. flour
1 tsp. salt

- Pour the milk into a small nonreactive saucepan. Add the onion, thyme, parsley, and peppercorns. Scald the milk. Remove from heat and allow to rest for 30 minutes. Strain and reheat before adding to the roux, below.
- Heat the butter in a heavy saucepan. Add the flour and cook over medium, stirring, for 2 minutes. Whisk in the heated milk and cook, stirring, until the mixture thickens. Add salt.

To scald milk, heat it in a nonreactive pan until bubbles form around the edges. Do not allow it to come to a full boil.

A "nonreactive" pan simply refers to a pan made from a material that will not have a chemical reaction with foods containing acid. For example, an unlined aluminum pan is unacceptable for cooking any tomato or milk dishes. The tomatoes will have an unpleasant metallic taste and the milk turns an unattractive gray color. Unlined cast iron is also not a good choice for cooking foods containing acid. Stainless steel, any material with a nonstick lining, and porcelain-clad cast iron are good choices.

Homemade Spinach-Ricotta Ravioli with Tomato Sauce

A favorite recreational cooking activity of mine is making ravioli. I have an interesting collection of gadgets designed for making the perfect geometrical ravioli, but I find myself reverting back to my free-form ravioli. Start by laying a fresh pasta sheet, right out of the pasta machine, onto waxed paper sprinkled with semolina. (So it won't stick.) Randomly spoon on dollops of the filling and top with a second sheet of pasta. Drape the top sheet loosely so you can press it around the little mounds of filling, allowing you to cut the individual raviolis without stretching or tearing the pasta. Simply go between those little mounds of filling with a pasta-cutting wheel that simultaneously cuts and seals (available in any kitchen store). You can make perfect geometric shapes or be creative with all sorts of odd ones. Pop them into a large pot of boiling, salted water (according to directions at the beginning of this chapter). Lift out the cooked ravioli with a large mesh scoop or slotted spoon so that the water can drain back into the pot. The sauce should be heated and ready to go so you can serve the ravioli as soon as it is done. Try it! Have a ravioli party and get the guests in on the action.

Homemade Pasta (see index)
Filling (see below)
Simple Tomato Sauce (see index)

- Roll pasta into sheets and place a sheet over a ravioli form. Fill and top with a second sheet of pasta. Form and cut the raviolis.
- Heat a large pot of water. Add salt and drop in the ravioli. Cook for about 2 minutes or until tender. Remove with slotted spoon.
- Serve topped with sauce.
- Serves 6-8.

Filling

2½ lb. fresh spinach
2 eggs
1 lb. ricotta cheese
1 cup freshly shredded Parmigiano-Reggiano
1 tsp. salt
¼ tsp. freshly ground pepper
⅛ tsp. freshly ground nutmeg

- Wash the spinach thoroughly. Lift from the water and place in a large pot. (It will cook in just the water that clings to the leaves.) Season to taste with salt and cook until just wilted. Cool, drain, and squeeze.
- Place the spinach with the eggs and cheeses in the food processor. Pulse on and off to mix together. Season with salt, pepper, and nutmeg.

Fettuccine with Porcini and Prosciutto Sauce

In my opinion porcini is the most elegant mushroom in the world. These round plump mushrooms that can grow to be as large as a dinner plate have never been domesticated. They grow wild in the forests in Italy and France (where they call them cèpes). I have been in Italy several times in the fall season when these wonderful mushrooms pop up on the forest floor and I have savored them in some wonderful Italian dishes. Dried porcini maintain their marvelous flavor, which becomes concentrated as they are dried. It doesn't take many to make a very tasty dish. Please note the directions for preparing the dried mushrooms and follow them exactly. Porcini grow in sandy soil and they are understandably not washed before they are dried, so they are very gritty. The hot water used to re-hydrate them is almost always reserved in order to add aromatic flavor to the dish. So, don't discard the soaking water. I first learned to strain it through several layers of cheesecloth, but have long since discovered that a single Microwave Bounty paper towel works even better for trapping all of that grit. Be sure to rinse the mushrooms long enough with plenty of water so they are completely grit free.

> 2 oz. dried porcini mushroom slices
> 3 cups boiling water
> 6 oz. prosciutto, cut into julienne strips
> 2 large shallots, finely chopped
> 4 tbsp. extravirgin olive oil
> 2 cups heavy cream
> Salt and pepper, to taste
> Freshly grated nutmeg
> 1 lb. fresh or dried fettuccine
> 1 cup freshly grated Parmigiano-Reggiano
> Chopped flat-leaf parsley

- Place the mushrooms in a bowl and pour over the boiling water. Soak for 30 minutes. Lift the mushroom from the water, squeezing out as much water as possible.

- Rinse the mushrooms thoroughly under cold water, making sure they are free of all grit. Place on soft white paper towels to drain. Chop finely and set aside. Line a strainer with a soft white paper towel and pour through the mushroom-soaking liquid. Reserve strained liquid.

- In a skillet over high heat, sauté the prosciutto and shallots in the oil for 3 to 4 minutes. Add the porcini mushrooms and sauté 2 to 3 minutes more, stirring.

- Add the reserved porcini liquid. Reduce to ½ cup liquid.
- Add the cream and season with salt, pepper, and nutmeg. Cook over medium heat, uncovered until mixture reduces by half— about 20 to 25 minutes. Stir often.
- Meanwhile, cook the pasta in a large pot of salted boiling water until "al dente." Drain and toss with the sauce. Sprinkle with cheese and parsley. Serve immediately. Pass extra cheese at the table.
- Serves 6-8.

Fettuccine with Leeks, Carrots, and Prosciutto

The carrot "ribbons" are important for the success of this easy dish. If you have a thin slicing disc on your food processor, place the carrots in sideways and hold them firmly in place with the center of the feed tube as they are sliced into ribbons. A mandolin with the slicing blade set on the thin setting works well too.

Leeks grow in sandy soil. Washing them properly and thoroughly is important. Cut away the tough part of the green top (save for the stockpot). Trim the root end. Place the trimmed leek on a cutting board and cut lengthwise three-fourths of the way through. Soak in lukewarm water for a few minutes. Hold under a steady stream of lukewarm water, pulling apart the layers with your thumbs.

2 tbsp. extravirgin olive oil
1 tbsp. unsalted butter
3 leeks, trimmed, washed, and thinly sliced
6 large carrots, peeled, halved, and sliced into ribbons
½ lb. prosciutto, thinly sliced and cut into small strips
¼ cup dry white wine
1 cup chicken stock
Salt and freshly ground black pepper, to taste
½ cup chopped flat-leaf parsley
1 lb. fettuccine, cooked al dente and drained
1 cup freshly grated Parmigiano-Reggiano

- Heat the oil and butter together in a large heavy skillet. Sauté the leeks, stirring, for 5 minutes.
- Add the carrots and sauté, stirring, for 2-3 minutes. Toss in the prosciutto and cook a couple minutes more. Add the wine and cook over high until wine is reduced by half.

- Stir in the chicken stock and simmer on low for 5 minutes. Season with salt and pepper. Toss in the parsley.
- Toss together the carrot mixture with the just-drained pasta. Toss in the cheese and serve immediately.
- Serves 4-6.

Fettuccine with Spring Onions and Asparagus

I love asparagus, as long as it's not too skinny. I don't think those skinny little spears have much to offer in either taste or texture. I think this dish deserves some nice plump asparagus spears. It is prettier with the asparagus cut on the diagonal as directed.

1 lb. fettuccine, dried or fresh
2 bunches green onions
1 lb. fresh asparagus, medium to large spears
4 tbsp. unsalted butter (½ stick)
Salt and freshly ground white pepper
1 cup heavy cream
3 tbsp. chopped flat-leaf parsley
½ cup freshly grated Parmigiano-Reggiano

- Cook the pasta, following directions at the beginning of the chapter.
- Trim the ends from the onions and cut away all but about 2" of the green tops. Wash, dry, and slice very thinly.
- Wash the asparagus and break away the tough ends. Cut on the diagonal into 1" pieces. Blanch in 3 or 4 cups of boiling water, salted with 2 tsp. of salt, for 2 minutes. Drain and refresh in ice water. Drain well and set aside.
- Melt the butter in a large heavy skillet. Sauté the sliced onions, stirring, for 2 to 3 minutes. Add the asparagus and cook 2 minutes more. Season to taste with salt and pepper.
- Add the cream and cook over high until the cream is reduced by one-third.
- Toss in the parsley, drained hot pasta, and cheese. Toss until the pasta absorbs the sauce. Serve immediately.
- Serves 6.

Pappardelle with Elegant but Easy Tomato Sauce

I love wide pasta! It is easier to cook because it doesn't overcook as quickly as the skinny stuff and it just tastes better. I have a well-used pappardelle attachment on my favorite pasta machine, but you can simply roll out your sheets of pasta, place them on a board sprinkled with semolina, and cut them into ribbons about ¾" to 1" wide. That's the way Italian home cooks have done it for centuries. This is a good winter recipe because you don't have to depend on fresh tomatoes for the sauce. In fact, you can toss this sauce on all sorts of pasta and even use it as an easy sauce for lasagna. The flavor can be changed slightly by substituting fresh thyme sprigs for the rosemary and you can use a good extravirgin olive oil instead of the butter.

> 1½ cups chicken stock
> 2 shallots, peeled and sliced
> 3 sprigs flat-leaf parsley
> 1 bay leaf
> 3 sprigs rosemary
> ½ tsp. whole black peppercorns
> 4 tbsp. unsalted butter (½ stick)
> 28-oz. can plum tomatoes, chopped (with juice)
> Homemade Pasta pappardelle (see index) (or 1
>   lb. dried pappardelle cooked according to
>   pkg. directions)
> ⅔ cup freshly grated Parmigiano-Reggiano

- Pour the stock into a small pan. Add the shallots, parsley, bay leaf, rosemary, and peppercorns. Bring to a boil.

- Simmer on low for 5 minutes. Set aside and allow to steep for 20 minutes. Strain.

- Melt the butter in a large heavy skillet. Add the stock and tomatoes. Cook, uncovered, over medium heat until mixture is reduced by half.

- Meanwhile, cook the pasta in a large pot of boiling, salted water for 3 to 4 minutes or until firm, but tender. Drain immediately. Add the cheese to the sauce and toss with the pasta. Serve immediately.

- Serves 4-6 as a main course or 7-8 as a pasta course.

Rigatoni with Roasted Vegetables

As I mentioned in the introduction to this chapter, the sauce must match the pasta. Chunky macaroni shapes such as rigatoni or penne are perfect to go with some chunky roasted vegetables. I like rigatoni because it is fat enough for the sauce to get trapped inside. This hearty vegetarian dish is great to make in the summer when all of these vegetables are at their peak. In warm weather, grill the vegetables on your outdoor grill.

1 small eggplant, cut into julienne strips
2 red bell peppers cut into julienne strips
2 Vidalia onions, halved and sliced
2 to 3 small zucchini, thinly sliced
8 Roma tomatoes, halved
Extravirgin olive oil
Coarse sea salt
1 lb. imported rigatoni
½ cup chopped flat-leaf parsley
½ cup chopped fresh basil
½ cup pitted and halved kalamata olives
Freshly ground pepper, to taste
¾ cup freshly shredded Parmigiano-Reggiano

- Preheat the oven to 500 degrees. Toss the vegetables on a large baking sheet with just enough olive oil to coat very lightly. Add sea salt to taste. Roast for 10 to 15 minutes in the preheated oven. Stir and check for doneness every 3 minutes.

- Meanwhile cook the rigatoni in a large pot of boiling salted water until al dente—according to package directions.

- When the vegetables are roasted, remove them from the oven and immediately toss with the parsley, basil, olives, and pepper to taste. Toss with the hot, drained pasta and toss in the Parmigiano-Reggiano. Serve immediately.

- Serves 6-8.

Rigatoni with Roasted Garlic and Toasted Walnut Sauce

You should always have a package of rigatoni in your pantry. On a busy day you can make an easy and satisfying dish with what you find in your refrigerator and cupboards. I like a sauce that can be made in the time it takes to cook the pasta. Rigatoni takes longer than some so there are all sorts of creative possibilities. This is one on my favorites that qualifies as "comfort food." Yes, you can substitute light cream, but the sauce won't be as creamy and tasty. I propose just eating a smaller portion.

> 1 cup walnuts
> 4 large cloves roasted garlic
> 1½ cups cream
> ½ tsp. salt
> ¼ tsp. freshly ground black pepper
> ½ cup freshly shredded Parmesan
> 1 lb. rigatoni, cooked al dente
> 2 tbsp. chopped flat-leaf parsley

- Spread the walnuts on a baking sheet and toast in a preheated 350-degree oven for 8 to 10 minutes. Cool.

- Chop the walnuts in the food processor. Add the garlic and cream and process to a sauce. Add salt, pepper, and cheese and blend.

- Drain the cooked pasta well. Immediately toss the sauce into the hot drained pasta. Add the parsley. Taste and correct the seasonings. Serve immediately.

- Serves 4-6.

Penne with Veal Sauce

Giuseppe Bovo, a native of Venice, is a busy, successful artist and photographer who still finds time to cook dishes from his homeland whether in his kitchen in New York or in Paris. This is one of his own recipes that has become a favorite of his friends. It is a good one to make when you have a busy schedule because all of the work is done ahead. Giuseppe actually prefers making it ahead because it tastes best. Substitute rigatoni or fusilli for the penne.

> **2 tbsp. olive oil**
> **1 tbsp. butter**
> **1 large onion, chopped**
> **1 cup dry white wine (heated, but not boiling)**
> **1 lb. ground veal**
> **2 or 3 large tomatoes, cored and chopped**
> **Salt and pepper, to taste**
> **1 clove garlic, finely chopped**
> **1 lb. penne pasta**
> **1 cup grated Parmigiano-Reggiano**

- In a skillet, heat olive oil and butter over medium heat until combined. Sauté chopped onion until tender, about 5 minutes. Add ¼ cup of the wine and cook until reduced.

- Stir in the veal and ¼ cup more wine. Cook, stirring, until the veal is cooked.

- Stir in the tomatoes and the remaining wine. Season with salt and pepper to taste. Reduce heat to low and cook, stirring often, for 20 to 30 minutes. Remove, let cool, transfer to a covered dish, and store in refrigerator.

- The next day, add the garlic and reheat over medium for 10 minutes, stirring.

- Meanwhile cook the penne (see cooking pasta in the beginning of this chapter) "al dente," drain, and toss with the sauce. Pass the cheese to sprinkle over the top.

- Serves 6-8.

Spaghetti Puttanesca

This recipe came out of a class called "Quick and Easy Pasta Dishes." It is my favorite version of the Italian classic that has been around for a long time. I can't remember where I first ate this dish, but with my love for spicy food I couldn't wait to try making it myself. If you like bold flavors I think you're sure to like it. Adjust the amount of crushed hot peppers according to your taste. Be sure to use kalamata olives in this recipe. Substituting plain black olives won't give the sauce enough flavor.

$\frac{1}{4}$ **cup extravirgin olive oil**
3 large cloves garlic
$\frac{1}{2}$ **cup chopped yellow onion**
$\frac{1}{2}$ **to 1 tsp. crushed red chile peppers**
$\frac{1}{2}$ **tsp. salt**
28-oz. can plum tomatoes, chopped (with juice)
$\frac{2}{3}$ **cup pitted kalamata olives, halved**
2 tbsp. capers, drained and rinsed
1 lb. spaghetti, cooked "al dente"
$\frac{1}{2}$ **cup chopped flat-leaf parsley**
1 cup freshly grated Parmigiano-Reggiano

- Over medium high, heat the oil in a large skillet. Add the garlic and onion and cook, stirring, for about 3 minutes. Do not burn the garlic. Stir in the red pepper and salt.

- Add the chopped tomatoes, reduce to low, and cook for 10 minutes.

- Stir in the olives and capers and cook 5 minutes more. Taste and correct the seasonings.

- Drain the cooked pasta well. Toss into the sauce along with the parsley and sprinkle with the cheese.

- Serves 6.

Spaghetti with Shrimp and Green Olives

There are not many things I like better than olives and I confess to being an olive snob. I like treating myself to the very best imported olives and that's what I use for this recipe. You can also make this dish with just plain pimiento-stuffed green olives and it will still taste good.

1 lb. spaghetti
¼ cup extravirgin olive oil
1 cup chopped yellow onion
2 large cloves garlic, finely chopped
1 tsp. chopped fresh thyme leaves
1 lb. raw peeled and deveined medium shrimp,
  cut into 3 pieces
¼ cup dry white wine
½ cup chicken stock
1 cup chopped plum tomatoes (fresh or canned)
1 cup green olives in brine, sliced
3 tbsp. chopped flat-leaf parsley
¼ to ½ tsp. hot pepper sauce
1 tsp. salt, or to taste

- Cook the spaghetti according to package directions and the directions at the beginning of this chapter until "al dente." Drain well.

- Heat the oil in a large heavy sauté pan over medium-high heat. Add the onion and garlic and cook, stirring, for 10 minutes. Add the thyme leaves and shrimp and cook, stirring constantly, for 2 to 3 minutes or until the shrimp turns pink.

- Stir in the wine and cook over high for a minute or two. Add the stock and tomatoes and continue to cook for 6 to 8 minutes on high heat. Stir in the olives and parsley. Season with hot pepper sauce and salt. Toss in the cooked, drained spaghetti and serve immediately.

- Serves 6-8.

Spaghetti and Meatballs

This old family recipe comes from my friend Lana Santavicca, a cooking-school friend who thought we should have at least one classic spaghetti with meatballs recipe in this book. Lana with her great sense of humor is always a welcome addition to the cooking-school kitchen and we've shared some good laughs together.

> **6 slices white bread**
> **½ cup milk**
> **½ cup chopped onion**
> **2 cloves garlic, finely chopped**
> **2 tbsp. extravirgin olive oil**
> **2 lb. ground beef**
> **1 egg, beaten**
> **¼ cup finely chopped flat-leaf parsley**
> **1½ tsp. sea salt**
> **½ tsp. pepper**
> **1 tbsp. crushed oregano**
> **1½ tsp. cumin**
> **Flour**
> **Sauce (see below)**
> **Spaghetti (see below)**
> **Grated Parmigiano-Reggiano, to sprinkle on top**
> **Chopped flat-leaf parsley, for garnish**

- Trim the crust from the bread, tear into pieces in a bowl, and pour over the milk. Soak for 20 to 30 minutes. Press out the excess milk.

- Sauté the onion and garlic in 1 tbsp. of the olive oil until the onion is tender. Stir into the ground beef along with the soaked bread. Stir in the egg, parsley, and seasonings. Set aside for 30 minutes to allow flavors to blend.

- Form into 1½" meatballs and dust lightly with flour. Heat the remaining 1 tbsp. olive oil in Dutch oven and brown the meatballs. Drain the fat from the pan.

- Pour the sauce over the meatballs; cover and place in preheated 350-degree oven for 30 minutes.

- Serve the spaghetti on a heated platter topped with the sauce and meatballs. Sprinkle generously with grated Parmigiano-Reggiano. Garnish with chopped fresh flat-leaf parsley.

- Serves 8-10.

Sauce

2 tbsp. extravirgin olive oil
1 cup chopped onion
3 cloves garlic, finely chopped
¼ cup finely chopped flat-leaf parsley
2 28-oz. cans tomato sauce
2 tbsp. dried oregano
1 tsp. sugar
¼ cup grated Parmigiano-Reggiano
Dash hot pepper sauce
Sea salt and pepper, to taste

- Place the olive oil in a saucepan. Sauté the onions until tender, about 5 minutes. Stir in the garlic and parsley and sauté for an additional minute or two.
- Add the remaining sauce ingredients and simmer on low gently for 20 minutes, stirring occasionally.

Spaghetti

1 lb. spaghetti
2 tbsp. extravirgin olive oil
1 clove garlic, peeled and lightly crushed

- Prepare spaghetti according to package directions.
- Over medium high, heat the olive oil in a large, deep skillet. Stir in the garlic and cook just until the garlic starts to turn color. Remove the garlic with a slotted spoon and discard. Reduce heat to low.
- Add the cooked spaghetti to the oil and swirl to coat.

Linguini in Herb Sauce

Amy Tobin, who contributed this recipe, is director of the Culinary Sol Cooking School in Cincinnati, where we often work together. She shares my passion for good food and is a great cook. This is one of her favorites that she has made for her family and guests for a number of years.

1 tbsp. olive oil
3 shallots, thinly sliced
1 clove garlic, finely chopped
4 medium mushrooms, sliced
½ cup matchstick-size strips prosciutto
½ cup dry white wine
1 bay leaf
1 whole clove
1 can (13¾ oz.) beef broth
2 tbsp. tomato paste
¼ tsp. freshly ground black pepper, or to taste
8 oz. dried linguini
1 tbsp. butter
1 tbsp. each chopped fresh basil and parsley
1 tsp. dried oregano
½ cup freshly grated Parmigiano-Reggiano

- Heat the olive oil over medium heat and add the shallots, garlic, mushrooms, and prosciutto. Cook for 5 minutes, stirring.
- Add the wine and cook over high to reduce by half.
- Add the bay leaf, clove, broth, tomato paste, and pepper and simmer on low for 15 minutes.
- Cook linguini for half the time directed on the package. Drain.
- Strain the broth mixture and reserve the solids. Discard bay leaf and clove. Over high heat, bring the broth to a boil and finish cooking the linguini in it until tender, but still firm.
- Toss in the butter and the herbs. Top with the reserved ham mixture and the freshly grated cheese.
- Serves 2-4.

Grilled Eggplant Lasagna

I dislike most lasagna, but this is the exception. I learned a number of years ago in Italy that the only cheese you need in lasagna is Parmigiano-Reggiano. Instead of using ricotta (or cottage cheese) for the creamy layer, it is far better to make a flavorful béchamel sauce. Though time consuming, this is the ultimate make-ahead dish. Make it early in the day and all you have left to do is pop it into the oven. If you are wondering if it is OK to substitute packaged dry lasagna noodles for the fresh ones the answer is yes, but for best results buy the dried homemade style that is quickly cooked and has a more delicate texture than the thick noodles with curly edges. (Look for it in gourmet specialty stores.)

> **Homemade Pasta (see index)**
> **Béchamel Sauce (see index)**
> **2 or 3 small eggplants (about 2 lb.)**
> **Extravirgin olive oil**
> **Salt and freshly ground pepper**
> **2 cups grated Parmigiano-Reggiano**
> **Tomato-Beef Sauce (see below)**

- Roll pasta into thin sheets (#7 or 8 on the pasta machine). Cut into lengths that will fit into your lasagne pan. Bring a large pot of water (6 qt.) to a rolling boil. Add 3 tbsp. salt. Poach the lasagna noodles in the water for 2 to 3 minutes.

- Remove to a bowl of cold water. Place on soft towels and pat dry. Cover with plastic wrap to prevent drying.

- When the Béchamel Sauce is made, place a sheet of plastic wrap directly over the top to prevent a film from forming.

- Wash, trim the ends, and slice the eggplant into ¼" circles. (If the peel is tender, you do not need to peel them. If it seems tough, peel before slicing.) Brush both sides with the olive oil and season with salt and pepper.

- Grill over a hot grill for just a few minutes, turning once, until golden brown and tender. (Or broil under a broiler, just 4 to 5" from the heat source.) Remove to a dish.

- Grease a 13" x 9" x 2" baking dish generously with olive oil. Line bottom with some of the prepared lasagna noodles to cover. Spread with a thin layer of béchamel. Sprinkle over ⅓ of the cheese and top with a layer of 1/2 of the eggplant. Spoon over 1/2 of the meat sauce.

- Repeat with a second layer. Top the second layer with the remaining pasta. Spread with remaining béchamel and sprinkle with remaining cheese.

- Place in the center of a preheated 400-degree oven and bake for 25 minutes, if just assembled and still warm. Bake 10 to 15 minutes longer if the lasagna has been made ahead and chilled. Allow to sit for 10 to 15 minutes before cutting into squares to serve.

- Serves 8-10.

Tomato-Beef Sauce

1/4 cup extravirgin olive oil
1 cup finely chopped yellow onion
3 large cloves garlic, finely chopped
1/2 cup finely shredded carrot
1 lb. very lean ground beef
1/2 cup dry red wine
28 oz. can plum tomatoes, chopped (with juice)
1 tbsp. tomato paste
2 tsp. sea salt
1/4 tsp. cayenne pepper
1/4 cup chopped flat-leaf parsley

- Over medium-high heat, heat the oil in a large heavy skillet. Add the onion, garlic, and carrots. Reduce to medium and cook, stirring often, for 10 minutes.

- Stir in the beef and cook, stirring, until all of the red is gone.

- Pour in the wine and cook for 2 minutes over high.

- Add the tomatoes and tomato paste, reduce to low, and simmer, uncovered, for 15 minutes. Stir occasionally.

- Season with salt, pepper, and parsley. Taste and correct the seasonings.

- Makes enough for 1 lb. pasta.

Tomato-Basil Risotto

I will never forget the first time I had real risotto. It was in a charming little trattoria in Tuscany on a chilly, rainy day. I was tired and hungry and thought that rice dish was the best stuff I had ever tasted. I grew up eating a lot of rice and learned early on the proper way to cook it—in the pilaf style, where every grain remains separate and fluffy. But this rice was very different. That's because risotto is made from short-grain rice with grains that are almost as wide as they are long. The constant stirring and gradual addition of the hot stock is all for the purpose of developing the starch in the rice. It combines with the liquid to make this heavenly creamy dish.

The combination of basil and tomato is one of the great classic flavors from the Italian kitchen. You can make this with some good canned plum tomatoes, but there is no substitute for fresh basil. When basil is dried it loses all of its flavor.

5 cups chicken stock (canned or homemade)
1 cup white wine
3 sprigs thyme
1 tbsp. black peppercorns
4 tbsp. extravirgin olive oil
3 large shallots, finely chopped
2 cups Italian Arborio rice
2 large tomatoes, peeled and seeded (6 plum tomatoes)
½ cup finely shredded fresh basil
¾ cup freshly grated Parmigiano-Reggiano

- In a large saucepan bring the chicken stock, wine, thyme, and peppercorns to a boil. Reduce to low and simmer for 20 minutes. Strain and return liquid to the pot. Over high heat, bring to a boil and reduce to low. Keep the stock at a simmer.

- Over medium heat, heat 3 tbsp. of the olive oil in a heavy pot. Sauté the shallots, stirring, for 2 to 3 minutes or until they are tender. Add the rice and stir to coat well.

- Ladle in enough of the hot stock to just cover the rice. Cook, stirring constantly, until almost all liquid is absorbed. Keep the heat at medium to medium low just so the rice is constantly cooking but not boiling too rapidly.

- Ladle in the same amount of stock and cook until absorbed.

Wash fresh basil by submerging in cool water. Drain and spin dry in a salad spinner or pat dry with towels. Place in a plastic bag with a soft white paper towel to absorb extra moisture. Store in crisper drawer in the refrigerator until ready to use. To slice, gather together 3 or more leaves and roll them into a tight little roll. On a cutting board with a very sharp chef's knife, slice crosswise into tiny ribbons.

- Repeat for 18 to 20 minutes or until the rice is done, but still very firm. Chop the tomatoes and toss in with the basil. Stir the remaining tbsp. of olive oil into the cheese and stir into the rice until cheese is melted and rice is very creamy. Serve immediately.
- Serves 4-6.

Three Mushroom Risotto

This is another recipe that features the elegant flavor of mushrooms. The soaking liquid infuses the milder mushrooms with the rich taste of porcini.

> **1 oz. dried porcini mushrooms**
> **2 cups boiling water**
> **3 cups chicken stock**
> **½ cup dry white wine**
> **4 tbsp. olive oil**
> **2 tbsp. unsalted butter**
> **3 shallots, finely chopped**
> **1 large Portobello mushroom, washed and cut into small slices**
> **½ lb. medium to large white button mushrooms, sliced**
> **2 cups Arborio rice**
> **1 tbsp. chopped fresh sage**
> **½ cup chopped flat-leaf parsley**
> **Salt and freshly ground pepper, to taste**
> **1 cup freshly grated Parmigiano-Reggiano**

- Place the dried mushrooms in a bowl and pour over the boiling water. Allow to sit for at least 30 minutes. Lift the mushrooms from the cooled water and rinse thoroughly. Drain on paper towels and chop finely; set aside. Strain the mushroom liquid through a strong white paper towel.
- In a saucepan mix together the mushroom liquid, chicken stock, and wine. Heat to boiling and turn to a slow simmer on low.
- Heat 2 tbsp. of the olive oil and 1 tbsp. of the butter together in a heavy skillet. Sauté the shallots over high heat, stirring, for 3 to 4 minutes. Add both fresh mushrooms and sauté for 3 to 4

minutes. Stir in the chopped dried mushrooms. Cook a minute more and set aside.

- In a heavy saucepan over medium heat, heat the remaining oil and butter. Stir in the rice and cook, stirring, until the rice is coated with oil. Add 1 cup of the hot stock to the rice. Cook, stirring constantly, until the rice has absorbed almost all of the liquid. Add more liquid and continue cooking over medium-low heat. Repeat the procedure until the rice is tender, but still firm—the cooking time should be 18 to 20 minutes.

- During the last couple of minutes of cooking time, stir the mushroom mixture, sage, and parsley into the rice. Season with salt and pepper. Stir in the cheese until melted and serve immediately.

- Serves 6-8.

Risotto with Roasted Radicchio and Toasted Pine Nuts

Radicchio, the dark-red, coarse-textured bitter lettuce, is good in salads, but I like it best cooked. Roasting brings out its elegant flavor and the slightly bitter taste is just perfect with the rich creamy flavor of this risotto. I've made a lot of different risottos in my classes, but this is a students' favorite.

> 1 cup pine nuts
> 4 small heads radicchio, washed and quartered
> Extravirgin olive oil
> Coarse sea salt
> 3 large shallots, finely chopped
> 2 tbsp. extravirgin olive oil
> 2 cups Arborio rice
> 5 cups flavorful chicken stock, boiling
> ½ cup dry white wine
> ½ cup chopped flat-leaf parsley
> 1 cup freshly grated Parmigiano-Reggiano
> ¼ tsp. crushed red chile peppers

- Place the pine nuts in a small shallow baking pan. Toast in a preheated 350-degree oven for 4 to 5 minutes or until lightly toasted. Set aside.

- Raise oven temperature to 500 degrees. Place the radicchio wedges, cut side up, on a baking sheet. Lightly drizzle with olive oil and lightly sprinkle with coarse sea salt. Toss lightly to evenly coat with the oil. Roast in the preheated oven for 10 minutes. Cool, cut into strips, and set aside.

- Sauté the shallots in a heavy saucepan in the olive oil for 3 minutes, stirring. Stir in the rice and stir to coat with the oil.

- Stir the wine into the hot chicken stock. Ladle about 1 cup into the rice. Cook over medium heat, stirring, until liquid is absorbed. Repeat, continuing to add liquid, and cook until rice is tender, but still firm—18 to 20 minutes.

- Stir the pine nuts, radicchio, parsley, cheese, and peppers into the rice. Taste and correct the seasoning, adding salt if necessary. Serve immediately.

- Serves 6-8.

Elegant but Easy Seafood

Easy Pan-Fried Fish

Salmon Cakes
with Chipotle
Remoulade Sauce

Fish Tacos
with Cherry Tomato Salsa

Mediterranean Tuna
with Almond Rice Pilaf

Broiled Fish Fillets
with Mustard Butter

Baked Fish
with Garlic Breadcrumbs

Easy Grilled Swordfish

Southwestern
Marinated Fish

Poached Salmon
with Herb Vinaigrette

Baked Orange Roughy
with Lemon Parsley Sauce

Quick Crab Cakes

Cornmeal Fried Oysters
with Remoulade Sauce

Boiled Shrimp

Sassy Scallops

I can't remember teaching a class on seafood when I didn't have a room full of eager students. I've so often heard them express their fear of failure where cooking seafood is concerned. What they perceived as "fancy fish dishes" was something cooked by an expert chef to be ordered off of a restaurant menu. I suspect this sort of fish-cooking mystique exists particularly here in the Midwest, where fish had long been something frozen in a hard block from the frozen-food case. This is happily no longer the case, since we now have many fresh seafood markets in every part of our country, even when you live far from the ocean. We still don't get shrimp just off the shrimp boat or soft-shell crabs just out of the water like the days when I lived and cooked in New Orleans, but there is plenty of good fresh seafood. The first thing you have to learn if you are one of the many Americans who live a goodly distance from the ocean is to be flexible. If you go to the market looking for a specific type of fresh fish you may be disappointed. Instead, look first to see what is available and then decide how you will prepare it. My seafood seminar that I call "The Art of Cooking Fish" has always emphasized basic knowledge and methods for seafood. The good news, as is quickly apparent to my students, is that cooking fish is amazingly simple and quick as well. Most of the recipes in this chapter are well suited for busy lifestyles and several of them can go from grocery bag to table in 20 minutes.

The Basics for Cooking All Types of Fish

For grilling, broiling, and pan frying fish:

- Cook for 10 minutes per inch of thickness, turning once about two-thirds of the way through the cooking time. It is important not to overcook fish.

- When fish is grilled, broiled, sautéed, or pan fried, cook over high heat so that it cooks quickly, is seared, and is browned on the outside and moist and tender inside.

For breading and frying fish:

- Season the fish with desired seasoning (salt and pepper or other seasonings).
- Dredge in all-purpose flour, just enough to coat.
- Dip into egg wash (composed of 1 tbsp. water per egg and beaten just until well mixed).
- Place on a dish and chill in the refrigerator for at least 30 minutes or as long as 1 hour.
- The fish is ready to fry. The chilling process sets the breading so that it won't come off during the frying.
- Fry in vegetable oil. Use a fat thermometer to determine the correct temperature, between 360 and 375 degrees.
- When the fish is brown on one side, turn and cook until the second side is a deep golden brown.
- For moist, flavorful fried fish, turn only once. Take care not to overcook.
- Remove the fried fish to a paper-towel-lined dish to quickly drain before serving.
- May be held in a warm oven (175 to 200 degrees) for about half an hour. Don't reheat in the microwave.

There is no longer a hard and fast rule about what wine to serve with what food. White wine goes with most fish dishes, but there is no reason not to serve red if you or your guests like it better. Some fish dishes with hearty sauces are better with a light red wine. See the reference guide to matching food and wine at the beginning of this book.

Easy Pan-Fried Fish

Here is another example where all you need for a tasty dish is some good fresh food and a few seasonings. There are no secrets to this one—just flavorful fresh fish cooked to perfection. Since fish cooks so quickly you can have this on the dinner plate in no time.

Salt and pepper (and/or other seasoning such as
Cajun or Creole seasoning)
Fish fillets
All-purpose flour
Butter and/or olive oil
Sauce (if desired)
2 or 3 tbsp. finely chopped dill, parsley, chervil,
or tarragon
Slice lemon

• Season fish. Dredge in flour to coat. Over medium-high heat, heat butter and oil (equal parts) or one or the other in a heavy skillet—just enough to coat the bottom of the pan.

• Quickly pan fry the fish, turning only once. Remove to a side plate.

• Drizzle sauce over the fish before serving, if desired. Sprinkle with one of the fresh herbs. Garnish with lemon.

Sauce

1 medium onion, 1 bunch green onions, or 2 or 3
shallots, finely chopped
Dry white wine

• After the fish is removed from the pan, sauté the onion, stirring, just until it is tender, about 5 minutes. Pour over a large splash of wine and cook over high, stirring to reduce the wine by about $1/2$.

Salmon Cakes
with Chipotle Remoulade Sauce

It is no secret that chipotle, the dried and smoked jalapeño pepper, has become one of the most popular spicy flavors. This recipe uses "chipotle in adobo," or reconstituted chipotle peppers that are canned in adobo sauce, a spicy Mexican-style tomato-chile sauce. These piquant little canned chiles are an easy flavor addition to all sorts of dishes. You'll find them in small cans in the Mexican section of the supermarket or in specialty stores.

1 lb. fresh salmon fillets
2 tbsp. coarse sea salt
2 tbsp. brown sugar
Olive oil
Salt and pepper, to taste
1 cup finely chopped red Spanish onion
1 cup finely chopped red bell pepper
½ cup finely chopped celery
¼ cup finely chopped roasted mild green chiles
⅔ cup mayonnaise
1 cup fresh breadcrumbs
1 egg, beaten
1 tsp. Worcestershire sauce
½ tsp. Tabasco
2 tbsp. fresh lemon juice
¼ tsp. cayenne pepper
2 tbsp. chopped cilantro
1 tsp. salt
Vegetable or olive oil, for frying
Chipotle Remoulade Sauce (see below)

- Skin the salmon. Remove any small bones with tweezers. Mix together the salt and sugar. Rub onto both sides of the salmon.

- Wrap tightly in plastic wrap and place in a shallow dish. Chill for 1 hour (not longer). Remove and rinse well under cool running water. Pat dry with paper towels.

- Brush the salmon with oil. Season with salt and pepper. Grill or broil, turning once, until cooked through. Cool.

- Put 2 tbsp. olive oil in a skillet and sauté the onion, pepper, and celery for 2 minutes, stirring. Remove and cool.

- Stir together the onion mixture, chiles, mayonnaise, crumbs, beaten egg, and seasonings. Flake the salmon into large flakes and gently fold into the mixture. Form into 8 patties.
- Over medium heat, heat just enough oil to cover the bottom of a nonstick pan and cook the salmon cakes until golden brown and crisp, 6-8 minutes. Turn and cook on second side until golden brown. Drain on paper towels and serve hot with the Chipotle Remoulade to spoon on top.
- Makes 8.

Chipotle Remoulade Sauce

2 canned chipotle chiles in adobo, finely
  chopped
1 tsp. adobo sauce (from the canned chiles)
1 cup mayonnaise
1 tbsp. fresh lemon juice
¼ cup sour cream
2 tbsp. chopped cilantro
Salt, to taste

- Gently whisk together until smooth.
- Makes about 1½ cups.

Fish Tacos
with Cherry Tomato Salsa

I'm not sure where fish tacos started, but I had my first one in Texas. It was made with some unidentifiable fried fish, but in combination with the fresh corn tortilla and great salsa I thought it was the tastiest "junk food" I'd had in a long while. I have since seen a number of fish tacos made with marinated fish fillets that were fancier than catfish, but I really like making my fish tacos like this. If you haven't tried farm-raised catfish from Mississippi you are missing out on a treat. It has a mild flavor and delicate texture. This has to be made with corn (versus flour) tortillas.

Cherry Tomato Salsa (see below)
1 lb. farm-raised catfish fillets
1 large clove garlic, peeled
1 tsp. salt
2 tbsp. vegetable oil
1 tsp. paprika
½ tsp. cayenne pepper
8 corn tortillas
1 small head Romaine
Flour, for dredging
Vegetable oil, for frying
Sour cream (optional)

Cherry tomatoes are usually good year round. Use them for salsa and other recipes that call for fresh tomatoes when tomatoes are out of season. They can also be combined with canned plum tomatoes to add a fresh touch.

- Make the Cherry Tomato Salsa and chill.

- If fish is frozen, thaw in refrigerator. Rinse quickly with cold water and pat dry with paper towels. Put the garlic on a cutting board and spoon the salt over it. Using the blunt end of a table knife, scrape the garlic into a paste, using the salt to help turn it into a creamy mixture. Mix the paste with the oil. Stir well and set aside for a few minutes for the flavor to infuse.

- Add the paprika and cayenne to the oil mixture. Stir to mix well. Rub both sides of the fish with the flavor mix.

- Place the tortillas tightly on heavy-duty foil. Sprinkle lightly with water and seal tightly. Before serving, place in a 350-degree oven for 15 minutes or until warmed.

- Wash the Romaine leaves, dry, and chill. Shred into fine shreds and keep chilled.

- Dredge the fish in the flour, shaking off the excess. Heat about

½″ vegetable oil in a large nonstick skillet. Fry the fish over medium heat until golden brown and cooked through, turning only once. Drain on paper towels.

- Put a fish fillet in a warmed tortilla. Top with some Romaine and a spoonful of salsa. Add a dollop of sour cream if desired. Roll and eat warm.
- Makes 8.

Cherry Tomato Salsa

1 pt. cherry tomatoes
½ cup chopped cilantro
2 tbsp. fresh lime juice
2 tbsp. olive oil
½ cup chopped sweet salad onion
1½ tsp. salt, or to taste

- Wash and chop the tomatoes by pulsing on and off in the food processor and stir together all of the salsa ingredients. Cover and chill until ready to serve.
- Makes 2½ cups.

Mediterranean Tuna
with Almond Rice Pilaf

One of my own creations that I often teach in my seafood classes, this recipe was inspired by some of the great fish dishes I've eaten on trips to southern France and Italy. Start with the best tuna you can find. I often use sushi grade for this recipe and think it is worth the extra cost. Rich, fruity olive oil is also key to the flavor. In the summertime I usually cook this on the grill, but it tastes great baked in a hot oven. This is a good time to use your instant-read thermometer so you cook it to your desired doneness. I recommend medium rare to rare, but cook it the way you enjoy it most. Just don't overcook it or it will be dry.

½ **cup extravirgin olive oil**
2 **cloves garlic, finely chopped**
6 **fresh tuna fillets**
Sea salt and freshly ground black pepper
¼ **cup fresh lemon juice**
2 **tbsp. finely chopped flat-leaf parsley**
6 **to 8 large basil leaves, cut into very fine strips**
Lemon wedges and basil leaves, for garnish
Almond Rice Pilaf (see below)

- Take out 2 tbsp. of the olive oil and set aside. Stir the garlic in the remainder, crushing with a fork to release the garlic flavor.

- If baking, preheat the oven to 500 degrees. Place the fish in a shallow dish. Drizzle over the oil, turning the fish to coat on all sides. Season well with salt and pepper.

- Bake for 15 to 20 minutes, depending on desired doneness. Remove from oven. Pour over the lemon juice, distributing evenly on the fish. Drizzle over the reserved olive oil, coating evenly. Sprinkle with the parsley and basil and serve garnished with the lemon wedges and basil leaves.

- If grilling, place the seasoned fish on a hot grill and grill over high heat until outside is well seared and the inside is cooked to desired doneness. Remove to a serving dish and complete as above.

- Serve with Almond Rice Pilaf.

- Serves 6.

Almond Rice Pilaf

1 cup slivered almonds
¼ cup extravirgin olive oil
¼ cup finely chopped shallots (or ½ cup onions)
2½ cups long-grain white rice (or Basmati rice)
5 cups chicken stock
½ tsp. sea salt, or to taste
¼ tsp. cayenne pepper
½ tsp. finely chopped lemon zest
¼ cup chopped flat-leaf parsley

- Spread the almonds in one layer on a sheet pan. Place in a pre-heated 350-degree oven for 8 to 10 minutes, stirring a couple of times, until the almonds are golden brown. Remove and cool.
- Heat the oil in a heavy pot with lid. Sauté the shallots for 3 minutes, stirring. Stir in the rice, just to coat with the oil.
- Add the stock, salt, and pepper. Bring to a boil. Cover tightly. Cook for 15 minutes for Basmati rice, 20 minutes for long-grain white rice.
- Remove from heat and allow to rest for 10 minutes. Toss in the almonds, lemon zest, and parsley and serve.
- Serves 6-8.

Broiled Fish Fillets
with Mustard Butter

This is a general, quick and easy recipe using ingredients that you are likely to have on hand. It comes from my seafood seminar. You can use this with any good fresh, firm fish, from halibut to salmon.

6 fresh fish fillets (5 to 6 oz. each)
6 tbsp. butter
½ cup finely chopped onion (or ¼ cup shallots)
3 tbsp. Dijon mustard
2 tbsp. fresh lemon juice
1 tsp. sweet paprika
Salt and freshly ground black pepper
¼ to ½ tsp. hot pepper sauce
Chopped fresh parsley or dill

- Skin the fish and remove any small bones. Rinse fish quickly under cold water and pat dry with paper towels.
- Melt butter over low heat. Add the onion and sauté for 3 to 4 minutes, stirring.
- Whisk in the mustard, lemon juice, paprika, salt, pepper, and hot sauce, whisking until well blended. Remove from heat.
- Dip the fillets into the mixture to coat one side. Place, buttered side down, in a shallow skillet or baking pan that can go under the broiler. Spoon over the remaining sauce.
- Broil about 4″ from heat, 4 to 6 minutes on first side (depending on thickness). Turn and cook 4 to 5 minutes on second side.
- Spoon over pan juices and sprinkle with parsley or dill to serve. Serve hot.
- Serves 6.

Baked Fish
with Garlic Breadcrumbs

This is another standby from my seafood seminar. I love to make this when I have nice fresh sea bass, but it tastes great on plain cod. It works best with thick fillets so I like to make it with those types of firm white fish. It is important to use fresh breadcrumbs and not the commercial toasted ones. Any firm-textured white bread can be tossed into the food processor and quickly processed into crumbs for this recipe.

> **6 fresh fish fillets (4 to 5 oz. each and cut about**
>   **1″ thick)**
> **Salt and pepper, to taste**
> **3 tbsp. butter**
> **3 tbsp. olive oil**
> **3 large cloves garlic, finely chopped**
> **1½ cups fresh breadcrumbs**
> **¼ cup chopped fresh parsley**
> **6 lemon slices**

- Season fish with salt and pepper.
- Heat the butter and oil together in a glass measuring cup in the microwave with the garlic. Heat on high for about 1 minute—or until very hot.

- Mix together the crumbs and parsley. Dip fish into the butter mixture and then coat with crumb mixture.
- Bake in a preheated 450-degree oven in a shallow baking dish for 10 to 15 minutes or until done through. Garnish with lemon slices.
- Serves 6.

Easy Grilled Swordfish

This is one of my simpler recipes that can be adapted to other types of fish. I especially like to grill swordfish with this easy mayonnaise method. It has so much delicious meaty flavor I don't think it needs a lot of extra ingredients—just a bit of salt, pepper, and fresh lemon to perk it up a bit. The mayonnaise keeps the surface moist as the fish grills and adds some flavor too.

> **6 swordfish steaks, 1" thick**
> **Mayonnaise**
> **Salt and freshly ground black pepper, to taste**
> **Fresh lemon wedges**

- Brush each side of the fish with a generous amount of mayonnaise. Season with salt and pepper to taste. Grill over high heat (or broil) for 10 to 15 minutes—turning once.
- Serve garnished with lemon wedges or top with your favorite salsa.
- Serves 6.

Southwestern Marinated Fish

Here is another basic and versatile recipe that can be used for most any firm, mild fresh fish fillets. You can also marinate shrimp and scallops in this piquant marinade. The secret is to use the very best chili powder you can find. My first preference is ancho because I like its rich flavor without too much hot-pepper taste. If you'd like the flavor to be a little hotter and with more of a smoky barbecue character, use chipotle chili powder or one or two canned chipotle chiles in adobo and add a bit of the adobo sauce along with the tomato sauce.

**6 fish fillets (any firm fish, e.g., halibut, sword-
   fish, tuna, etc.)**
1 cup tomato sauce (8 oz.)
1 to 2 fresh jalapeño peppers, finely chopped
1 tsp. ancho chili powder
½ cup olive oil
¼ cup lime juice
2 tsp. salt
¼ cup chopped cilantro
Lime slices and cilantro sprigs

• Put the fish into a shallow dish or heavy-duty plastic bag with
recloseable top. Stir together the tomato sauce, peppers, chili
powder, oil, juice, salt, and chopped cilantro and pour over the
fish. Marinate in the refrigerator in the covered dish or sealed
plastic bag for at least 2 hours.

• Remove fish from the marinade and grill over a hot grill for 10
to 15 minutes or until done through and lightly browned. Turn
only once. Garnish with lime slices and cilantro sprigs.

• Serves 6.

Poached Salmon
with Herb Vinaigrette

*This summertime favorite can be an elegant lunch anytime of the year.
Allowing the poaching stock to simmer is important so the flavors have
time to develop. Poaching fish takes a relatively short period of time and
it should start in this tasty stock so the flavor can infuse the fish. The
parchment paper, buttered on the side that rests on the fish, functions to
hold the heat in the pan. It is better than covering with a tight lid and
building too much heat in the pan, which is likely to overcook the fish,
making it dry and hard versus moist and delicate. I have also made this
recipe with fresh halibut fillets. I normally serve the fish chilled over a
bed of tender greens, but try it warm. Spoon the warm vinaigrette over
the fish. The warm version is delicious with some fresh spinach that has
been lightly sautéed in a bit of olive oil.*

2 cups dry white wine
2 cups water
1 rib celery, chopped

Cook with wine
that you enjoy
drinking and that is
appropriate for the dish you
are making. For example, for
poaching fish use a light, dry
white wine such as a Sauvignon
Blanc that you might also serve
with the finished dish.

1 medium onion, coarsely chopped
1 bouquet garni composed of:
   2 sprigs thyme
   2 sprigs parsley and 1 large bay leaf
$\frac{1}{2}$ tsp. hot pepper sauce
Pulp of $\frac{1}{2}$ lemon
2 tsp. salt
6 fresh salmon fillets (5 to 7 oz. each)
Parchment paper, buttered
Herb Vinaigrette (see below)

- In a large, nonreactive skillet (large enough to hold fish in a single layer), combine wine, water, celery, onion, bouquet garni, hot pepper sauce, lemon pulp, and salt. Bring to a boil over high heat and allow to simmer on low for 15 minutes.
- Add the fish. Cover with buttered parchment paper and poach over gentle heat for 5 to 7 minutes or just until fish is cooked through. Remove from liquid and serve with Herb Vinaigrette.
- Serves 6.

Herb Vinaigrette

$\frac{1}{4}$ cup white wine vinegar
$\frac{1}{4}$ cup dry white wine
2 tbsp. finely chopped shallots
$\frac{3}{4}$ cup extravirgin olive oil
1 tbsp. Dijon mustard
1 tbsp. each finely chopped fresh chives, flat-leaf parsley, and tarragon
$\frac{1}{2}$ tsp. freshly ground black pepper
1 tsp. salt

- In a non-aluminum saucepan, heat together the vinegar, wine, and shallots. Boil until the mixture is reduced to 2 tbsp.
- Whisk in the oil and mustard, whisking until well blended.
- Stir in the herbs, pepper, and salt.
- Makes about $1\frac{1}{2}$ cups.

Baked Orange Roughy
with Lemon Parsley Sauce

This is an example of simple, but tasty baked fish for the busy cook. Orange roughy is available frozen in almost every store. Fresh fillets are, of course, even better. Try this with some fresh sole or trout fillets. It's quick and delicious.

> 2 lb. orange roughy fillets
> ¼ cup chopped flat-leaf parsley
> ½ cup melted butter
> 1 tbsp. fresh lemon juice
> 1 tsp. salt
> ½ tsp. white pepper
> Lemon wedges and parsley sprigs, for garnish

- Rinse fillets; pat dry. Arrange in a single layer in a shallow baking pan. Sprinkle with chopped parsley.

- Combine butter and lemon juice; drizzle over fish. Sprinkle with salt and pepper. Cover pan with foil and chill until ready to bake.

- Uncover and bake in a preheated 400-degree oven for 10 to 15 minutes, or until done through. Serve garnished with lemon wedges and parsley sprigs.

- Serves 6.

Quick Crab Cakes

This is not only a quick but also very simple recipe for this popular seafood dish. There are many fancier ones around, but I like this because it has a lot of crab with just enough bread mixture to hold it together. Try to find fresh, chilled crabmeat versus the canned crabmeat on the shelf. Fresh crabmeat is sometimes packed in cans, and has been pasteurized for longer shelf life, but it will always be refrigerated and the flavor and texture are good. Make these into bite-sized cakes for a first course. For a lunch or light supper entrée, form them into larger cakes (4" in diameter) and serve them on a bed of shredded greens with a bit of creamy dressing of your choice drizzled over the top.

15 to 16 oz. fresh lump crabmeat
½ cup thinly sliced green onions
1 cup fresh breadcrumbs
2 eggs, slightly beaten
½ tsp. salt
¼ to ½ tsp. hot pepper sauce
Vegetable oil

- Toss the crabmeat with the onions. Mix the breadcrumbs with the egg and add to the mixture. Season with salt and hot pepper sauce. Form into small patties.
- Heat about ¼" vegetable oil in a large skillet over medium heat until hot. Add the crab cakes and cook for 5 to 6 minutes on the first side. Turn and cook 4 to 5 minutes on the second side or until golden brown.
- Serves 4 as a main course (more if made smaller as appetizers).

Cornmeal Fried Oysters with Remoulade Sauce

The first thing I eat when I go back to New Orleans is oysters. I like them raw and any way they are cooked, but I admit a weakness for fried oysters. It isn't true that you should only buy oysters in the months that have an r, but they do taste best when the weather is cooler. Purchase the plumpest ones you can find to make this dish.

1½ pt. large "select"-size fresh oysters
Salt and cayenne pepper, to taste
Flour
2 eggs
¼ cup milk
Cornmeal
Vegetable or peanut oil, for frying
Remoulade Sauce (see below)

- Drain the oysters. Season. Dredge in flour to lightly coat.
- Whisk together the eggs and milk. Dip the oysters in the egg mixture. Dredge in cornmeal to coat.
- Place on a waxed-paper-lined tray and chill for 20 to 30 minutes.

- Heat 2" oil in a heavy skillet to 365 degrees. Fry the oysters until golden brown, 6 to 8 minutes, depending on size. Drain on a soft white paper towel. Serve immediately with Remoulade Sauce.
- Serves 6.

Remoulade Sauce

¼ cup horseradish Dijon mustard
½ cup tarragon vinegar
2 tbsp. catsup
1 tbsp. paprika
1 tsp. salt
1 clove garlic, peeled
½ cup coarsely chopped green onions
½ cup coarsely chopped celery
¼ cup flat-leaf parsley leaves
½ tsp. cayenne pepper
1 cup vegetable oil

- Blend together all ingredients, except oil, in the food processor or blender. With motor running, pour in the oil in a steady stream. Process until mixture is blended.

Boiled Shrimp

There is hardly a better treat for seafood lovers than a big bowl of chilled boiled shrimp—that is, if they have been properly cooked so that they are flavorful, tender, and juicy. When I went to my first cocktail party in the Midwest and saw a beautiful bowl of boiled shrimp on the table I thought I was in for a treat. How disappointing to discover that the shrimp only looked pretty. The only flavor I detected was the cocktail sauce. And that's a shameful way to treat these tasty crustaceans. For my secret for great boiled shrimp, simply follow these directions.

6 to 8 qt. water
1 cup salt or more
1 pkg. shrimp or crab boil seasoning
1 large onion, peeled and quartered
1 lemon, halved
1 to 3 lb. shrimp

- Bring water to a boil in a large pot. Add enough salt to make the water as salty as ocean water (6 percent solution; about 1 cup salt for 6 qt. water).
- Add shrimp or crab boil, onion, and lemon. Allow the broth to boil for at least 20 minutes to infuse the water with the flavors.
- Add the shrimp into the rapidly boiling water. Cook until shrimp turns pink and curls slightly. Do not overcook. Cooking time depends on size of shrimp and its temperature when added (whether it is fresh or frozen).
- Drain shrimp in a colander as soon as it is done. Chill until ready to serve. Serve in shell or peel and devein before serving.
- Serves 8-10 as an appetizer, 4-6 as a main course.

Sassy Scallops

You need plump sea scallops as fresh as you can find them to make this recipe. Serve 2 or 3 as the appetizer course with French bread to soak up the sauce. For a quick and easy main course, serve with rice or couscous. To make the scallops even "sassier," add some more cayenne.

1½ lb. fresh large sea scallops
¼ cup soy sauce
¼ cup dry sherry
¼ cup vegetable oil
1 tbsp. finely chopped gingerroot
2 cloves garlic, finely chopped
¼ tsp. cayenne pepper
Extra oil for cooking
Chopped parsley, for garnish

- Rinse and drain the scallops. Place in a shallow glass dish.
- Whisk together the soy sauce, sherry, oil, ginger, garlic, and cayenne. Pour over the scallops. Cover and chill for 1 hour.
- Remove the scallops from the marinade. Reserve marinade. Pat the scallops dry with white paper towels.
- Heat just enough oil to lightly cover the bottom of a skillet. Over high heat quickly sauté the scallops for just a couple of minutes on each side, turning once, until hot through. (Do not overcook.)

Scallops are always cooked quickly over high heat. As soon as they are seared on the outside and have time to get hot through they should be taken off of the heat. When cooked properly they are velvet textured, juicy, and delicious. Overcooking makes them tough and rubbery.

One to three hours is long enough to marinate most fish. If fish is marinated too long it can take on too much of the marinade and you will lose the flavor of the fish itself. The texture is also affected by the acidity in the marinade and the cooked fish will not be as tender and succulent as it should be.

- Remove from the skillet to a side dish. Pour half of the marinade into the skillet and bring to a rolling boil. Simmer on low for 10 minutes.
- Add the scallops and cook a couple minutes longer. Sprinkle with parsley. Serve hot with crusty French bread.
- Serves 10-12 as an appetizer.

Cooking Terms:
Deep fry: to cook submerged in hot fat.
Fry: to cook in hot fat.
Pan fry: to cook in a moderate amount of fat in an uncovered pan.

Cooking Chicken and Turkey

**Apricot-Rice-Stuffed
Chicken Breasts**
with Apricot Sauce

Creamy Curried Chicken
(with Parsley Rice Pilaf)

**Spicy Fried Boneless
Chicken Breasts**

Chicken Rosemary

Creole Chicken Supreme

Chicken Mexicana

Supreme of Chicken
with Porcini Mushroom Sauce

**Old-Fashioned
Oven-Fried Chicken**

**Quick and Easy
Chicken Burritos**

Soft Chicken Tacos
with Great Guacamole

Roast Turkey

Turkey Stock

White Wine Turkey Gravy

**Three-Onion
Bread Stuffing**

**Southern Cornbread-Pecan
Stuffing**

I couldn't even estimate how many classes I've taught around the theme of cooking chicken. I've taught many a workshop where the students and I boned, pounded, stuffed, roasted, carved, and sauced. All that fuss over a mere chicken. Now my most popular poultry class is "The Versatile Chicken Breast," featuring quick and easy preparations for that popular cut, the boneless, skinless chicken breast. I used to begin that class by teaching the proper technique for boning a chicken breast. Now I skip the boning step and start, as everyone these days seems to do, with boneless and skinless chicken breast. It is easy to understand why this cut of chicken, called a "supreme" in the French kitchen, is so popular with cooks. It is healthy, high in protein, low in fat, and quick and easy to cook. I have included several of my favorite recipes for making good use of this most versatile cut. Though there is little work required, there are still a few quick steps needed for the proper preparation of a boneless breast. You will find that information here.

Not all of my chicken recipes call for the boneless, skinless chicken breast. A few other recipes made it into this chapter. I hope some of these recipes, the everyday easy ones as well as some more festive company recipes, will join your list of favorite chicken recipes.

I've also included what I hope will be everything you need to know to roast your next delicious holiday turkey.

By the way, if you're wondering where the cranberry sauce is—I couldn't put everything in this book so allow me to refer you to my Cranberry Chutney recipe in *Cooking with Marilyn*.

Basic Chicken Cookery

For roasting a chicken:

Cut off wing tips. Trim excess fat. Press the chicken back together tightly with the legs against the breast.

Place fresh thyme and parsley (or tarragon and parsley), a slice of onion, and a chunk of butter in the cavity. Thread a large threading needle with a long length of fine kitchen twine, pass it through the back just at the base of the wings, and tie the wings together. Pass the needle through the tail and tie the legs together.

Oil the outside generously with vegetable oil. Place the chicken, breast side up, on an oiled rack covering a pan with about ½" water in the bottom. Roast in a preheated 400-degree oven, for about 1 hour or until a thermometer placed into the thickest part of the thigh (without touching bone) reads 180 to 185 degrees.

Here are some options and alternate roasting method. For lemon-flavored chicken, place a whole lemon that has been pierced several times with a fork in the cavity with the other ingredients.

Start the chicken breast side down on a *V*-shaped rack and turn halfway through the cooking time. Chicken roasted on this rack is likely to be juicier.

Form a large mound of celery (with leaves), parsley, and quartered onions in the center of the roasting pan. Place the chicken, breast side up, on the vegetables to elevate it instead of using a rack. Add a small amount of water or white wine to the bottom of the pan. When the chicken is done, strain the juices, pressing all liquid from the vegetables, and reserve for making a sauce.

For frying a chicken:

Cut up a 2½- to 3-lb. frying chicken. Rinse it thoroughly in cool water and pat dry. Rub a generous amount of salt and black pepper on all sides of the chicken. Dredge it in flour to coat well. Heat about 1" vegetable oil (or vegetable shortening) over medium heat in a very heavy skillet with a tight-fitting lid until hot (350 to 360 degrees). Put in the chicken, skin side down, a piece at a time (so as not to cool the oil too much). Fry until the skin side is a deep golden brown. Turn over and brown the second side. Turn again and cover skillet with the lid. Cook until the chicken is done through, 30 to 40 minutes. Remove the lid and continue to turn the chicken about every 5 minutes. Test for doneness with a fork. When the juices run clear the chicken is done. Remove it to a paper-towel-lined plate to drain.

To debone a chicken:

Use a very sharp boning knife with a flexible blade. Cut off the wing tips. Cut down the backbone from neck to tail. Cutting as close to the bones as possible, scrape the "oysters" that are located in the small cavity on the back just below the neck. Cut

A good all-around sauce for chicken dishes (especially casseroles) is Béchamel Sauce (see index). Substitute chicken stock for the milk and it becomes "Velouté Sauce."

out the oysters and reserve. Leave the shoulder blade on the carcass. Cut around the wishbone. Cut around one thigh, cutting the tendons. Scrape down and work out one drumstick. Trim around the end of the drumstick so the bone comes out easily when inverted. When one-half is removed, repeat on the other side. Be very careful when detaching the meat at the top of the breastbone. It is best to cut through the cartilage, leaving some cartilage attached to the meat, and cut it off after all of the chicken is off of the bones.

Apricot-Rice-Stuffed Chicken Breasts with Apricot Sauce

My talented colleague Sharon Shipley, of Mon Cheri Catering and Cooking School in Sunnyvale, California, has taught as many classes as I have and has assembled a massive file of good chicken recipes. She chose this one to share with us. She uses canned chicken broth for this recipe. For perfectly cooked wild rice, see the tip.

½ **cup uncooked wild rice**
1½ **cups dried apricots**
1½ **cups apricot brandy (or regular brandy)**
½ **cup uncooked long-grain white rice**
1 **cup chicken broth**
2 **shallots, finely chopped**
2 **tbsp. butter**
Salt, to taste
Cayenne pepper, to taste
8 **whole boneless chicken breasts, with skin on**
1 **cup chicken broth**
2 **cups heavy cream**

- Follow tip for preparing the wild rice in advance.
- Cut the apricots into a small dice (the size of green peas) and soak in the brandy overnight.
- The second day, simmer the long-grain rice in 1 cup chicken broth for 18 to 20 minutes or until tender, but firm. Allow to sit for 10 minutes. Fluff with a fork and mix with the wild rice.
- Sauté the shallots in the butter. Stir the shallots and ⅓ of the marinated apricots into the rice mixture and season with salt and pepper to taste.
- Rinse the chicken with cool water and dry. Place each breast on a board with the skin side up. Loosen the skin from the sides and stuff approximately ⅓ cup of the filling under the skin. Tuck the skin and meat under the breast, forming a domed shape.
- Place stuffed chicken breasts in a shallow baking dish and pour over 1 cup chicken broth. Cover with parchment paper and foil and bake for 25 minutes in a preheated 375-degree oven. Remove paper and foil and bake 10 to 15 minutes longer, or until golden brown. Remove chicken and keep warm.

The day before cooking wild rice, rinse it and place in a large bowl. Cover with 2 or 3" boiling water. Allow to sit at room temperature overnight. In the morning, drain and repeat with the boiling water. Allow to sit for several hours. Drain, place in a container that will go into the microwave oven, and cover with cool water. Cook, uncovered, in the microwave for 12 to 15 minutes or until rice is tender. Do not overcook or rice will become mushy.

- Strain the liquid in the pan and reserve 1 cup. In a saucepan, reduce the reserved chicken stock to ½ cup.

- In a second saucepan, reduce the cream to 1½ cups.

- Stir the remaining marinated apricots into the chicken stock and process in the food processor or blender until smooth. Add to the reduced cream and heat until hot. Season to taste with salt and pepper. Spoon the sauce over the chicken.

- Serves 8.

Creamy Curried Chicken (with Parsley Rice Pilaf)

This is an elegant dinner in a dish that can be made ahead for easy entertaining. For company I make this with the heavy cream, but you can substitute all light cream. (The fat-free "half and half" will work too, since the cornstarch thickens it.) Unsweetened coconut tastes best in this recipe, but you can use the sweetened kind.

4 whole skinless, boneless chicken breasts
3 large Roma tomatoes
6 tbsp. clarified butter
1 cup chopped onion
1 clove garlic, finely chopped
1 tsp. pure chili powder (not a blend)
½ tsp. turmeric
½ tsp. cumin
¼ tsp. cayenne pepper
1 tbsp. finely chopped gingerroot
1 cup chicken broth
½ cup chopped macadamia nuts
½ cup shredded coconut
2 tbsp. cornstarch
1 cup heavy cream
1 cup light cream
2 tsp. salt, or to taste

- Rinse, dry, pound chicken to a consistent thickness, and cut into small strips.

- Peel, core, seed, and coarsely chop the tomatoes.

- Heat half of the butter over high heat in a large, heavy skillet.

If you want to have boneless, skinless chicken breast in your freezer for convenience, buy the quick-frozen ones and store them for no longer than 3 months. I don't recommend freezing fresh chicken breasts in your home freezer. They freeze too slowly and that affects both flavor and texture. Always thaw any frozen chicken overnight in the refrigerator.

For clarified butter, heat the butter in a small open pan (or in a glass measuring cup in the microwave) until melted and starting to bubble. Remove from heat and allow to sit for about 30 minutes or until all the solids sink to the bottom. Carefully skim the foam off the top and ladle or pour off the clear butter, leaving the milky liquid behind. The clear "clarified" butter is best for sautéing over high heat. It has a higher smoke point because it is the solids that burn at a lower temperature. It is also used in sauces or as a dipping sauce for lobster and other foods.

Boneless chicken breasts, whether cooked whole, halved, or cut into pieces, should be flattened so they will cook evenly. Place the rinsed and dried chicken between two sheets of plastic wrap. Pound with a veal pounder or some heavy smooth object just until the chicken is a consistent thickness. After the chicken is pounded keep it encased in the plastic and place in the refrigerator until ready to cook.

Add the chicken and quickly sauté just until browned on all sides. Remove to a side dish.

- Add the remaining butter. Stir in the onion and garlic and sauté until tender, about 5 minutes, stirring.
- Stir in the chili powder, turmeric, cumin, and cayenne. Cook on high heat, stirring constantly, for 1 minute.
- Return the chicken to the pan. Stir in the tomatoes and ginger and cook for 2 minutes, stirring.
- Add the chicken broth, nuts, and coconut. Whisk the cornstarch into the combined creams and stir into the skillet, stirring until it comes to a boil and thickens. Season to taste. Serve with Parsley Rice Pilaf.
- Serves 8.

Parsley Rice Pilaf

I serve this easy and delicious rice dish with many different chicken dishes. The cooking time varies according to the kind of rice you use. This recipe is for parboiled long-grain white rice. Some varieties of long-grain white rice will take as long as 25 minutes. Basmati rice is a good choice for curried dishes and has a delicious nutty flavor. It's a timesaver too, because it cooks in only 15 minutes.

> **4 tbsp. butter (½ stick)**
> **1 clove garlic, finely chopped**
> **½ cup chopped onion**
> **2 cups long-grain white rice**
> **4 cups chicken stock**
> **½ cup chopped parsley**

- Melt butter in a heavy saucepan. Stir in garlic and onion and cook for 5 minutes over medium heat or until onion is tender.
- Stir in rice, stirring until well coated. Add stock; stir and bring to a boil.
- Cover and cook on low about 20 minutes or until liquid is absorbed.
- Remove from heat and allow to rest, covered and undisturbed, for 10 minutes.
- Toss in parsley and serve.
- Serves 8.

Spicy Fried Boneless Chicken Breasts

This is my own eclectic version of crispy fried boneless chicken breasts with a Louisiana-style seasoning mix and Japanese breadcrumbs. I guess it's a recipe that came out of my love for the great schnitzels I've eaten in Germany and the chicken fried steak with cream gravy of my childhood. Find the crumbs in an Asian market or in the Asian section of the supermarket. You can use fresh coarse breadcrumbs, but the chicken won't be as crisp and crunchy. For the schnitzel version, serve it with the lemon slices. If you want the Southern comfort-food version, make the gravy.

> **6 skinless, boneless chicken breast halves**
> **1 tbsp. Hungarian sweet paprika**
> **1 tbsp. fine sea salt**
> **½ tsp. cayenne pepper**
> **¼ tsp. black pepper**
> **1 tsp. thyme leaves**
> **1 tsp. brown sugar**
> **⅔ cup flour**
> **2 large eggs**
> **2 tbsp. water**
> **2 cups Japanese breadcrumbs (Panko crumbs)**
> **Vegetable oil**
> **Lemon slices or Cream Gravy (see below)**

- Rinse and trim the chicken. Place between two sheets of plastic wrap and flatten to ¼" thickness. Mix together all of the seasonings and rub generously on both sides of the chicken.

- Put the flour in a shallow dish.

- Beat the eggs with the water in another shallow dish.

- Pour the crumbs in a dish.

- Dredge chicken in the flour, shaking off the excess. Coat with the egg wash and coat well with the crumbs. Place on a tray and chill, uncovered, for 30 minutes.

- Heat about 1" oil in a large heavy skillet over medium heat until very hot, but not smoking (about 365 degrees). Fry the chicken about 5 minutes on the first side, then turning and cooking 3 to 4 minutes on the second side or until golden brown. Remove to a paper-towel-lined tray to drain.

Breaded chicken or meats and vegetables should be placed in a single layer on a tray and chilled for 30 minutes before frying. This chilling time sets the breading and prevents it from coming off in the skillet. Don't chill longer than an hour or the breading can become soggy.

Use fresh chicken within 2 or 3 days after you purchase it. Remove it from the grocery-store package and wrap in plastic wrap. Store in the meat drawer.

- If you plan to make the gravy, pour off all but 3 tbsp. of the oil and return the skillet to the range.
- Serve hot topped with lemon slices or nap with Cream Gravy.
- Serves 6.

Cream Gravy

3 tbsp. oil (in pan from frying the chicken)
¼ cup flour
2 cups milk, heated
1 tsp. salt, or to taste
½ tsp. freshly ground black pepper

- Heat the oil over medium heat. Stir in the flour, stirring to incorporate well. Cook, stirring constantly, for 2 to 3 minutes.
- Whisk in the hot milk, stirring until mixture is creamy. Season with salt and pepper. Serve hot.
- Makes 2 cups.

Chicken Rosemary

Glance through my recipe files and you know that rosemary is a favorite herb. I like it on chicken as well as lamb and pork. This is an easy recipe for entertaining because you can brown the chicken breasts ahead, coat them with the herbs, and have them ready to go into the oven.

6 skinless, boneless chicken breast halves
2 tsp. fine sea salt
1 tsp. freshly ground black pepper
Flour
½ cup extravirgin olive oil or vegetable oil
¼ cup finely chopped fresh rosemary leaves
½ cup chopped flat-leaf parsley
½ cup dry white wine
Rosemary sprigs, for garnish

- Rinse and dry the chicken breasts. Place between two sheets of plastic wrap and flatten to about ½" thickness. Season on both sides with salt and pepper and dredge in flour to coat. On high, heat the oil in a large heavy skillet and sauté the chicken until golden brown, about 3 minutes on the first side, then turning and browning the second side 2 to 3 minutes.

- Mix together the rosemary and parsley and roll the chicken in the herbs to coat. Place in a shallow baking dish and pour over the wine. Just before serving bake for 20 to 25 minutes (depending on size and whether the chicken has cooled)—in a preheated 450-degree oven.

- Garnish with sprigs of rosemary. Serve with Parsley Rice Pilaf or Parmesan Mashed Potatoes (see index).

- Serves 6.

Creole Chicken Supreme

My own modern version of a famous Louisiana dish goes together quickly and is quite a tasty dish. Substitute canned plum tomatoes that are drained and chopped when tomatoes are out of season or to save time. Use less cayenne pepper when seasoning the chicken for a milder-flavored dish.

6 skinless, boneless chicken breast halves
2 tsp. fine sea salt
½ tsp. cayenne
Flour
¼ cup extravirgin olive oil
2 medium yellow onions, thinly sliced
2 cloves garlic, finely chopped
½ cup thinly sliced celery
1 medium red bell pepper, cut into small strips
1 medium green pepper, cut into small strips
2 large ripe tomatoes, peeled, seeded, and
    coarsely chopped
1 tsp. dried thyme leaves
1 cup chicken broth
½ cup chopped flat-leaf parsley

Store paprika, chili powder, and cayenne pepper in the freezer to maintain freshness and flavor. If they are packed in glass, seal tightly and put into freezer. If they are packed in tins, place the tins into a small plastic freezer bag, seal, and freeze. The spices do not have to be thawed before using.

- Rinse, dry, and flatten the chicken. Cut, across the grain, into ½"-wide strips. Season with salt and cayenne pepper. Dredge in the flour just to coat lightly.

- Heat the oil in a large heavy skillet. Sauté the chicken, stirring, for 4-5 minutes. Remove to a side dish.

- Add the onion, garlic, celery, and peppers to the skillet. Cook, stirring, for 5 minutes.

- Stir in the tomatoes, thyme, and chicken broth. Return the chicken. Cook, uncovered, for 10 minutes. Stir occasionally.
- Taste and correct the seasonings. Garnish with sprinkled parsley. Serve with Parsley Rice Pilaf or just fluffy white rice.
- Serves 6.

Chicken Mexicana

For a heartier dish make this with all dark-meat pieces of chicken. You can use a combination to have everyone's favorite or make it a bit more elegant for company by using all chicken breasts (bone in and skin on). You may make this ahead and reheat it. Adjust the amount of the canned chipotle chiles according to the spice level you desire. If you really like it hot you can use more than three.

> 2½ to 3 lb. meaty chicken pieces
> Salt and pepper
> ¼ cup vegetable oil
> 1 large yellow onion, thinly sliced
> 2 cloves garlic, finely chopped
> 28-oz. can chopped plum tomatoes
> 2 to 3 chipotle chiles in adobo, finely chopped
> 1 tbsp. adobo sauce
> 1 tsp. dark brown sugar
> 1 tbsp. fresh lime juice
> 3 tbsp. chopped cilantro

You cannot substitute boneless chicken breasts in a recipe that calls for chicken breasts with bones and skin. The cooking time and temperature are not the same.

- Rinse and pat the chicken dry. Season with salt and pepper.
- Heat the oil in a large skillet. Brown the chicken over medium heat, turning, for 10 to 15 minutes. Remove to a side dish.
- Stir the onion and garlic into the skillet. Cook, stirring, for 1 to 3 minutes.
- Stir in the tomatoes, chiles, adobo sauce, and sugar. Cook, stirring occasionally, for 10 minutes.
- Return the chicken to the sauce. Cover the skillet and simmer on low for 45 minutes, or until chicken is done through.
- Add the lime juice and cilantro. Taste and correct the seasonings. Serve with rice.
- Serves 6.

Supreme of Chicken
with Porcini Mushroom Sauce

Dress up an everyday chicken breast and take it to an elegant dinner party. This rich and flavorful porcini sauce does just that. I like to serve this with wild rice or little roasted potatoes. You can substitute 1 cup heavy cream for the crème fraiche.

8 skinless, boneless chicken breast halves
1 oz. dried porcini mushrooms
2 cups boiling water
2 tsp. fine sea salt
½ tsp. freshly ground black pepper
Flour
½ cup clarified butter
2 shallots, finely chopped
1 lb. fresh white mushrooms, thinly sliced
¼ cup dry Marsala
1 cup crème fraiche
3 tbsp. finely chopped parsley

- Rinse, trim, and flatten the chicken breasts. Chill until ready to use.
- Pour the boiling water over the dried mushrooms and allow to sit for ½ hour.
- Season the chicken breasts with the salt and pepper. Dredge to lightly coat in the flour.
- In a large heavy skillet over medium high, heat half the butter. Sauté the chicken breasts for 8 to 10 minutes or until lightly browned and cooked through. Remove to a side dish.
- Lift the dried mushrooms from their soaking water and strain the water through a soft white paper towel. Reserve 1 cup of the strained liquid. Rinse the reconstituted mushrooms thoroughly. Dry and chop.
- Put the remaining butter in the skillet and sauté the shallots until tender.
- Stir in the sliced fresh mushrooms. Sauté for 2 to 3 minutes over high heat. Add the chopped mushrooms, the mushroom liquid, and wine.

- Cook, uncovered, over high heat to reduce the liquid to ¼ cup.
- Add the crème fraiche and cook, stirring, until slightly thickened. Return the chicken breasts and cook 1 minute longer. Season to taste and sprinkle with parsley.
- Serves 8.

Old-Fashioned Oven-Fried Chicken

For those of you who don't want to stand over a hot stove to cook fried chicken, this is a tasty alternative. This recipe can be easily doubled or tripled in a large heavy baking pan if you are cooking for a crowd. It's been done at many a church supper down home. Instead of buying a whole chicken, it is more efficient to buy meaty breasts, thighs, and drumsticks.

> 3 lb. meaty chicken pieces, with skin on
> 1 cup flour
> 1 tbsp. salt
> 2 tsp. black pepper
> 1 tbsp. sweet paprika
> ½ cup vegetable oil

- Rinse chicken with cool water and pat dry with white paper towels.
- Mix flour, salt, pepper, and paprika in a gallon-sized plastic bag. Shake 2 or 3 pieces of chicken at a time in the bag to coat thoroughly.
- Pour the oil in a 13" x 9" x 2" baking pan. Place in a preheated 400-degree oven to heat the oil.
- Place the chicken, skin side down, in a single layer in the hot oil. Return the pan to the oven and bake for 30 minutes.
- Remove and turn over the chicken pieces. Bake 20 minutes longer or until the juices run clear when chicken is pierced with a fork.
- Serves 6-8.

Quick and Easy
Chicken Burritos

This is a recipe I invented for a Sunday-night supper to use up some chicken breasts. It turned out beautifully and so I shared it with my cooking students in a class called "Dinner in a Hurry." You may use either regular or reduced-fat sour cream. Any favorite brand of commercial tomato salsa will do just fine. If you happen to have some fresh homemade salsa it will taste even better. I've used both a mild New Mexican red chili powder and chipotle chili powder. It depends on your taste. Just use a pure chili powder and not a blend from the grocery store.

12 small flour tortillas
2 whole skinless, boneless chicken breasts
3 tbsp. pure chili powder
1 tbsp. cumin
2 tsp. salt
¼ tsp. cayenne pepper, or to taste
3 tbsp. olive oil
½ cup finely chopped onion
1 cup sour cream
3 tbsp. tomato salsa
½ cup chopped cilantro
Extra salsa

- Wrap the tortillas in heavy-duty foil. Place in a preheated 350-degree oven to heat until warmed through, 5-10 minutes.

- Trim, rinse, and dry the chicken. Flatten between two sheets of plastic wrap to ¼" thickness. Cut, across the grain, into ½"-wide strips.

- Mix together the chili powder, cumin, salt, and cayenne. Dredge the chicken in the spice mixture to coat lightly.

- Heat the oil in a large skillet. Sauté the chicken, turning once, for 5 to 6 minutes or until done through. Do not overcook. Remove to a side dish.

- Add the onions to the skillet and sauté, stirring, for 5 minutes, or until tender.

- Stir in the sour cream and heat until bubbly.

- Stir in the salsa. Return the chicken pieces and cook, stirring gently, for 3 minutes or just until chicken is heated through.

- Add the cilantro. Place a large spoonful of the chicken mixture in the center of a warmed tortilla. Fold and roll up burrito style. Serve with more salsa for spooning over the top.
- Serves 4-6.

Soft Chicken Tacos with Great Guacamole

I think a soft taco has far more appeal than a crisp fried one. It's easier to eat, too. Use only corn tortillas for this recipe. You will find good ones in Mexican specialty stores or the Mexican/Southwest section of the supermarket. Making your own is fun and the best of all. Buy a bag of "masa harina" (Mexican corn flour) and follow the directions for making tortillas. You will need a tortilla press, available at most kitchen stores. I recommend the simplest non-electric ones.

> 1 lb. boneless chicken breast
> 1 tbsp. extravirgin olive oil
> 2 large garlic cloves, finely chopped
> 1 tsp. cumin
> ½ cup finely chopped onion
> 2 large fresh jalapeño peppers, finely chopped
> ½ tsp. crumbled dried oregano leaves
> 1 tsp. sea salt
> ¼ tsp. cayenne pepper
> ⅓ cup chopped cilantro
> 12 corn tortillas
> 2 ripe medium tomatoes, finely diced
> 1 cup shredded Romaine lettuce
> Great Guacamole (see below)

- Wash and dry the chicken. Flatten between two sheets of plastic wrap to ¼" thickness. Cut, across the grain, into strips (2" x ¼").
- In a large, nonstick skillet, heat the oil over medium-high heat. Add the chicken, garlic, and cumin. Sauté, stirring, for 5 minutes.
- Stir in the onion, jalapeño, oregano, salt, and pepper. Increase the heat to high and sauté until the chicken is cooked through, 3 to 4 minutes. Toss in the cilantro.

- Place a medium skillet over medium heat. Moisten each corn tortilla with drops of water on each side. Add the tortillas to the skillet, one at a time, and flip several times until hot and softened and the water has been absorbed.

- Spoon 2 tbsp. of the chicken filling across the center of each tortilla. Top with the tomatoes and lettuce and fold in half. Garnish with Great Guacamole.

- Serves 6-12.

Great Guacamole

3 medium ripe avocados
½ cup finely chopped sweet salad onion
2 tbsp. fresh lime juice
½ tsp. salt
½ tsp. hot pepper sauce, or to taste
1 medium ripe tomato, cored and chopped
3 tbsp. chopped cilantro

- Peel, seed and mash avocados. Stir in the remaining ingredients. Cover and chill for at least 1 hour. Serve chilled.

- Makes about 2½ cups.

Roast Turkey

Several years back I did my first annual "Turkey Repair" radio show on Thanksgiving morning. My erstwhile radio colleague and sidekick, Jan Mickelson, had moved to WHO in Des Moines and he invited me to call in on Thanksgiving morning and repair turkeys in Iowa. He came up with the show's name. (The car-repair show followed, so it seemed appropriate.) Thus my annual turkey talk show began and it continues today. I've repaired a lot more gravy than turkey, but there have been a few turkey crises (such as the novice cook who had just taken his bird out of the freezer that morning and wondered why it hadn't thawed in 5 hours).

So, that is how I came to be the local turkey expert, though I hesitate to label myself with that lofty title. I have always told my listeners that no one learns more than I on my cooking show. I will have to say I've collected an impressive stack of information and turkey recipes with all of the trimmings.

I always start with a fresh turkey because I like the flavor and

Plan on 1 lb. of turkey per person. You'll have plenty plus some leftovers.

Don't reheat turkey in the microwave oven. Wrap it securely in heavy-duty foil and heat in a 350-degree oven or place in a pan with the leftover gravy and reheat on the range top.

texture better. I soak it overnight in brine as I describe below and the results are a flavorful, tender, and juicy turkey. Skip the brining step if you have a frozen turkey. If you do roast a frozen bird, follow the directions below for thawing it properly.

Both of the following roasting methods can result in a beautiful, tasty turkey. I prefer the traditional 325-degree method for a larger bird and for one that is stuffed. For a turkey up to 15 lb. the shorter method with higher temperature gets perfect results. I prefer to roast a turkey unstuffed and serve the stuffing (or "dressing" as we call it down South) in a separate casserole with a crisp brown top and fluffy interior. If you have been intimidated by the stuffing procedure or don't want to get up so early to do it, just skip it and bake the stuffing on the side.

I include two of my favorite stuffing recipes. If I have good eaters coming to dinner I make both. The bread stuffing is for the local traditionalists and the cornbread is for those of us who grew up Southern, because we know it's not Thanksgiving without some cornbread dressing.

One question I often get concerns making stuffing ahead. You can make it ahead and spread it into a shallow baking dish to chill overnight. You *cannot* stuff the stuffing into the bird ahead. It has to go in just before the turkey goes into the oven.

Here is some other essential advice.

- Be sure to have a thermometer so you can determine when the turkey is done. Even if you have a frozen turkey with a pop-up thermometer, it is a good idea to double check the internal temperature.

- I prefer roasting a turkey in an open roasting pan. Invest in a large, heavy-duty *V* rack and a heavy-duty roasting pan with sturdy handles on the end. Your turkey will turn out better and it is much easier and safer to take in and out of the oven.

- Note that I say below that basting is optional. (That has caused a lot of discussion on the show.) After the turkey is in the oven long enough for the skin to brown, the basting stock will simply run down into the bottom of the pan. None of it goes into the turkey. The only thing you accomplish is to let out a lot of oven heat and lengthen the roasting time. But if it makes you feel better to baste your turkey, go right ahead. It will do no harm.

- When dinner is over, remove all stuffing from the turkey into a dish. Cover and store in the refrigerator immediately. It is best to carve all of the meat from the turkey and store it well covered in the refrigerator. If you plan to boil the carcass for soup, wrap it in foil and chill. Use within a day or two.

Turkey Preparation

For brining:

Twenty-four hours before roasting a fresh turkey, soak it in brine. For a medium to large bird (16-24 lb.), first dissolve 2 cups pickling or kosher salt and 1 cup sugar in 3 qt. boiling water. Cool. For extra flavor, add 3 bay leaves, 1 tbsp. peppercorns, 3 to 4 sprigs of rosemary and/or sage, and 3 cloves peeled garlic to the hot water to infuse while it cools.

Next, remove giblets from both the main cavity and the neck cavity. (Save in refrigerator, if desired.) Wash turkey in cool water.

Place turkey in a large stockpot or roasting pan (of nonreactive material). Pour over the brine concentrate and then add enough cool water to just cover the turkey. Cover and refrigerate. (If the weather is very cold, you can brine the turkey in a protected unheated area such as the garage or a porch. The temperature must be no warmer than 35 to 40 degrees.)

When you are ready to cook, remove turkey from the brine. Rinse and pat dry, inside and out, with soft white paper towels.

For thawing frozen turkey:

Leave in its original wrap. Allow 24 hours in the refrigerator for each 5 pounds.

For no brine:

Remove giblets from both cavities. Rinse the turkey thoroughly, inside and out, with cool water. Pat dry with soft white paper towels.

For stuffed turkey:

Spoon the stuffing into both cavities just before time to start roasting. Seal the cavity with small metal skewers with pointed ends or with a large needle and fine kitchen twine.

For unstuffed turkey:

Season cavities liberally with freshly ground black pepper. If turkey is not brined, add 1 tbsp. kosher or coarse sea salt in the large cavity and 1 tsp. in the neck cavity. Put 6 tbsp. butter, cut into three pieces, into the large cavity. Loosely stuff with fresh sage, parsley, and thyme sprigs; chopped celery and leaves; or coarsely chopped onion, shallots, or leeks (or some of each). Apples may also be used.

For both stuffed and unstuffed turkey:

Tuck the wings and tie the legs together with kitchen twine. Brush outside of turkey generously with olive or vegetable oil.

Roasting Method 1

Preheat the oven to 450 degrees. Place the turkey on a *V*-shaped heavy-duty rack placed in an open roasting pan. Pour some water in the bottom of the pan (not touching the turkey) to prevent burning and preserve the drippings for gravy. Place in the oven so top of turkey is as near center as possible. Roast for 30 minutes at preheated temperature. Turn oven down to 375 degrees for the remaining time (see below). For more even roasting start with the legs pointing to the back of the oven. For about the last hour of roasting, turn the pan so that the legs are pointing toward the front of the oven.

Roasting Method 2

Preheat the oven to 325 degrees. Follow above directions, but roast the entire time at the same temperature. Basting is optional for both methods.

Roasting Times

For unstuffed turkey:
About 12 minutes per pound.
For stuffed turkey:
Between 16 and 18 minutes per pound.

Doneness Check

Check for doneness by moving a drumstick up and down. If it moves easily in the joint, the turkey is likely to be done. The best way to be sure about doneness is to test with an instant-read thermometer placed in the center of the inside thigh muscle (above the drumstick). Don't touch the bone with the thermometer. It is done when the thermometer reads 180 degrees. When roasting just the turkey breast, the thermometer should read 170 degrees when placed in the thickest part of the breast without touching bone.

Allow a turkey to rest on a platter for 20 to 30 minutes (according to the size) before carving. Turkey breast should rest 15 to 20 minutes.

Turkey Stock

6 cups water
6 cups canned chicken broth
1 cup dry white wine
Neck from turkey (and giblets, if desired)
1 bay leaf
3 large sprigs each parsley, thyme, sage, and
    rosemary
1 cup coarsely chopped celery, including leaves
1 cup coarsely chopped onion
1 large carrot, coarsely chopped
1 tsp. black peppercorns

- Bring all to a boil in a large pot. Simmer on low, uncovered, for 2 hours. Strain through a fine sieve. Season with salt to taste.

- Makes 13 cups.

White Wine Turkey Gravy

6 tbsp. butter
3 large shallots, finely chopped
½ cup flour
Turkey drippings
1½ cups dry white wine
3 to 4 cups Turkey Stock
Salt and pepper, to taste

- Melt the butter in a large heavy saucepan. Sauté the shallots until tender.

- Stir in the flour and cook, stirring, for 3 minutes.

- Add the warm drippings to the white wine and whisk into the roux, whisking until smooth. Whisk in 3 to 4 cups of the turkey stock until the gravy is desired consistency. Season to taste.

- Makes 4-5 cups.

Three-Onion Bread Stuffing

10 cups lightly toasted cubed bread (white or a mixture of white and whole wheat)
6 to 7 cups Turkey Stock
2 sticks butter
1½ cups chopped red onion
1 cup chopped green onions
½ cup finely chopped shallots
3 cloves garlic, finely chopped
2 cups chopped celery
½ cup chopped celery leaves
1 cup chopped flat-leaf parsley
2 tbsp. finely chopped fresh sage leaves (2 tsp. dried)
1 tbsp. chopped fresh thyme leaves (1 tsp. dried)
2 tsp. sea salt, or to taste
1 tsp. freshly ground black pepper, or to taste

- Place the bread cubes in a large mixing bowl and pour over the stock to moisten. It should be thoroughly moistened but not soggy.

- Melt the butter in a large skillet. Sauté the onions, shallots, garlic, and celery in the butter, stirring until celery is "crisp tender."

- Remove from heat and stir in the herbs. Toss into the bread. Add the salt and pepper. Taste and correct the seasonings.

- Stuff into the turkey. Makes enough to stuff an 18- to 20-lb. turkey.

- To bake the stuffing as a casserole, toss in 3 beaten eggs and pour into 2 2-qt. greased baking dishes. Bake in a preheated 375-degree oven until hot through and lightly browned—45 minutes to 1 hour.

Southern Cornbread-Pecan Stuffing

2 sticks butter
3 cups chopped onion
2 cups chopped celery
2 bunches green onions, sliced
Cornbread (see below)
2 tsp. dried thyme leaves
1 tbsp. dried sage leaves
Salt, black pepper, and cayenne pepper, to taste
½ cup chopped parsley
Stock, just enough to moisten
3 eggs, beaten
2 cups toasted pecans

- Melt the butter in a large skillet. Over high heat, cook the onion, celery, and green onions, stirring, for 5 minutes. Pour into a large mixing bowl.
- Add the cornbread, herbs, and seasonings. Stir in enough stock to moisten and the eggs. Toss in the pecans.
- Pour into a well-greased shallow 3-qt. baking pan (or 2 smaller pans) and bake in a 375-degree oven for 45 to 50 minutes or until hot through and golden brown on the top. Serve topped with gravy.
- Serves 10-12.

Cornbread

2 cups cornmeal
1 tsp. salt
2 tsp. baking powder
½ tsp. baking soda
2 cups buttermilk
3 eggs, beaten
4 tbsp. olive or vegetable oil

- Preheat oven to 450 degrees.
- Stir together the dry ingredients. Stir buttermilk into eggs and stir into the dry ingredients. Do not over mix.
- Heat the oil in a heavy baking pan (9″ x 13″). Pour in the batter. Bake until golden and toothpick inserted in the center comes out clean—about 20 minutes.
- Cool and tear into coarse chunks into a large mixing bowl.

For Cornbread Oyster Stuffing, omit the pecans and add 1 pt. medium-sized fresh oysters with their liquor.

To taste something with raw eggs or raw meat or poultry to correct the seasonings before cooking, remove a spoonful and cook it in the microwave oven. Cool and taste.

Mainly Meats

Brown Sauce

Roasted Rib Roast
with Sauce Madeira and
Yorkshire Pudding

**Ginger-Lime Beef
Tenderloin**
with Apple Pear Chutney

Marilyn's Zesty Meatloaf

Barbecued Brisket

**Roasted Citrus Pork
Tenderloin**

Pork Medallions
with Apple and Cabbage

Cincinnati Chili Chops

**Garlic Roasted
Leg of Lamb**

You may be hosting your most elegant party or just throwing a picnic in the backyard. Chances are you'll plan either menu around a main dish selected to fit the occasion. In this chapter you'll find recipes for both of those parties, plus a number of other meat dishes to serve both your family and your favorite guests.

A simple beef roast with a tasty sauce and vegetable side dishes remains a trend-proof menu. Following are recipes and directions for roasting standing rib roast and beef tenderloin. They both come from the rib section making them naturally tender and juicy. A rib roast with bones can be roasted slowly because the bones insulate and keep the meat moist while contributing a rich flavor. Always position this cut of beef with the fat side up so it bastes as it roasts. A boneless rib or "rib-eye" roast is roasted at slightly higher temperature, 350 degrees. With its generous amount of marbling this boneless cut can be roasted at this moderate temperature and finish moist and tender. Beef tenderloin, the leanest cut, has little or no marbling and should be trimmed of all external fat and brushed with oil before it goes into a very hot oven, 450 to 500 degrees, to roast in a relatively short period of time. Roast all tender cuts of beef uncovered. Place on a rack in a shallow pan so the heat can surround the meat on all sides, and start with a preheated oven. If you want to infuse the meat with flavor before roasting, use a flavorful dry or wet rub. (See grilling chapter for more rubs and marinades.) In that case, a sauce is optional. For example, I serve chutney as a side condiment rather than saucing the flavorful marinated beef tenderloin.

A good cut of tender beef can be simply seasoned with salt and pepper and sauced before serving. Pour some beef stock and/or red or white wine under the rack (not touching the meat) so the drippings fall to the bottom of the pan into the liquid. Those pan juices make a fine sauce or gravy. Another option is to make one of the sauces that follow and have it ready when the meat comes out of the oven.

The most popular "less tender" cuts of beef roasts are: brisket, chuck, round, sirloin tip, rump, and eye of the round. They have less marbling and are generally not as tender. They are only cooked with dry heat after being marinated for several hours. Braising is the preferred method, as in "pot roast," so named because these cuts are cooked in a covered pot and often with vegetables, herbs, and flavors added. When making a pot roast:

• Brown the meat first for best flavor and color.

• Roast in a pot with a heavy bottom and a tight-fitting lid.

• May be roasted on top of the range or in the oven, but keep the temperature low to moderate.

• Add just enough liquid to add moisture. Don't boil the meat by adding too much liquid.

• Add a flavorful liquid, stock, and/or wine, rather than water.

• Toss in a bouquet garni composed of some flavorful herbs (thyme, rosemary, etc.) for extra flavor.

Follow the same rules for beefsteaks as for the larger cuts. Tender cuts can be simply seasoned and grilled, sautéed, or broiled using high heat. The less tender cuts need to be marinated or braised.

The pork people have done a great job informing us about today's pork that is much leaner than what our mothers and grandmothers cooked. Please note the temperatures for cooking pork in the recipes that follow.

We have an elegant leg of lamb for you to try too, and this chapter wouldn't be complete without my husband's favorite meat dish, meatloaf.

Brown Sauce

A flavorful sauce can turn the simplest cut of meat into an elegant dish fit for your most discriminating guest. Following is a classic sauce that can do wonders for a grilled beefsteak or a plain slice of roast beef or veal. Add it to other sauces for instant flavor and body. For example, sauté a beef fillet in a bit of clarified butter to the desired doneness. Remove from the skillet and deglaze the pan with some red wine. Whisk in a large spoonful of brown sauce with a splash or two extra wine or water to thin it to the desired consistency and it's finished. Busy cooks don't usually have time to make fancy sauces from scratch, but this is a sauce to make ahead when you have some creative time to spend in your kitchen. It will keep, tightly sealed, for a couple of weeks in the refrigerator and months in the freezer. Pack the frozen sauce in small amounts ready to go directly into the pan. It can also be thawed quickly in the microwave oven. Make this sauce in stages. Start by making the Beef Stock (see index). It can be made ahead, chilled, and finished a day or so later. Make the Brown Sauce in a heavy pot so it can slowly cook without scorching. Chop the vegetables to a very fine dice and brown them well for the best flavor. When it is finished, you may reduce this sauce by half to a very concentrated sauce called "demi-glace." It takes up very little space in the refrigerator, keeps for months, and a small spoonful will add a magic flavor touch to many dishes.

> **Brown Roux (see below)**
> ¼ **cup chopped carrots**
> ¼ **cup chopped celery**
> ½ **cup chopped onion**
> ¼ **cup extravirgin olive oil**
> **2 large sprigs thyme**
> **1 bay leaf**
> ½ **cup dry white wine**
> **3 tbsp. tomato paste**
> **8 cups hot Beef Stock**

- Make the Brown Roux.
- Slowly cook the vegetables in the olive oil in a heavy pan over medium-low heat for 15 to 20 minutes or until they turn golden brown. Stir often.
- Tie the thyme and bay leaf together with kitchen twine. Add to the pot with the wine. Whisk in roux.

- Add tomato paste and gradually stir in stock, making sure there are no lumps. Bring to a boil over high heat, stirring, and reduce heat to very low. Simmer for 2 hours, stirring frequently and skimming fat. The sauce is complete when it is reduced by half.
- Makes about 4 cups.

Brown Roux
¼ cup clarified butter
5 tbsp. flour

- Heat the butter in a small heavy saucepan. Whisk in the flour. Stir over low heat and cook for 5 to 6 minutes, stirring constantly, until it turns a light brown color.

Roasted Rib Roast with Sauce Madeira and Yorkshire Pudding

The elegant standing rib roast has graced many a holiday table in this country, but in England it stars almost always at the Christmas dinner table, as well as on other special occasions. A typical and tasty preparation for this succulent cut of beef is the one that follows: napped with a hearty Madeira Sauce and accompanied by a crispy Yorkshire Pudding. The Yorkshire Pudding comes from my good pal Chris Hassall's mum, Jo Hassall, who shared her recipe all the way from her home in England.

3 tbsp. olive oil
1 tbsp. sea salt
1 tsp. finely chopped fresh garlic
1 tsp. freshly ground black pepper
1 standing rib roast (4 to 6 lb.)

- Preheat oven to 325 degrees. Mix together the oil, salt, garlic, and pepper. Rub on surface of roast.
- Place fat side up on a rack in a shallow roasting pan. Place in preheated oven and roast for 15 to 18 minutes per pound for medium rare or 20 to 25 minutes per pound for medium well to well done. Check for doneness by sticking the instant-read meat thermometer sideways into the center of the meat. Don't go through the fat layer or touch the bone.

Always allow large cuts of just-roasted meat to sit for 30 minutes before carving.

To make your standing rib roast easier to carve into uniform slices, ask your butcher to cut the meat away from the bones and tie it back together. When roasting is completed, cut the string, place the meat on a carving board, and carve cutting against the grain. Save the bones for soup or stock.

You can make this sauce hours ahead and reheat it. It is best made with a good homemade beef stock, but it can be made with canned beef consommé.

- Remove from the oven and allow to sit for 30 minutes before carving. Slice between the ribs into thick slices.
- Serves 6-8.

Sauce Madeira

3 tbsp. Madeira
1 cup beef stock
3 tbsp. butter
¼ cup flour
Salt, to taste
Dash white pepper

- Add 1 tbsp. Madeira to the beef stock and bring to a boil in a small saucepan. Keep warm.
- In a separate heavy saucepan, melt the butter and add the flour. Stir over medium heat for 3 to 4 minutes. (The flour should take on a pale brown color.)
- Whisk in the warm stock. Reduce to low and simmer for 3 minutes and finish with remaining Madeira. Season to taste.
- Makes 1½ cups.

Yorkshire Pudding

All of the pan drippings from the roast beef
1 cup flour
1 tsp. salt
4 eggs
2½ cups milk

- Preheat the oven to 450 degrees.
- Pour the pan drippings into a 9" x 13" x 2" baking pan.
- Sift flour and salt into a bowl. Make a well in center and break eggs into well. Add half of the milk. Mix and beat thoroughly.
- Add remaining milk and mix into a smooth thin batter.
- Place the pan in the preheated oven just long enough to heat the pan drippings until they are hot and bubbling—but not smoking.
- Remove and pour in the batter. Place in the center of the oven and bake until puffed and dark golden brown—40 to 45 minutes. Make the Yorkshire Pudding after the roast beef has been removed from the oven and while the gravy is being made.
- Serves 4-6.

Madeira, Vermouth (white and red), Sherries, Port, and Marsala are wines often used for flavor in sauces and marinades. They are all fortified wines with higher alcohol content, giving them a shelf life of several months after they are opened. Keep the bottle tightly closed and store in a cool, dark cabinet.

The Yorkshire Pudding is always made after the roast comes out of the oven since the pan drippings are an essential ingredient. Mix the batter just before the roast is done. Remove the roast from the oven and allow it to rest on the carving board. Get the pudding in the oven while the roast rests and is being carved.

Easy blender method for Yorkshire Pudding: pour the milk in first, add the eggs and finally add the dry ingredients and the remaining pan drippings. Process until the mixture is smooth and pour into the pan.

Ginger-Lime Beef Tenderloin with Apple Pear Chutney

Beef tenderloin is a year-round favorite to serve at a dinner party and is delicious hot or cold. The advantage of a marinade like this one is that you can simply slice the meat and serve it without any sauce. A side condiment such as chutney adds flavor and interest. This easily made chutney can be prepared days ahead and is also delicious with ham and pork roast. It keeps for weeks in the refrigerator. Store in a tightly sealed glass container.

3 to 4 lb. beef tenderloin
¼ cup extravirgin olive oil
1 tbsp. finely chopped gingerroot
2 large cloves garlic, finely chopped
2 tbsp. fresh lime juice
1 tsp. lime zest
1 tbsp. coarse sea salt
½ tsp. cayenne pepper
1 tbsp. honey

- Trim all of the fat and skin off of the tenderloin. Place beef in a large heavy-duty plastic bag with a zip top.
- Stir together all of the remaining ingredients until well mixed. Rub onto all sides of the meat. Press out the air and seal the bag. Place in refrigerator for 24 hours.
- Place the tenderloin on a rack in a shallow roasting pan. Roast in a preheated 500-degree oven for 20 to 30 minutes or until the thermometer registers desired doneness. Remove from oven and allow to rest 10 minutes before slicing.
- Serve warm with the Apple Pear Chutney spooned on the side.
- Serves 6-8.

Apple Pear Chutney

3 large tart cooking apples, peeled and cubed
3 large pears, peeled and cubed
½ cup red wine vinegar
2 cups sugar
2 tbsp. Worcestershire sauce
1 tsp. Tabasco sauce
2 tbsp. finely chopped gingerroot
1 tsp. hot curry powder
1 cup golden raisins
1 tsp. salt

To freeze beef, wrap in moisture-proof wrap, press out air, and freeze in a freezer that is no warmer than 0 degrees. Store large cuts up to 1 year, steaks up to 6 months, and ground beef up to 3 months. Thaw in the refrigerator.

For generous servings of roast beef (and probably left-overs), figure on 6 to 8 oz. trimmed boneless raw meat per person. For a roast with bones, figure on 12 oz. to 1 lb. per person.

- In a heavy, nonreactive saucepan over medium-high heat, stir together the apples, pears, vinegar, and sugar until sugar is dissolved. Reduce to low and simmer, uncovered, for 20 minutes.
- Add the remaining ingredients and simmer 20 minutes longer or until the fruit is very tender.
- Cool. Cover and chill until ready to serve.
- Makes 3½-4 cups.

Marilyn's Zesty Meatloaf

I think anyone who likes meat fancies a meal of really good meatloaf with mashed potatoes. A successful meatloaf depends on fresh ingredients and proper cooking technique. In my kitchen the only way to cook a meatloaf is to first mold it in a loaf pan and then invert it into a shallow baking pan. I always top mine with a glaze to make it look prettier and to keep it moist and more flavorful as it bakes. To make this meatloaf even zestier, simply add more cayenne pepper. Serve with Parmesan Mashed Potatoes (see index).

> 3 tbsp. extravirgin olive oil
> 1½ cups chopped onion
> 2 large cloves garlic, finely chopped
> 2 lb. ground sirloin
> 2 eggs
> 2 tbsp. milk
> 1 cup fresh breadcrumbs
> ¼ cup chopped flat-leaf parsley
> 2 tbsp. finely shredded fresh basil
> 1½ tsp. salt
> ¼ tsp. cayenne pepper, or to taste
> 1 tbsp. orange zest
> ¾ cup chile sauce
> 3 tbsp. dark brown sugar
> 1 tbsp. Dijon mustard
> 1 tbsp. fresh orange juice
> ½ tsp. hot pepper sauce
> Orange slices, for garnish (optional)

- Heat the olive oil in a small skillet and sauté the onion and garlic for about 3 minutes, stirring.

For best flavor, onions and garlic should be lightly cooked before they are added to meatloaf or hamburgers.

Fresh ground beef is bright red on the outside, but dull red in the center because the center is not exposed to light.

For a very lean meatloaf, buy a center-cut chuck steak or top round steak. Cut the well-chilled beef into cubes and finely chop in the food processor.

Fresh breadcrumbs make a moister meatloaf than dry bread or cracker crumbs.

Dark brown sugar has more molasses in it and lends more flavor than light brown sugar.

- Remove from heat, cool slightly, and toss with a fork into the ground beef.
- Whisk together the egg and milk and pour over the bread-crumbs. Add the breadcrumb mixture, parsley, basil, salt, pepper, and orange zest to the beef. Toss lightly to mix well.
- Gently press the mixture into a loaf pan. Run a flexible metal spatula or knife blade between the meatloaf and the sides of the pan. Invert into a lightly greased shallow baking pan.
- Make the glaze by stirring together the chile sauce, sugar, mustard, orange juice, and hot sauce. Spoon it over the top of the meatloaf, spreading evenly. (Some glaze will run down the sides.)
- Bake in a preheated 350-degree oven for 1 hour and 15 minutes or until done through. Let cool a few minutes before slicing. Garnish with a thinly sliced orange, if desired.
- Serves 6-8.

Barbecued Brisket

I have so many friends who are exemplary cooks. I extended an invitation to as many as I could to contribute to this book. Richard Roth is an expert bread baker who prides himself on being a pretty darn good grill chef. Smoked brisket is one of his specialties. If you have a smoker with a water pan, Dick suggests using a can of beer instead of water.

⅓ **cup red wine vinegar**
¼ **cup catsup**
¼ **cup soy sauce**
2 tbsp. oil
1 tbsp. Worcestershire sauce
½ **tsp. dry mustard**
1 large clove garlic, finely chopped
1 tsp. salt
¼ **tsp. pepper**
1 large onion, chopped
1 tbsp. pure chili powder
5 lb. beef brisket

Marinating meats in a plastic bag is convenient because you can simply toss away the bag. Be sure to use a heavy-duty bag or two regular bags. Always place the bag in a shallow dish before placing it in the refrigerator.

- To make the marinade, mix together all of the ingredients except the brisket.
- Trim the fat from the brisket and place in a shallow glass dish or a large heavy-duty plastic bag with a zip top.

- Pour over the marinade, coating the beef well. Cover the dish tightly or press out the air and seal the bag. Place in the refrigerator and marinate 24 hours.
- Smoke brisket in a smoker or gas grill set at 200 to 250 degrees for 8 hours.
- Remove beef from the smoker and wrap securely in heavy-duty foil. Place in a preheated 225 degree oven for 2 hours or until very tender. Test with fork for doneness.
- To serve, blend the cooked meat juices with your favorite barbecue sauce. Brush on the brisket and glaze quickly on the grill or under the boiler. Pass the remaining sauce.
- Serves 6-8.

Roasted Citrus Pork Tenderloin

Easy, quick and delicious: what more can you ask from a dinner entrée? This pork tenderloin delivers on all three counts. Marinate it at least 8 hours to allow enough time for the pork to be infused with this fresh-flavored marinade. Be sure to roast it on a rack and take care not to overcook it. For a nice presentation, slice on the diagonal into about 2" slices. Serve plain or add your favorite mustard sauce with some orange peel stirred into it. It is tasty hot or cold.

> **2 pork tenderloins**
> **¼ cup extravirgin olive oil**
> **2 tbsp. fresh lemon juice**
> **2 tbsp. fresh orange juice**
> **1 tsp. lemon zest**
> **2 tsp. orange zest**
> **2 large cloves garlic, finely chopped**
> **2 tbsp. chopped fresh thyme leaves**
> **2 tsp. kosher salt**
> **1 tsp. coarsely ground black pepper**

- Preheat oven to 500 degrees. Thoroughly trim the pork of all fat and skin. Mix together all of the remaining ingredients and rub the mixture onto all surfaces of the meat. Place in a zip-lock plastic bag. Chill for at least 8 hours in the refrigerator.
- Place pork on a rack in a shallow pan. Roast for 25 to 30 minutes in the preheated oven, or until the internal temperature is 150 degrees. Let sit for a few minutes before slicing.
- Serves 6-8.

Pork Medallions
with Apple and Cabbage

This quickly cooked dish is fun to eat because it's simply bursting with rich flavor. Serve it on a chilly day with just some crusty bread and a glass of good wine. Use your veal pounder or the bottom of a heavy glass to flatten these pork tenderloin slices into quick-cooking "medallions." Slice the apples very thin so they will be "crisp tender" by the time the cabbage cooks. This is the time to bring out some really good, well-aged balsamic vinegar. You may substitute dry Sherry or Madeira for the dry Marsala.

> 1 medium head green cabbage
> 2 large Granny Smith apples
> 4 tbsp. butter (½ stick)
> 4 shallots, finely chopped
> 1 tsp. fine sea salt, or to taste
> ½ tsp. freshly ground black pepper, or to taste
> 2 tbsp. balsamic vinegar
> 1 pork tenderloin
> Fine sea salt and freshly ground black pepper
> Flour
> 2 tbsp. unsalted butter
> 3 tbsp. vegetable oil
> ¼ cup chicken stock
> 1 cup heavy cream
> ¼ cup dry Marsala
> 1 tbsp. Dijon mustard
> Chopped fresh parsley

- Cut the cabbage into quarters and slice each into coarse shreds.

- Peel, core, and halve the apples. Cut into thin slices.

- Melt the butter in a large skillet. Sauté the shallots and cabbage, stirring over high heat for 5 minutes.

- Stir in the apple slices. Season with salt and pepper. Reduce heat to medium and continue cooking, uncovered, for 10 minutes or until apples are just tender and the cabbage is limp.

- Stir in the vinegar. Taste to correct seasonings. Cover and keep warm until pork is ready.

- Trim all of the fat and skin from the pork. Slice into ¼" slices.

Place the slices between 2 layers of plastic wrap and pound until very thin (⅛"). Mix together the salt and pepper and lightly season the meat, then dredge in flour to coat.

- Heat the butter and oil over medium-high heat in a heavy, large skillet. Sauté the pork medallions for 1 minute on each side. Transfer to a platter and keep warm.

- Pour excess fat from skillet and add the stock, cream, and Marsala. Cook over high heat to reduce by one-half. Whisk in the mustard. Taste to correct seasonings.

- Spoon the sauce over the pork and surround it with the apple-cabbage mixture. Sprinkle with chopped parsley. Serve immediately.

- Serves 6-8.

Cincinnati Chili Chops

Be advised that Cincinnati's famous and unique style of chili has nothing to do with the Tex-Mex dish, but Cincinnatians love it. Try this recipe and you will see why. My friend Chuck Martin, food editor of the Cincinnati Enquirer, *submits here one of his pork-chop recipes that represents the "Queen City" in proper fashion. With their town called "Porkopolis" in the nineteenth century, Cincinnatians, many with German heritage, ate a lot of pork. Chuck recently helped to revive the pork tradition when he declared "The Year of the Pork Chop" in the "Taste" section of the Sunday paper. This recipe was one of many flavorful pork recipes he created for his culinary campaign.*

> **4 rib or loin pork chops, cut about 1½" thick**
> **Olive oil**
> **Cincinnati Chili Rub (see below)**
> **Cincinnati Chili Sauce (see below)**
> **½ cup grated cheddar cheese**
> **Canned French-fried onions (optional)**

- Rub pork chops lightly on both sides with olive oil. Sprinkle about 1 tsp. chili rub on each side of pork chops and press until spices adhere. Cover chops and allow to rest at room temperature no longer than 1 hour or refrigerate overnight.

- Grill or broil chops until internal temperature is 150 to 155 degrees and allow to rest for 5 minutes.

- Divide the chili sauce equally among 4 plates and scatter about

1 tbsp. grated cheese over top of each portion of chili. Place a chop on top of the cheese. If desired, sprinkle French-fried onions over top of chops as garnish.

• Serves 4.

Cincinnati Chili Rub

1 tsp. each black pepper, allspice, cinnamon, cayenne pepper, and whole cumin
½ tsp. white pepper
⅛ tsp. ground cloves
1½ tsp. salt
½ tsp. cocoa powder

• Combine all ingredients except salt and cocoa powder in sauté pan over medium heat. Shake pan until spices are fragrant, 3 to 5 minutes.

• Remove pan from heat and add spices, along with salt and cocoa, to electric spice grinder. Blend until cumin seeds are roughly ground and spices are mixed well.

Cincinnati Chili Sauce

1 medium onion, finely diced
½ medium green bell pepper, ribbed, seeded, and finely diced
2 tbsp. olive oil
Salt and pepper, to taste
2 15-oz. cans crushed tomatoes, with juice
2 cups kidney beans, cooked or canned
1 tbsp. Worcestershire sauce
2 tbsp. cider vinegar
2 garlic cloves, finely diced
2 tbsp. chopped parsley
2 tsp. hot pepper sauce, or to taste

• Sauté diced onion and bell pepper in olive oil over medium heat until onions are transparent, about 7 minutes.

• Add salt and pepper to taste along with the crushed tomatoes, and simmer on low, uncovered, 15 to 20 minutes.

• Stir in beans. (If using canned beans, rinse and drain first.) Add Worcestershire, vinegar, diced garlic, chopped parsley, and hot pepper sauce, and simmer 10 minutes.

• Taste and correct seasoning. Keep chili warm while cooking chops.

To best preserve color and flavor, store condiments such as catsup, hot pepper sauce, and Worcestershire sauce in the refrigerator.

Store whole garlic in a container that is well ventilated, such as a basket. Place in a cool, dark place and not in the refrigerator.

Garlic Roasted Leg of Lamb

For the best lamb dish, start with the best lamb you can find. Fresh is important. I've never had any imported frozen lamb that was really good. When preparing your good, fresh lamb, trim away as much fat as possible. Even those who say they are not fond of lamb flavor will change their minds when it is properly trimmed. Infusing it with garlic and other good flavors also helps to win over those who think they don't enjoy lamb. Roast this bone-in leg to a perfect golden brown, then carve it on the diagonal into thin, succulent slices. Serve with some pretty roasted vegetables and a glass of good red wine.

> **5 to 6 lb. leg of lamb**
> **3 large cloves garlic, peeled and thinly sliced**
> **2 tbsp. Dijon mustard**
> **¼ cup extravirgin olive oil**
> **2 tsp. coarsely ground black pepper**
> **1 tbsp. kosher salt**
> **1 tbsp. fresh lemon juice**

- Trim all of the fat from the outside of the lamb. Using a small sharp knife, make small incisions in the surface of the lamb and fill each with a sliver of garlic, using the tip of the knife blade to push the garlic into each slit.
- Mix together the mustard, olive oil, pepper, salt, and lemon juice. Spread the mixture over the top and sides of the lamb. Place in a shallow dish. Cover securely with plastic wrap and place in the refrigerator overnight.
- To roast, place on a rack in a shallow roasting pan. Place in a preheated 450-degree oven for 15 minutes.
- Reduce heat to 325 degrees and roast for about 1 hour for medium rare (longer if you prefer medium to well).
- Place the lamb on a large platter and garnish with lemon slices and parsley sprigs, if desired.
- Serves 8.

Use a knife with a long, thin blade for carving meat. Look for "slicing knife" or "carving knife." A boning or fillet knife is used for boning and has a very thin, flexible blade.

Cooking Terms:
Braise: to cook, covered, in a small amount of liquid, usually after preliminary browning (for meats and poultry) or to cook certain vegetables in a small amount of liquid without browning.

Broil: to cook with radiant heat from above.

Deglaze: to add liquid to a sauté pan or other pan, stirring or swirling over heat to dissolve the particles of food remaining in the pan—the liquid is usually used as a sauce or to flavor a sauce.

Pan broil: to cook, uncovered, in a skillet without fat.

Roast: to cook foods by surrounding with hot, dry air in an oven or covered grill (meats, poultry, seafood, and vegetables).

Great Grilling

**Ginger-Pepper Steak
Marinade**

Honey-Lime Marinade

Red Wine Marinade

Bourbon Marinade

Herbed Mustard Marinade

Lemon-Dill Rub

**Zesty Dry Rub
for Pork and Beef**

**Santa Fe Dry Rub
for Pork, Beef, and Chicken**

Savory Seafood Dry Rub

**Grilled Vegetable Dip
with Basil**

Great Grilled Salmon

**Grilled Fish and
Vegetable Kebabs**

**Lime-Marinated
Chicken Kebabs
with Roasted Corn Salsa**

Russ's Grilled Chicken

**Quick Southern
Barbecued Chicken**

Grilled Chicken Salad

**Rosemary-Lemon
Pork Chops**

**Barbecued Pork
Tenderloin**

Grilled Orange Pork

In the past few years I've taught a number of classes featuring foods from the grill. A popular summer class, "Meals from the Grill," appears every year in my class schedule with a new menu every year. Grilling suits the kind of casual entertaining that defines how so many of us enjoy spending our leisure time and the cooking is often part of the fun. Another driving force of the ever-increasing interest in grilling is the evolution of the appliance itself. Large, fancy, state-of-the-art grills are replacing the typical backyard charcoal grill. There are, of course, exceptions. My good pal Russ Wiles, who shares his wonderful recipe for whole chickens from the grill in this chapter, still insists that charcoal-grilled food tastes better. However, even traditionalists like Russ have upgraded their grills to fancy new models that have features such as gas starters for the charcoal and more accurate heat control. Today's grills are generally larger, fancier, and easier to use and that just means more fun for the "al fresco" chef.

Basic Outdoor Grill Cookery

Begin by preheating your grill, whether that means turning on the gas or starting the fire. Adjust the heat according to what is being cooked. Even with charcoal grills, where there is no control for regulating the heat, it is fairly simple to cook perfectly done food because you can control where to place the food on the grill. A whole chicken or large cut of meat, for example, can be seared and browned directly over the fire on one side of the grill, then moved aside to finish with indirect heat.

Foods that are grilled (as opposed to roasted or smoked) should have constant high heat under them. Keep the grill lid open and tend the food. But don't be too attentive and keep turning it. Beef and fish steaks, small chops, and burgers are best turned only once about two-thirds of the way through the cooking time. Pressing the burger with the spatula causes the juices to run out and produces a dry burger.

• A necessary tool for precise grilling is the instant-read thermometer. Not designed to leave in the food during the entire cooking time like the cooking thermometers of the past, the small probe is inserted into the center of the food when you are ready to check for doneness and you get an immediate temperature reading. These little cooking thermometers are found in every cooking store and are relatively inexpensive. There is even a cooking fork that gives you the internal temperature when plunged into the food. Knowing the internal temperature is, of course, imperative for poultry since it must be fully cooked, 170 degrees for the breast and 180 degrees (or until the juices run clear) for the dark meat on the thigh and leg portions.

- Pork is cooked until done inside (150 to 160 degrees). We used to cook it to a much higher 185 degrees, but pork is leaner now and dries out very quickly if overcooked. For large cuts of pork such as a whole loin, the temperature will continue to rise after the meat has been removed from the grill. Remove these larger cuts at 150 degrees.

- Beef can be cooked to your desired doneness, but because of food safety many of us are cooking our beef longer. For instance I never serve burgers rare (125 to 130 degrees) anymore, but continue to cook them until they are at least medium (140 degrees) and usually medium well (150 degrees). The fancy cuts such as beef tenderloin are often seared over high heat with a rare internal temperature (125 degrees). Tender beefsteaks (filet mignon, rib eye, etc.) are also grilled over high heat and can be served from rare to well done. Medium-rare internal temperature for tender beefsteaks is 135 degrees, medium 140 degrees, medium-well 150 degrees, and well-done 155 to 160 degrees.

- For "less-tender" cuts of beef such as beef brisket and pork butt that you want to cook until they literally fall apart in the barbecue sauce, the thermometer should go all the way to 180 to 185 degrees.

- Judging the doneness of fish and seafood is a bit easier. The general rule is 10 minutes cooking time per inch of thickness. Turn it only once. Another test for doneness is when it easily flakes with a fork. Take care not to overcook fish. For fish such as salmon and tuna that is often seared over high heat with a browned outside but left rare to medium-rare inside, the thermometer is essential for accuracy.

Gourmet Burgers
with Béarnaise Mayonnaise

**Flank Steak in Spicy
Southwest Marinade**

Grilled Lamb Chops
with Shallot-Parsley Butter

**Grilled Butterflied
Leg of Lamb**

Ratatouille in a Package

Grilled New Potatoes

Grilled Fennel

Grilled Asparagus

Grilled Corn on Cob
with Chili Lime Butter

Spicy Baked Pinto Beans

- Just like the well-equipped kitchen, having the right grilling tools helps you to turn out a better product, besides making the whole process easier and more fun. Treat yourself to some proper tools designed for cooking on the grill. They have longer handles that protect you from the high heat and heavy-duty potholders and mitts protect your hands and arms.

Grill and Food Safety

- Place your grill in a well-ventilated area.
- When using a charcoal grill be cautious with lighter fluid. Never add it to coals after the fire is started.
- Be sure all fires are out when you finish cooking.
- Keep poultry, meats, and seafood chilled until ready to put on the grill.
- Place poultry, meats, and seafood on a clean, dry plate and take a second clean plate for the cooked food when it comes off of the grill. You contaminate the cooked food when you put it on a plate that contains raw juices.

Marinades and Rubs

There are several approaches to infusing flavor into foods from the grill.

- Marinades: Usually a combination of oil, some acid ingredients such as fruit juice, vinegar, or alcohol, and spices and herbs, marinades infuse with flavor. The oil lubricates and enhances browning when the food is cooked. The acid ingredients enhance the flavor absorption by meats, poultry, and fish and have some tenderizing effect. Food can remain in a marinade as short a time as 30 minutes or as long as 24 hours, depending on what is being marinated. Fish and chicken need less time than beef and pork. All seafood, meats, and poultry should be marinated in the refrigerator. When the food is very cold, you can save time by marinating for short periods of time—30 to 45 minutes—at room temperature. After that, place in the refrigerator. Marinate in dishes made from nonreactive materials, such as glass. The most convenient "container" is a heavy-duty plastic bag with a recloseable top. (Double the bags if you don't have the "freezer-weight" or heavy-duty ones.) Remove the food from the bag and toss the bag away. Marinades are used only once. If you plan to baste the grilled food with a marinade, set aside what you need for basting before adding the raw meats, fish, or poultry.

- Dry Rubs: The most common type of rub is a dry mixture of spices and herbs, sometimes seasoned with salt and a bit of sugar for flavor. For lean cuts of poultry, meats, and fish, spray or rub oil onto the surface before rubbing on the dry rub. Spraying or brushing on more oil before the food is placed on the grill helps the rub adhere and sears the outside more efficiently. There are many ready-to-use dry rubs to purchase, but it is easy and more economical to make your own. Make them with the freshest spices and herbs (not those that have been sitting in your cabinet for a couple of years). Store, tightly sealed, in glass jars in a cool, dark cabinet. This type of rub can be used for everything from ribs to fish.

- Wet Rubs: I refer to the recipes of oil-based mixtures that often contain fresh garlic and fresh herbs as "wet rubs," and they end up looking more like a flavorful paste. Olive oil is usually the base for my wet rubs, because I like the flavor of the oil itself. If the rub has strong flavors such as pepper and piquant spices, I recommend using a regular bland vegetable oil as the base. This type of rub can be used for everything from fish fillets that need only an hour or so to be infused with flavor to pork loin that is always marinated overnight.

Ginger-Pepper Steak Marinade

Though many of the recipes in this chapter have their own seasonings and marinades, I begin with some multipurpose marinades and rubs. Experiment to see which flavors you like best. Try these recipes with a variety of meats, poultry, and seafood. Correct the seasonings to your own palate. All grilled food tastes better when it's infused with great flavors before grilling. I usually use the one below on flank steak, but it is also good for a thick-cut top sirloin or sirloin strip steaks.

2 tbsp. finely chopped gingerroot
1 tsp. freshly ground coarse black pepper
2 large cloves garlic, chopped
2 tbsp. lemon juice
2 tbsp. brown sugar
¼ cup soy sauce
2 tbsp. dry sherry
¼ cup vegetable oil

- Stir together all ingredients until mixed. Place the beef in shallow glass dish or recloseable heavy-duty plastic bag. Pour over the marinade. Cover tightly and refrigerate for 24 hours. Remove from marinade and grill to desired doneness.
- Makes about 1½ cups.

Honey-Lime Marinade

This is my favorite flavor combination for chicken and pork. I also marinate duck breasts in this. It tastes good, too, on salmon, tuna, and other very flavorful, meaty fish.

¼ cup fresh lime juice
1 tbsp. lime zest
2 tbsp. finely chopped gingerroot
2 tbsp. chopped cilantro
2 tbsp. honey
3 tbsp. extravirgin olive oil (or vegetable oil)
¼ tsp. cayenne pepper
2 tsp. salt
Fresh lime slices and cilantro sprigs

- Mix together all ingredients. Place chicken or pork in a heavy-duty plastic bag and pour over the marinade. Pork (loin, tenderloin, or chops) should be marinated 24 hours, chicken with bones overnight, and boneless breasts at least 2 to 3 hours—all in the refrigerator.
- Makes about ¾ cup.

Red Wine Marinade

I've flavored butterflied leg of lamb with this delicious marinade. Use it too for beef cuts such as flank steak or a whole eye of the round roast or to marinate thick pork chops or a whole pork loin. Dark-meat chicken pieces and game birds as well as venison are other good candidates for this marinade.

> 1½ cups Merlot or Cabernet Sauvignon (or any
>   hearty dry red wine)
> ¼ cup olive oil
> 1 large yellow onion, sliced
> 3 large cloves garlic, peeled and crushed
> ½ cup chopped flat-leaf parsley
> 1 tbsp. chopped fresh rosemary leaves
> 1 tsp. Dijon mustard
> ½ tsp. hot pepper sauce
> ½ tsp. freshly ground black pepper
> 2 tsp. salt

- Combine all ingredients for the marinade. Pour into a large, heavy-duty plastic bag. Place the meat in the marinade, seal, and place in the refrigerator. Marinate for 24 hours, turning occasionally.
- Makes about 2 cups.

Bourbon Marinade

This marinade enhances any cut of beef: flank steak, top round, center chuck steaks and eye of the round steaks or roast. It is also good for pork, dark-meat chicken pieces, and game.

> ½ **cup light soy sauce**
> 3 **tbsp. vegetable oil**
> 2 **medium onions, sliced**
> 3 **large cloves garlic, chopped**
> 2 **tbsp. finely chopped gingerroot**
> 2 **tbsp. dark brown sugar**
> ½ **to 1 tsp. hot pepper sauce**
> ½ **cup bourbon**

- In a heavy-duty gallon-size plastic bag with a zip top, mix together all ingredients. Add the meat and marinate overnight.
- Makes about 1¾ cups.

Herbed Mustard Marinade

This fresh-flavored marinade adds zip to seafood as well as pork and white meat of chicken.

> ½ **cup extravirgin olive oil**
> ½ **cup Dijon mustard**
> 2 **to 3 large cloves garlic, finely chopped**
> 2 **tbsp. white wine vinegar**
> 1 **tbsp. fresh lemon juice**
> 2 **tsp. sea salt**
> ½ **tsp. freshly ground black pepper**
> 1 **tbsp. chopped fresh thyme leaves**
> 1 **tbsp. chopped fresh tarragon leaves**
> 2 **tbsp. chopped flat-leaf parsley**

- Whisk together all ingredients. Pour over the food in a shallow glass dish, cover tightly with plastic, and chill for 1 to 12 hours, depending on what is marinated. Or place food in a heavy-duty recloseable plastic bag and pour over the marinade. Seal and chill for the appropriate time.
- Makes about 1¼ cups.

Lemon-Dill Marinade

Here is a good wet rub to use on any kind of fish for the grill. Fish fillets need only 1 to 2 hours to marinate with this rub and they are ready to grill. Try a whole salmon with this: rinse the inside of the fish thoroughly with cool water. Pat dry and rub inside with this mixture. Close, wrap in plastic wrap, and chill for at least 3 hours or as long as 8 hours. Brush the outside of the fish with vegetable oil and grill over medium heat—or wrap in heavy-duty foil and grill over a hot grill—just until fish flakes (time depends on size of the fish). Serve garnished with lemon wedges and dill sprigs.

> **Juice and zest of 2 large lemons**
> **¼ cup chopped fresh dill (1½ tbsp. dried)**
> **½ cup chopped onion**
> **½ cup extravirgin olive oil**
> **¼ tsp. coarsely ground black pepper**
> **1 tsp. salt, or to taste**
> **½ tsp. brown sugar**

- Mix together the marinade in a heavy-duty zip-top plastic bag. (Or double two regular bags.) Add the seafood to the marinade. Place in the refrigerator and allow to marinate for at least 3 hours if using whole fish.
- Makes about 1½ cups.

Zesty Dry Rub for Pork and Beef

> **2 tbsp. sweet paprika**
> **1 tbsp. onion powder**
> **1 tbsp. garlic powder**
> **2 tbsp. fine sea salt**
> **1 tsp. coarsely ground black pepper**
> **1 tsp. cayenne pepper**
> **2 tsp. thyme leaves**
> **1 tsp. brown sugar**

- Stir together all ingredients. Store in a glass jar with a tight-fitting lid.
- Makes ½ cup.

Santa Fe Dry Rub for Pork, Beef, and Chicken

3 tbsp. pure chili powder (ancho or chipotle)
1 tbsp. green chili powder (jalapeño)
2 tbsp. hot paprika
1 tsp. cayenne pepper, or to taste
1 tbsp. garlic powder
2 tsp. ground cumin
1 tsp. ground coriander
1 tbsp. oregano leaves
2 tbsp. fine sea salt
2 tbsp. dark brown sugar

- Stir together all ingredients. Store in a tightly closed glass jar.
- Makes 1 cup.

Savory Seafood Dry Rub

2 tbsp. onion powder
2 tbsp. garlic powder
1 tbsp. dried thyme leaves
¼ cup dried dill
2 tbsp. sea salt
1 tbsp. coarsely ground black pepper
1 tbsp. white pepper
1 tbsp. sugar

- Stir together all ingredients. Store in a glass jar with a tight-fitting lid.
- Makes about ⅔ cup.

Dry herbs have a shelf life of no longer than 1 year. Store them in a cool place away from light. Crush dried-leaf herbs between your thumb and forefinger to release the flavor before adding to your food.

Grilled Vegetable Dip
with Basil

Take the heat out of the kitchen and let the grill do the work for more than just burgers. Start an informal summertime meal with this dip. It tastes best when made ahead. Serve it with tortilla chips or keep it lighter and healthier with crisp veggies for dipping. Note that each onion is cut lengthwise so that the root end holds it together, preventing it from separating while on the grill.

1 small eggplant (½ to ¾ lb.)
Extravirgin olive oil
Salt, to taste
5 ripe Roma tomatoes
2 large Vidalia onions
1 cup sour cream
3 oz. cream cheese
2 tbsp. mayonnaise
½ cup finely shredded fresh basil
2 tsp. sea salt
1 tsp. hot pepper sauce
Extra basil leaves, for garnish

- Peel the eggplant and cut into ½"-thick slices. Brush both sides with olive oil and sprinkle with some salt.

- Core the tomatoes and cut in half lengthwise. Brush both sides with olive oil and sprinkle cut side with some salt.

- Peel the onions and cut each into 4 or 5 thick, lengthwise slices. Brush with olive oil and sprinkle with some salt.

- Place all of the vegetables on a preheated hot grill and grill, turning once, for about 15 minutes or until the eggplant is fork tender and the tomatoes are cooked and start to give up their juices. The onion slices should be "crisp tender." Remove from grill and cool.

- Remove peeling from tomatoes and chop all of the vegetables in the food processor, pulsing on and off to chop coarsely. Do not purée.

- Whisk together the sour cream, cream cheese, and mayonnaise. Fold in the vegetables and shredded basil. Season with salt and hot pepper sauce. Chill until ready to serve. Garnish with basil leaves and serve with crisp vegetables, tortilla chips, or pita crisps.

- Serves 10-12 as an appetizer.

Great Grilled Salmon

Grilled salmon can be such a treat when properly done. Try this brining method for grilled salmon with great flavor and a firm, but moist, texture. Start with the freshest salmon you can find. Fresh salmon has almost no aroma, so beware of a strong fishy smell. You can substitute coarse sea salt for the kosher salt, but don't use regular fine table salt. For a Southwest flavor, substitute cilantro for the dill and add a spoonful of good-quality, pure chili powder to the salt and sugar mixture. Follow the exact timing on this recipe. One hour in the refrigerator is long enough.

> **6 salmon fillets (approximately 6 oz. each)**
> **2 tbsp. kosher salt**
> **2 tbsp. sugar**
> **¼ cup chopped fresh dill**
> **¼ cup extravirgin olive oil**
> **2 lemons**
> **Extra chopped dill**
> **Lemon slices and dill sprigs, for garnish**

- Remove skin and any small bones from the salmon. Mix together the salt, sugar, and dill. Rub into the sides of the salmon. Wrap salmon tightly in plastic wrap. Place in a shallow dish and chill for 1 hour.

- Quickly rinse the fillets with cool water to rinse off all of the salt-sugar rub. Pat dry with paper towels.

- Brush with oil on both sides. Grill over a hot grill, turning only once, for 10 to 15 minutes, depending on thickness of fillets.

- Remove fillets and squeeze over some lemon juice. Sprinkle with chopped dill. Serve garnished with lemon slices and dill sprigs.

- Serves 6.

Grilled Fish and Vegetable Kebabs

Kebabs right off the grill are perfect for an outdoor meal. You can have everything prepped ahead, ready to pop on the grill. They cook quickly and all you need to complete a light summer supper is a tossed green salad and some crusty bread. Bamboo skewers are handy and disposable, but remember to use two per kebab to hold it firmly and make turning easier. Soak in water to prevent them from catching fire on the hot grill.

> Metal or bamboo skewers
> 1½ lb. fresh firm fish fillets (halibut, tuna, or salmon), cut into 2"-3" cubes
> 18 Portobello mushroom slices (¼")
> 2 red bell peppers, seeded and cut into 2" pieces
> 1 sweet salad onion, peeled, quartered, and layers separated
> 1 fennel bulb, trimmed, quartered, and layers separated
> Marinade (see below)

- If bamboo skewers are used, soak for 30 minutes in cold water. Use 2 skewers, side by side, for each kebab.
- Thread the fish and vegetables in an attractive, alternate pattern on the skewers. Place in a shallow glass or ceramic dish in a single layer. Pour over the marinade. Cover and chill for at least 2 hours or as long as overnight.
- Strain the marinade and boil it for 5 minutes.
- Grill kebabs over a hot grill, turning and basting with the boiled marinade. Cook for 10 to 15 minutes. Do not overcook. Fish should be cooked through, but veggies "crisp tender."
- Serves 6.

Marinade

> ½ cup extravirgin olive oil
> 1 tbsp. fresh lemon juice
> ¼ cup chopped onion
> 2 cloves garlic, finely chopped
> ½ tsp. coarsely ground black pepper
> 1 tsp. coarse sea salt
> ¼ cup chopped fennel fern
> ¼ cup chopped flat-leaf parsley

- Stir together.

Lime-Marinated Chicken Kebabs with Roasted Corn Salsa

These chicken kebabs boast a great fresh flavor. Grill the corn and make the salsa as long as a day ahead. Serve this versatile corn salsa with grilled salmon, chicken, and pork too.

> **4 whole skinless, boneless chicken breasts**
> **¼ cup fresh lime juice**
> **1 tsp. lime zest**
> **1 tbsp. finely chopped gingerroot**
> **2 tbsp. chopped cilantro**
> **1 tbsp. honey**
> **2 tbsp. vegetable oil**
> **¼ tsp. cayenne pepper**
> **½ tsp. salt**
> **Bamboo skewers, soaked in cold water for at**
> **least 30 minutes**

- Cut each chicken breast into 2 halves and trim well. Rinse in cool water and pat dry with paper towels. Place between 2 sheets of plastic wrap and flatten with a veal pounder (or some flat heavy object). Cut the chicken breasts into 1" cubes. Place in a heavy-duty recloseable plastic bag.

- Mix together the lime juice, zest, ginger, cilantro, honey, oil, pepper, and salt. Pour over the chicken in the bag. Seal and marinate for 2 to 6 hours.

- Thread the chicken onto the skewers. Grill over a hot grill, turning, for 5 to 6 minutes or until cooked through and browned. Serve with Roasted Corn Salsa.

- Serves 6-8.

Roasted Corn Salsa

> **5 medium ears corn**
> **3 tbsp. Infused Chile Oil (see below)**
> **1 cup chopped sweet salad onion**
> **1½ cups diced Roma tomatoes**
> **2 large fresh jalapeño peppers, finely chopped**
> **1½ tsp. sea salt**
> **2 tbsp. fresh lime juice**
> **¼ cup chopped cilantro**

- Place the corn in a large shallow dish. Pour over the oil and roll around to generously coat the surface of the corn with the oil. Grill over a hot grill with the corn 4" to 6" from the heat, turning several times for even roasting. Roast 15 minutes for medium ears.
- Remove, cool, cut corn from the cobs, and mix with the other ingredients. Serve at room temperature or slightly chilled.
- Makes about 3½ cups.

Infused Chile Oil

3 to 4 dried chile peppers (see tip)
1 cup olive or vegetable oil

- Place peppers in a 2-to 4-cup heatproof glass measuring cup. Pour in oil. Heat in the microwave oven for 2 to 3 minutes (depending on wattage) or until just begins to bubble. Don't overheat.
- Remove from oven and allow to sit on the countertop for 2 to 8 hours. Strain. Cover and chill any oil you don't use right away.

Chipotle is best for this salsa recipe, but you may use dried serranos or other small hot red chiles.

Russ's Grilled Chicken

Nobody I know is better at grill cooking than my good friend Russell Wiles. Russ is not only a master chef at the grill but a gracious host who enjoys giving great parties with his charming wife, Connie. Both wine experts, they excel at matching their creative food with just the right wine from their fabulous wine cellar. One of our favorite Russ specialties is the chicken he prepares on his grill with consistent perfection. Russ claims to have spent 25 years perfecting this recipe. There is no doubt in our minds that he has it figured out. Russ swears by his charcoal grill, but it should taste just fine from your gas grill.

1 whole roasting chicken (5 to 6 lb.)
2 large onions, coarsely chopped
4 ribs celery (with leaves), coarsely chopped
Zest of 1 large lemon
Salt and pepper, to taste
3 medium cooking apples
2 tbsp. kosher salt
2 tsp. black pepper
Olive oil
1 tbsp. fresh lemon juice

- Start by lighting 24 charcoal briquettes without using lighter fluid (to avoid the oily flavor it imparts). While the charcoal heats, prepare the chicken.

- Wash thoroughly in cool water and remove giblets. Discard or reserve liver for later use. Put the remaining giblets and neck in a large saucepan with the onions, celery, and lemon zest. Add enough cold water to cover by a couple of inches and bring to a boil.

- Simmer on low for 1 hour. Strain, season with salt and pepper, and use as a basting broth for the chicken.

- Cut the apples in half, remove the seeds, core, and then stuff the chicken with the prepared apples. Mix together salt, pepper and olive oil with the lemon juice. Rub on the chicken.

- The charcoal should be red hot. Divide the coals in half and move one half to each side of the grill. Put a drip pan in the middle.

- For best results place a *V*-shaped rack on top of the grill rack breast down. Close the grill lid. Open the vents on the lid about ⅔ open and cook for 45 minutes.

- With a soft basting brush, baste the chicken twice with the reserved basting broth, brushing over the entire surface and covering it well with broth.

- Raise the lid and add 8 new coals to each side. Turn chicken breast side up, and cook for 45 additional minutes, basting at least one more time.

- Remove chicken. Cover with foil and let sit for 20 minutes. Carve and serve.

- Serves 4-6.

Check temperature for doneness in a whole chicken or turkey by sticking the instant thermometer probe into the thickest part of the thigh without touching the bone. When the thermometer reads 180-185 degrees the chicken is done.

Quick Southern
Barbecued Chicken

Here is a page from one of my "Dinner in 20 Minutes" classes. Take care not to overcook this boneless chicken. Marinate the chicken and make the sauce ahead. Toss a salad, sauté a quick vegetable while the grill heats, and you really do have dinner on the table in 20 minutes. Be sure to flatten the chicken breasts so they will cook evenly.

> 1 tbsp. paprika
> 2 tsp. sea salt
> 1 tbsp. brown sugar
> ½ tsp. cayenne pepper
> ½ tsp. black pepper
> 1 tsp. onion powder
> 1 tsp. garlic powder
> 8 skinless, boneless chicken breast halves
> Oil
> Bourbon Barbecue Sauce (see below)

- Combine the dry ingredients to make a dry rub.
- Wash and trim the chicken. Place between 2 sheets of plastic wrap and pound lightly to flatten to same thickness. Brush the chicken breasts with oil and coat with the rub. Place in a plastic bag and chill for at least 1 hour or as long as all day.
- Preheat grill to high. Grill the chicken for 10 to 12 minutes or until done through. Turn only once after about two-thirds of the cooking time.
- During the last 2 minutes, baste with the reserved sauce (see below).
- Pass the warm barbecue sauce. Serve with Marilyn's Greens (see index).
- Serves 8.

Bourbon Barbecue Sauce

1 stick butter
2 cups finely chopped onion
3 cloves garlic, finely chopped
1/2 cup bourbon
1 cup bottled chile sauce
2 tbsp. cider vinegar
1/4 cup fresh lemon juice
1/2 cup dark brown sugar
1 tsp. black pepper
1 tbsp. sea salt

- Melt the butter and sauté the onions and garlic for 5 minutes.
- Add remaining ingredients and simmer on low for 40 minutes, stirring often.
- Remove some of the sauce to baste the chicken during the last 2 minutes of grilling. Warm remainder of sauce to spoon over the chicken at serving time.

Grilled Chicken Salad

I love to be invited to dinner at my friend Brett Stover's house. The food and company are always great. This chicken salad is one of the many dishes I have enjoyed there. Brett is a fine cook, but his real talent is eating—he is the most dedicated restaurant explorer I have ever met. On a recent trip to Paris, he ate the menu dégustation at three three-star establishments in four days. And somehow he stays trim.

3/4 cup real mayonnaise
1/4 cup honey
1/4 cup Dijon mustard
1 tbsp. chopped fresh tarragon leaves
4 skinless, boneless chicken breast halves
6 cups fresh salad greens (bagged greens from
    store save time)
1/2 cup sliced red radishes
1/2 cup sliced green onions

- Mix mayonnaise, honey, mustard, and tarragon together. Reserve 1/2 cup. Pour remaining mayonnaise mixture over chicken in shallow baking dish; cover.

- Refrigerate 20 minutes or overnight to marinate. Drain; discard marinade. Place chicken on grill over medium-hot coals. Grill, covered, 10-12 minutes total (about 6 minutes per side) or until tender.
- Toss salad greens with radishes and onions and arrange on server platter or individual plates. Slice chicken into strips; arrange over greens. Drizzle with reserved ½ cup dressing. Serve immediately
- Serves 4.

Rosemary-Lemon Pork Chops

A flavorful marinade is essential for juicy, tasty pork chops from the grill. The thick cuts are far preferable because they have time to brown and caramelize on the surface before the center is done. Check carefully with your thermometer and don't allow it to go beyond 155 degrees. These chops are so infused with flavor they don't need a sauce.

6 center-cut thick pork chops (2" thick)
Juice and zest of 2 lemons
¼ cup vegetable oil
2 cloves garlic, finely chopped
1 tsp. salt
½ tsp. pepper
2 tbsp. finely chopped fresh rosemary leaves

- Trim any fat from edge of chops.
- Mix together all of the remaining ingredients. Place pork chops in a shallow glass or ceramic dish. Rub both sides with the wet rub. Cover and chill for 2 to 8 hours.
- Grill chops over a medium-hot grill, turning two or three times, until browned and cooked through (about 18-20 minutes or until the instant thermometer registers 155 degrees). Do not overcook.
- Serves 6.

Barbecued Pork Tenderloin

Pork tenderloin is perfect for grilling because it's thick enough to remain juicy and tender, yet small enough to cook quickly. Rub and marinate the meat overnight in the refrigerator. Make the sauce ahead too. It will taste better and your work is mostly done. Serve with Spicy Baked Pinto Beans and grilled corn.

> **2 tsp. sea salt**
> **1 tsp. freshly ground black pepper**
> **¼ tsp. cayenne pepper**
> **1 tsp. paprika**
> **½ tsp. dried thyme leaves**
> **2 tsp. dark brown sugar**
> **2 pork tenderloins, well trimmed**
> **Sauce (see below)**

- Mix together the dry seasonings. Rub into the surface of the tenderloins. Place in a dish, cover, and chill for at least 2 hours, or as long as overnight.

- Place the pork on a preheated hot grill and grill, turning once or twice for even cooking, until the thermometer reads 155 degrees, about 15 to 20 minutes, depending on the weight of the meat. During the last 5 minutes of grilling time, constantly baste the pork with the sauce. The outside should be well glazed and browned.

- To serve, slice on the diagonal, across the grain, into thin slices. Pass the warm sauce.

- Serves 6-8.

Sauce

> **½ cup chopped onion**
> **2 cloves garlic, finely chopped**
> **3 tbsp. vegetable oil**
> **½ cup cider vinegar**
> **¼ cup honey**
> **2 cups chile sauce**
> **1 tbsp. Worcestershire sauce**
> **1 tsp. hot pepper sauce**

- Sauté the onion and garlic in the oil for 2 to 3 minutes. Stir in the remaining ingredients and simmer on low for 10 minutes, stirring often. Cool. Set aside one-half of it to warm for passing at the table.

Grilled Orange Pork

Basting with some of the reserved marinade accents the flavor while it glazes this delicious pork loin. Place, hot from the grill, onto a carving board. Slice and serve with grilled potatoes and fennel or asparagus (see recipes below). Thinly slice cold leftovers and serve on top of a hearty tossed green salad.

3½ to 4 lb. boneless pork loin
3 tbsp. extra-virgin olive oil
3 cloves garlic, finely chopped
2 medium onions, chopped
1 tbsp. orange zest
1 cup fresh orange juice
¼ cup fresh lemon juice
1 tsp. salt
1 tbsp. brown sugar
½ tsp. coriander
½ tsp. cayenne pepper
¼ cup chopped cilantro
Fresh orange slices and cilantro sprigs, for garnish

- Trim fat from the pork.
- Heat the oil and lightly sauté the garlic and onions, about 3 minutes. Add zest, juices, salt, sugar, coriander, cayenne, and chopped cilantro. Measure out ½ cup of this marinade and put into a covered container. Store in the refrigerator to use for basting the pork while it cooks.
- Place the pork in a large shallow glass or ceramic dish. Pour over the marinade. Cover tightly with plastic wrap and marinate in the refrigerator for 24 hours.
- Remove the pork from the marinade. Discard this marinade. Grill pork over a medium-hot grill for about 40 minutes or until the internal temperature is 155 degrees. Baste with the reserved marinade during the last 10 minutes of cooking time.
- Remove and cut into thin slices to serve. Garnish with orange slices and sprigs of cilantro.
- Serves 10-12.

Gourmet Burgers
with Béarnaise Mayonnaise

Béarnaise sauce with filet mignon is certainly a tried and true favorite. So, why not the same blend of flavors on a burger? Admittedly this burger recipe is not the quickest to make, but you can speed it up a bit by using lean ground beef from the market rather than grinding your own in the food processor. Please note that it is important to chill the beef so that it is very cold before grinding in the processor or meat grinder. It is a good idea to check the internal temperature of the cooked burgers with an instant thermometer. Always cook them to at least 140 degrees. Be sure to use real mayonnaise for this sauce.

Chop garlic and shallots quickly by dropping them into a clean, dry food-processor bowl fitted with the cutting blade with the motor running. (Don't use this method with onions.)

2 lb. very lean center-cut chuck steaks or roast, cut into 2" cubes
4 tbsp. extravirgin olive oil
1 medium sweet salad onion, finely chopped
2 cloves garlic, finely chopped
$\frac{1}{4}$ cup dry white wine
2 tsp. Dijon mustard
1 tbsp. balsamic vinegar
2 tsp. fine sea salt
$\frac{1}{2}$ tsp. freshly ground pepper
Fresh buns
Béarnaise Mayonnaise (see below)
Crisp lettuce leaves

- Chill the beef until very cold. Grind in the food processor (with steel blade) and return, covered, to the refrigerator.

- Heat the olive oil in a heavy skillet. Add the onion and garlic and sauté over high heat, stirring, for 2 minutes. Pour in the wine and cook over high to reduce by half. Remove and cool.

- Toss the cooled onion mixture, mustard, vinegar, salt, and pepper into the ground beef. Form into 6 to 8 patties, taking care to use the gentlest touch possible when forming the burgers. Grill or cover and chill until ready to grill.

- Grill over a hot preheated grill to desired doneness, about 20 minutes for medium well. Turn only once about two-thirds of the way through the cooking time. Don't press with the spatula while cooking.

- Serve on a fresh bun topped with a dollop of Béarnaise Mayonnaise and a crisp lettuce leaf.
- Serves 6-8.

Béarnaise Mayonnaise

2 large shallots, peeled and finely chopped
⅓ cup white wine vinegar
½ tsp. salt
¼ tsp. hot pepper sauce
1 tsp. Dijon mustard
2 tbsp. finely chopped flat-leaf parsley
2 tbsp. finely chopped fresh tarragon leaves
1 cup mayonnaise

- In a small nonreactive saucepan, bring shallots and vinegar to a boil. Boil until vinegar is reduced to 1 tbsp. Remove and cool.
- Stir the shallot mixture, salt, hot pepper sauce, mustard, and herbs into the mayonnaise. Chill until ready to use. Best used within 24 hours.
- Makes about 1 cup.

Flank Steak in Spicy Southwest Marinade

I tossed this marinade together one evening over a bottle of wine with my good pal Rita Burnett. I didn't write down the ingredients but Rita did, so we have it to share with you. The success of this marinade depends on the quality of the chili powder you use. It is imperative to use a good-quality, pure, and fresh chili powder (as opposed to the generic chili mixes in the spice section of the supermarket). Rita and I have only used this for flank steak, but try it on other cuts of beef and on pork as well. This makes enough marinade for 1 large flank steak or 2 small steaks.

Juice of 2 limes
1 tbsp. pure chili powder (chipotle or ancho)
¼ cup extravirgin olive oil
2 large cloves garlic, finely chopped
1 tbsp. coarse sea salt
1 tsp. honey
1 large flank steak

- Mix together the juice, chili powder, oil, garlic, salt, and honey. Place the steak in a heavy-duty gallon-size plastic bag. Pour over the marinade. Seal the top and place the bag in a shallow dish to refrigerate for at least 8 hours, or as long as 24 hours.

- Remove the meat from the marinade and discard the marinade. Grill over a hot grill to desired doneness, about 15-18 minutes, turning only once. (Best not cooked longer than medium—140 degrees internal temperature in the thickest part of the steak.)

- Place on a cutting board and cut with a very sharp slicing knife on the diagonal and across the grain into very thin slices.

- Serves 4-8, depending on size of steak.

Grilled Lamb Chops
with Shallot-Parsley Butter

This dish is a special treat at my house for my favorite guests and a recipe I like sharing with my students. Buy the best lamb you can find. In my opinion that's Jamison Lamb from the Jamison Farm in Latrobe, Pennsylvania. (Jamison Farm ships lamb all over the U.S. Their toll-free number is: 1-800-237-LAMB.) Don't forget the important step of trimming the fat from the edge of the chops.

> 8 lean lamb chops, about 1½" thick
> Olive oil
> Sea salt and freshly ground black pepper, to
>   taste
> 1 stick unsalted butter
> 2 large shallots, finely chopped
> ½ cup chopped flat-leaf parsley
> Parsley sprigs, for garnish

- Trim most of the fat from the edge of the chops. Brush chops generously with the oil and season with salt and pepper.

- Melt the butter. Add the shallots and parsley to the butter. Simmer over low heat for 10 minutes. Do not allow the butter to brown. (May do this on the grill or heat on kitchen range and keep hot over grill while lamb is cooking.)

- Grill the lamb chops over a hot grill for 10 to 12 minutes or to desired doneness. Turn once after about two-thirds of the cooking time. Place on a platter and spoon over the butter. Garnish with parsley sprigs and serve immediately.

• Serves 4-8, depending on serving size.

Grilled Butterflied
Leg of Lamb

This lamb is high on the list of my favorite grilled meats, and I've made it for many friends and students. It's quick, easy to prepare, and easy to carve and serve. It's also a bit out of the ordinary for summer grill fare and everybody always raves about how delicious it is, even those who don't particularly like lamb.

> **1 butterflied leg of lamb (3 to 4 lb.)**
> **½ cup extravirgin olive oil**
> **4 large cloves garlic, finely chopped**
> **1 tbsp. finely chopped fresh rosemary leaves**
> **2 tbsp. kosher salt**
> **1 tsp. freshly ground black pepper**
> **1 tbsp. Dijon mustard**
> **2 tbsp. balsamic vinegar**
> **Rosemary sprigs, for garnish**

For the most flavorful marinades and dressings, use balsamic vinegar that has been aged at least 6 years.

• Trim all visible fat from the lamb. Place lamb in a shallow dish.

• Mix together oil, garlic, chopped rosemary, salt, pepper, mustard, and vinegar and coat both sides of the lamb with the mixture. Cover tightly and chill for 8 to 24 hours.

• Place on a medium-hot grill and cook for 40 to 45 minutes until a meat thermometer registers desired doneness.

• Let sit for 5 to 10 minutes before serving. Slice across the grain. Garnish with sprigs of fresh rosemary and serve.

• Serves 6-8.

Ratatouille in a Package

The famous French vegetable dish is made easy by tucking everything into a heavy-duty foil packet. Because these are individual servings, they cook quickly and are easy to serve. Caution your guests to open their packet with care since the steam can be very hot. Small, tender, and firm eggplants work best for this recipe.

> **2 ¼″ slices unpeeled eggplant**
> **4 ¼″ slices zucchini**
> **2 ¼″ slices unpeeled tomato**
> **1 thin-sliced red bell pepper**
> **1 thin-sliced green bell pepper**
> **2 ¼″ slices onion**
> **¼ tsp. finely chopped garlic**
> **1 tbsp. extravirgin olive oil**
> **1 tbsp. chopped flat-leaf parsley**
> **Sea salt, to taste**
> **Hot pepper sauce, to taste**
> **1 large sprig fresh basil**

- Arrange the eggplant, zucchini, tomato, pepper, and onion slices alternately on a large square of heavy-duty aluminum foil.

- Mix the garlic into the oil and sprinkle over the vegetables. Sprinkle with parsley and season with salt and a few drops of hot pepper sauce. Place a sprig of basil on top.

- Seal the foil tightly, leaving some air space at the top. Place in a hot covered grill. Cook for 20 minutes.

- Serves 1.

Grilled New Potatoes

Potatoes can, of course, be cooked entirely on the grill. But this method saves time and grill space because they can be finished on the grill after the meat is almost done or already removed to a carving board to rest.

 2 lb. small new potatoes
 Olive oil
 Sea salt and freshly ground pepper, to taste
 ½ cup chopped flat-leaf parsley

- Cover the potatoes with cold water and boil for about 15 minutes, or until they can be pierced with a knife tip but are still very firm.
- Cut each potato in half. Brush each half with olive oil and season with salt and pepper.
- Grill over medium-high heat, turning several times, brushing with more oil as needed until brown and fork tender. They should be ready in 6-8 minutes.
- Place into a bowl and toss with the parsley. Taste and correct seasoning.
- Serves 6-8.

Grilled Fennel

Fennel is a great vegetable for grilling. Not so long ago found only in specialty produce markets, this anise-flavored root is available in most supermarkets. It's quick and easy to prepare and delicious with some simple grilled fish while adding some pizzazz to your menu. When choosing fennel, look for the elongated bulbs.

 2 large fennel bulbs
 Extravirgin olive oil
 Coarse sea salt

- Cut off the fennel fronds even with the tops of the bulbs. (Some of the nice ones may be saved for garnish.) Trim a thin slice from each bulb bottom.
- Wash and dry bulbs. Slice, lengthwise, into ¼" slices. The solid section on the root end will hold each slice together.

- Brush with olive oil and sprinkle lightly with salt. Grill over a hot grill just until lightly browned, but still crisp tender, 12-15 minutes. Turn once. Serve warm.
- Serves 6.

Grilled Asparagus

There is nothing better in spring and early summer than fat, succulent asparagus spears from the grill. This is such a simple and delicious way to cook asparagus, but you must choose the thick spears. This method doesn't work with skinny asparagus (which I never buy anyway). Choose spears that are ¾" to 1" in diameter at the bottom.

> **2 lb. asparagus spears**
> **Extravirgin olive oil**
> **Coarse sea salt**

- Hold each asparagus in both hands and snap off the bottom. Discard bottoms. Wash the tip ends and place on soft paper towels to dry.
- Lay in a single layer in a shallow dish. Drizzle with oil and roll around to lightly coat with oil. Sprinkle with salt.
- Place on a hot grill. Grill for 12 to 15 minutes, turning often, until crisp tender. Serve immediately.
- Serves 6-8.

Grilled Corn on Cob
with Chili Lime Butter

Any of my regular students will attest to my fondness for most any-thing spicy. A favorite combination of mine is spicy and tart. That explains why I like this corn so much. If you prefer the natural flavor of the corn, follow this recipe but just put plain butter with some salt and freshly ground pepper over your grilled corn.

8 fresh ears corn, shucked and silks removed
Vegetable oil
1 stick unsalted butter, cut into pieces
2 large cloves garlic, finely chopped
1 tbsp. good chili powder (ancho or chipotle)
2 tsp. sea salt
2 tbsp. fresh lime juice

• Wash the corn in cold water. Rub lightly with oil. Place on a medium-hot grill. Grill for 18 to 20 minutes, turning often. Place in a shallow dish.

• Heat the butter with the garlic. Stir in the chili powder, salt, and lime juice. Pour over the corn. Serve immediately.

• Serves 8.

Spicy Baked Pinto Beans

Pinto beans give this vegetarian baked-bean dish a light touch. If your grill is large enough and has a cover, you can bake the beans outside and avoid heating the oven on a hot summer day. Simply preheat the grill and allow it to get up to 350 degrees and no hotter than 425 degrees. Put the beans in a metal casserole (such as a porcelain-clad cast-iron pot) or any Dutch oven that has heatproof handles. Assemble the dish according to the following directions and put into the preheated, covered grill. The beans will need at least an hour to cook, maybe a little longer, depending on how efficient and well insulated the grill is.

> 3 16-oz. cans pinto beans
> ¼ cup olive oil
> 1 cup chopped onion
> 3 large cloves garlic, finely chopped
> 1 8-oz. can tomato sauce
> ½ cup spicy tomato salsa, or to taste
> ½ cup molasses
> 2 or 3 chipotle chiles in adobo, to taste
> 2 tbsp. adobo sauce (from the chiles)
> 2 tsp. chili powder
> 1 tsp. ground cumin
> 1 tsp. salt
> Dash good bourbon

- Drain the beans into a colander and rinse. Allow to sit and drain well.

- Heat the oil in a skillet and lightly sauté the onions and garlic, about 2 minutes, stirring. Add the beans. Stir in the remaining ingredients.

- Pour into a pot with a tight-fitting lid that can be put into the grill. Bake in the preheated grill as directed above or bake in a preheated 350-degree oven for 1 hour.

- Serves 8-10.

Versatile Vegetables

Lemon Asparagus

White Asparagus

Sautéed Green Beans

Fresh Green Beans
with Herbed Egg Sauce

Brussels Sprouts
with Toasted Walnuts in
Mustard Sauce

Scalloped Celery
and Onions

Sautéed Corn
with Tomatoes and Cilantro

Southern Corn Pudding

Eggplant Sandwiches
with Fresh Tomato Sauce

Marilyn's Greens

Brie-Stuffed
Mushroom Caps

Creamy Poblano Crepes

Parmesan Mashed Potatoes

Buttered Parsley
New Potatoes

Spicy Sweet
Potato Casserole

Roasted Root Vegetables

Spicy Spinach Casserole

Stuffed Yellow Squash

Summer Squash Casserole

Tomato-Olive Tart

Zucchini Pancakes

Where I grew up, the vegetables were always an important part of the meal. There is definitely a Southern tradition of plenty of flavorful and attractive vegetable dishes on every dinner table. It was not unusual to have 5 or 6 vegetables at one meal. Many of the recipes in this chapter go back to those roots, where I learned to eat and enjoy a tremendous variety of vegetables.

Many of my inherited Southern recipes were pretty rich and heavy by today's standard of healthier eating, but over the years they have evolved as eating habits have changed. I have tried to lighten them without changing their delicious flavors. Some of them are intended to be special company fare when you don't mind a bit of extra indulgence and, in my opinion, shouldn't worry about it. I hope you will make lots of these yummy dishes for your guests and that you and your family will enjoy them too.

Not all the recipes in this chapter have a Southern character. When I started gathering these recipes together, I found that a surprising number of my favorites were collected from my travels (and studies) in Europe. There are also some great shared recipes from colleagues, radio listeners, and readers of my column. I am pleased to see how it all fused together to make what I think is a most colorful collection of veggie recipes. It is my hope that you will find this a useful reference as well as an idea source when you are searching for just the right addition to your menu.

Lemon Asparagus

Here is a good example of "the simpler, the better." Tender fresh asparagus never needs much dressing up. Take care not to overcook it. Cover with paper, rather than a tight-fitting lid, to preserve the bright green color.

2 lb. medium to thick asparagus spears
Water
½ stick unsalted butter
3 tbsp. fresh lemon juice
Sea salt and pepper, to taste

- Wash the asparagus. Break off the tough ends and discard them.
- Bring 2" to 3" water to a boil in a large skillet. Place the asparagus in the water and cover with parchment or a sturdy white paper towel. Cook 5 to 7 minutes (according to thickness of spears) or until crisp tender.
- Melt butter and add the lemon juice.
- Season the asparagus with salt and pepper. Just before serving pour over the butter mixture. Serve hot.
- Serves 4-6.

White Asparagus

White asparagus is my favorite vegetable. I learned to love it in Germany, where it seems to be everybody's favorite. It is always exciting when that first "Spargel" is harvested in late spring. It is available in the markets through most of June. We import some into our country, from Europe in the spring and South America in the winter. There is also some white asparagus grown here, but not to the extent it is cultivated in Europe. White asparagus is a creamy white color because it grows in mounds of sandy soil. Without the sunlight the chlorophyll never develops to turn it green. It also has a thicker peel and must always be peeled. It takes longer to cook white asparagus, so it is never served crisp like the green variety but should be tender with a velvet texture. The cooking method is simple and the result is so delicious. Serve it, as they do in Germany, with tiny boiled new potatoes with melted butter drizzled over both asparagus and potatoes.

When purchasing asparagus try to get them as uniform in size as possible so they will cook to the same doneness at the same time. Thick spears are more succulent and flavorful than the very thin ones.

Never cut the tough end from green asparagus. Hold the spear in both hands and break it apart with a snap. The part above where it snaps in two is the tender part to cook. Discard the bottom portion or tough end.

3 lb. white asparagus
Water
6 tbsp. butter
2 tsp. salt

- Wash the asparagus and cut 2″ to 3″ from the tough ends. Discard ends. Peel with a swivel peeler, starting about 1″ below the tip.

- Bring about 2″ to 3″ water to a boil in a deep skillet. Add 4 tbsp. butter and the salt. Lay in the asparagus spears on their side. The spears should be covered with water.

- Simmer on low for 18 to 25 minutes, depending on the size of the spears. Check for doneness with the tip of a sharp knife. It should be very tender, but still firm. (Don't overcook or it will become mushy.)

- Lift from the water and place on a serving platter. Melt the remaining butter, drizzle over, and serve hot.

- Serves 6.

White asparagus spears must always be peeled. Use a swivel peeler and start about 1″ below the tip. The very thick green asparagus spears are sometimes peeled, but it's for appearance only and not necessary.

Sautéed Green Beans

Fresh green beans fit into almost any menu and this simple preparation makes them so easy to add. The beans can be blanched as long as a day ahead. Place them in a plastic bag with a soft white paper towel to absorb the moisture and store in the crisper drawer. Sauté them just before you are ready to serve. You can substitute a couple cloves of garlic or a small onion for the shallots.

2 lb. fresh green beans (as small and tender as possible)
6 qt. water
3 tbsp. sea salt
¼ cup extravirgin olive oil
2 large shallots, finely chopped
Fine sea salt and pepper, to taste
3 tbsp. chopped fresh dill or fresh tarragon

- Wash and trim the beans.

- Bring the water to a rolling boil. Add the 3 tbsp. salt. Add the beans and blanch for 1 to 3 minutes, depending on size.

- Drain and refresh in ice water. Drain and pat dry on dishtowels or paper towels. Set aside until ready to serve. (Chill if done far ahead.)
- At serving time, heat the olive oil in a sauté pan. Add the shallots and sauté for 3 to 5 minutes, stirring, until the shallots are tender.
- Toss in the beans and cook, stirring constantly until hot through. (Beans should be "crisp tender.") Season with the salt and pepper to taste. Sprinkle with fresh dill or tarragon and serve.
- Serves 6.

Fresh Green Beans
with Herbed Egg Sauce

This green-bean recipe is done in two stages. The sauce adds a lot of flavor and color. Since these beans are a perfect side dish for fish, I often serve them with grilled salmon.

> **2 lb. fresh green beans (as small and tender as possible)**
> **4 qt. water**
> **2 tbsp. salt**
> **2 tbsp. unsalted butter**
> **2 tbsp. extravirgin olive oil**
> **1 large shallot, finely chopped**
> **½ cup dry white wine**
> **2 hard-cooked eggs, finely chopped**
> **¼ cup chopped green onions**
> **1 tbsp. capers**
> **3 tbsp. chopped fresh dill**
> **2 tbsp. chopped flat-leaf parsley**
> **Sea salt and freshly ground pepper, to taste**

- Wash the beans and trim the ends.
- Bring water to a rolling boil. Add the salt and return to a boil. Toss in the beans and blanch until crisp tender (as short as 2 minutes for *haricots verts*—tiny French beans—or as long as 5 minutes for larger beans). Drain and refresh in ice water. Drain and set aside.

- Heat 1 tbsp. each of the butter and oil in a skillet. Sauté the shallot, stirring until softened, about 5 minutes.

- Add the wine and cook over high heat until reduced to 2 tbsp.

- Remove from heat and stir in the eggs, green onions, capers, dill, and parsley. Season to taste with salt and pepper.

- To finish, heat the remaining butter and oil in a large skillet over high heat. Toss the green beans just until they are hot. Remove to a serving dish and spoon over the egg mixture. Serve immediately.

- Serves 6-8.

Brussels Sprouts with Toasted Walnuts in Mustard Sauce

Here is a dish from a Thanksgiving menu. I usually hear a groan or two from the back of the class when I mention Brussels sprouts. I know it is not a universally loved vegetable, but that is because it is so often improperly cooked. Nobody loves an overcooked Brussels sprout. Use the best imported Dijon mustard you can find for this sauce and cook the sprouts just until they are "crisp tender." You may be surprised when you taste them and see how delicious they can be.

1 lb. Brussels sprouts
⅔ cup walnut halves
5 tbsp. butter
1½ tsp. Worcestershire sauce
1½ tsp. fine sea salt
¼ tsp. cayenne pepper
1 tbsp. whole-grain Dijon mustard
1 tbsp. fresh lemon juice

- Wash, trim the ends, and halve the Brussels sprouts lengthwise. Steam them in a vegetable steamer 5 to 6 minutes or until crisp tender.

- Place the walnuts on a sheet pan. Melt 1 tbsp. of the butter and toss with the walnuts. Toast in a preheated 350-degree oven for 8 minutes. Cool and set aside.

- In a saucepan stir together the remaining butter, Worcestershire sauce, salt, pepper, mustard, and lemon juice. Heat until butter

The secret to perfectly cooked Brussels sprouts is to cut them in half lengthwise. They cook quickly and are the proper "crisp-tender" consistency inside and out.

When steaming broccoli, Brussels sprouts, or cauliflower, remove the lid of the steamer for 15 seconds about halfway through the cooking time. Allowing the steam to escape improves their color and flavor.

Sauces that contain acid such as lemon or vinegar should not be poured over Brussels sprouts, broccoli, green beans, or pea pods until just before serving. The acid in the sauce changes the bright green color to a dull green.

melts. Stir in the toasted walnuts. Pour sauce over warm sprouts just before serving.

• Serves 6.

Scalloped Celery and Onions

This is from an oft-taught class called "Thanksgiving Side Dishes." There have been very few holiday dinners at our house without this delicious dish. Blanch the celery just until it is "crisp tender."

1 stick unsalted butter
2 extralarge yellow Bermuda onions, peeled and thickly sliced (about ¼″)
2 cups coarsely sliced celery (about ½″ long)
3 tbsp. flour
1½ cups whole milk, heated
1 tsp. salt
½ tsp. black pepper
½ tsp. paprika
1 cup fresh breadcrumbs
¼ cup chopped fresh parsley
¼ tsp. black pepper

• Melt 3 tbsp. butter in a large, heavy skillet. Sauté the onions, stirring until crisp tender, about 5 minutes. Remove to a side dish.

• Blanch the celery in lightly salted, boiling water for 3 minutes. Drain and refresh in cold water. Drain thoroughly and add to the onions.

• Melt 3 tbsp. butter in a heavy saucepan and stir in flour. Cook on medium, stirring, for 2 minutes; do not brown.

• Add the milk, whisking until sauce thickens. Season with salt and pepper and fold into vegetable mixture. Spoon into a shallow, 2-qt. baking dish.

• Melt the remaining 2 tbsp. butter in a heavy saucepan. Stir in the paprika and stir over medium heat for a minute or two.

• Toss in breadcrumbs and stir to coat well with butter. Remove from heat and add the parsley and pepper. Sprinkle the topping over the vegetables. Bake in a preheated 350-degree oven for about 25 minutes or until bubbly and hot through.

• Serves 8-10.

Store potatoes and onions in separate containers, never together.

The easiest (and safest) way to slice an onion is to first cut in half cutting through the stem and root ends. Place a half, flat side down, on a cutting board and slice, cutting through the onion layers, which will naturally divide into strips.

Sautéed Corn
with Tomatoes and Cilantro

I developed this quick and easy recipe for a class called "Easy Summertime Vegetables." This fresh corn and tomato dish takes advantage of some of the best flavors of the season. Make it when the corn is in its prime and the tomatoes are vine ripened. If you use regular tomatoes you'll need 3 large ones. Peel and seed them before chopping. The larger tomatoes have more seeds and pulp than Roma tomatoes, which are usually best for cooking.

> 6 medium ears sweet corn
> 1 tbsp. butter
> 2 tbsp. extravirgin olive oil
> 1 cup thinly sliced green onions
> 2 large cloves garlic, finely chopped
> 1 jalapeño pepper, finely chopped
> 6 large Roma tomatoes, peeled, cored, and
>   coarsely chopped
> 1 tsp. sea salt, or to taste
> Hot pepper sauce, to taste
> 1 tbsp. fresh lime juice
> 3 tbsp. chopped cilantro

- Cut the corn from the cobs and set aside.
- In a large heavy skillet heat the butter and oil. Sauté the onions and garlic for 2 minutes, stirring.
- Add the jalapeño and tomatoes and cook, stirring, for 3 minutes.
- Stir in the corn and cook 4 to 5 minutes longer.
- Add the salt, hot pepper sauce, and lime juice. Taste and correct the seasonings. Stir in the cilantro just before serving.
- Serves 6-8.

   Note: for a heartier dish add 1 cup small strips of ham after the corn. Heat just until hot.

Southern Corn Pudding

Here is a Southern specialty right off of the Sunday dinner table. I bake this in a soufflé dish. Time your dinner so you are ready to serve this hot from the oven.

> **6 medium ears corn**
> **1 tbsp. sugar**
> **1 tsp. salt**
> **3 tbsp. butter, melted**
> **6 eggs, well beaten**
> **3 cups milk**
> **1 tbsp. cornstarch**
> **1 tbsp. water**

- Cut corn kernels from cobs, scraping cobs. Stir together the corn, sugar, salt, butter, eggs, and milk.
- Dissolve the cornstarch in the water and stir into the corn mixture. Pour into well-greased 2-qt. baking dish. Bake at 350 degrees for about 1 hour or until firm and browned.
- Serves 8.

Eggplant Sandwiches with Fresh Tomato Sauce

Versatile eggplant often replaces meat in a meal. This is one of my best examples of an eggplant dish that serves as a complete meal and no one misses the meat. Assemble these little sandwiches ahead. They need at least 30 minutes in the refrigerator to set the breading, but can chill as long as an hour before they are cooked.

For choosing the best eggplant, slender usually is preferable over a round shape. Look for a shiny, unblemished skin and a bright green stem. Check the weight of same-sized eggplants—the heavier, the better.

> **2 medium eggplants**
> **Salt**
> **Freshly ground pepper**
> **8 ¼" slices fresh mozzarella (rounds)**
> **8 fresh basil leaves, washed and dried**
> **2 eggs**
> **2 tbsp. water**
> **½ cup flour (approximately)**
> **2 cups fine fresh breadcrumbs**
> **Vegetable oil, for frying**
> **Fresh Tomato Sauce (see below)**

- Wash and trim the eggplants. Cut into ½" rounds. Sprinkle generously on both sides with the salt. Place in colander in the sink to drain for 30 minutes.
- Rinse quickly with cool water. Pat dry with paper towels. Sprinkle with pepper to taste.
- Place a slice of mozzarella and a basil leaf on an eggplant slice. Top with a second slice and press firmly together.
- Beat together the eggs and water.
- Dredge the eggplant sandwiches in flour, shaking off the excess. Dip into the egg wash, then coat well with the breadcrumbs, including the sides. Place on a baking sheet and chill for 30 minutes.
- Over medium high, heat about 2" oil in a heavy skillet. Fry the sandwiches for 2 to 3 minutes on each side or until golden brown. Drain well on soft white paper towels.
- Place on baking sheets and keep warm in a 275-degree oven until ready to serve for up to 30 minutes. Serve with a spoonful of Fresh Tomato Sauce on top.
- Serves 8.

Fresh Tomato Sauce

12 Roma tomatoes
3 tbsp. extravirgin olive oil
2 large cloves garlic, finely chopped
¾ cup finely chopped onion
1 bouquet garni composed of:
   3 sprigs fresh thyme
   2 sprigs rosemary
2 tsp. salt
½ tsp. hot pepper sauce
1 tsp. sugar
2 tbsp. finely shredded fresh basil

- Wash and core the tomatoes. Cut in half and chop finely in the food processor. Set aside.
- Heat the oil in a heavy skillet and sauté the garlic and onion until tender, stirring.
- Add the tomatoes and bouquet garni and cook on low, uncovered, for 15 minutes. Stir often.
- Remove the bouquet garni and season the sauce with the salt, hot pepper sauce, sugar, and basil. Cook 5 minutes longer. Serve hot.
- Makes about 3 cups.

To prevent fried or sautéed eggplant from absorbing too much oil, slice or cube the eggplant (according to the recipe) and place in a colander in the sink. Sprinkle over enough kosher salt to lightly coat all sides of all eggplant. Let sit for 30 minutes. Rinse with cool water and pat dry before proceeding with the recipe.

Marilyn's Greens

I used to think you had to grow up in the South to appreciate the wonderful flavor of all of these cooked greens. But lately I've noticed that some trendy American chefs have discovered them, and the word seems to be spreading that "a mess of greens" is not only good for you but tastes great too. This is obviously not my grandmother's recipe and is actually far more flavorful and better for you, with the olive oil replacing the bacon in the traditional dish.

> ½ **lb. fresh turnip greens**
> ½ **lb. fresh mustard greens**
> **1 lb. fresh collard greens**
> **3 tbsp. extravirgin olive oil**
> **2 large shallots, finely chopped**
> ⅔ **cup chicken stock**
> **2 canned chipotle chiles in adobo, finely**
>   **chopped**
> **1 tsp. hot pepper sauce, or to taste**
> **2 tsp. fine sea salt, or to taste**
> **1 tbsp. balsamic vinegar**
> **1 tbsp. fresh lime juice**

- Wash the greens thoroughly by submerging them in water and soaking. Remove to colanders and rinse well. For the large leaves (and all of the collard greens), cut the leaves away from the coarse center stem. Discard the stems.
- Roll the greens into small bundles and slice into 1" ribbons.
- Heat the oil in a large skillet (with a tight-fitting lid). Sauté the shallots, stirring, for 5 minutes.
- Add the greens and cook over medium heat, stirring often. When all of the greens are added and wilted, pour over the stock. Cover and cook for 15 minutes over low heat.
- Add the chiles, pepper sauce, and salt. Cook, covered, 5 to 10 minutes longer, or until tender but not mushy.
- Toss in the vinegar and lime juice. Serve hot.
- Serves 6-8.

Brie-Stuffed Mushroom Caps

Try this elegant preparation for mushrooms that can be completely assembled ahead and baked later. Serve them as a first course or as a side vegetable with a plain chop or fillet. For cocktail-party hors d'oeuvres, stuff small, bite-sized mushrooms. You will need three times as many for this amount of stuffing. Buy firm, very fresh Brie for this recipe.

> **12 large white mushrooms**
> **Juice of 1 lemon**
> **6 oz. Brie cheese, chilled**
> **4 tbsp. butter (½ stick)**
> **2 shallots, finely chopped**
> **1 clove garlic, finely chopped**
> **1 cup fresh breadcrumbs**
> **2 tbsp. Madeira**
> **1 tsp. salt**
> **¼ tsp. cayenne or black pepper**
> **½ tsp. fresh thyme leaves**
> **¼ cup chopped flat-leaf parsley**

- Wash mushrooms, remove stems, and chop stems finely.

- Toss caps with the lemon juice and set aside.

- Cut the white exterior from the Brie. Cut Brie into small cubes.

- Melt the butter in skillet and add chopped stems, shallots, and garlic. Sauté, stirring, for 8 to 10 minutes.

- Stir in the breadcrumbs. Add the Madeira, salt, pepper, thyme, and parsley and cook for 2 minutes, stirring.

- Stir in the cheese. Spoon the mixture into the mushrooms caps and place in a well-buttered shallow baking dish. Bake in a pre-heated 350-degree oven for 15 to 20 minutes. Serve hot.

- Serves 6.

Wash mushrooms by holding them under a steady stream of lukewarm running water. (Do not soak or they become saturated.) After washing away all soil, place on soft white paper towels to dry before cooking.

To make fresh breadcrumbs, tear up coarse-textured bread and process in the food processor. Slightly stale bread is good to use for breadcrumbs. You may use white or whole-wheat bread, or a combination of the two.

Creamy Poblano Crepes

This flavor-filled dish is from one of my Southwestern classes. It's a good main dish anytime of the year, but I especially enjoy serving this when the fresh peppers and corn are in season. It can be made in stages, starting days ahead with making and freezing the crepes. You can add this to your list of recipes for easy entertaining.

1½ cups milk
1 cup flour
¼ cup cornmeal
4 egg whites
2 eggs
½ tsp. salt
2 tbsp. extravirgin olive oil
Vegetable oil
Filling (see below)

- In exact order, place milk, flour, cornmeal, egg whites, eggs, salt, and olive oil in a blender jar. Cover and blend at top speed for 1 minute.
- Heat a 7" to 9" crepe pan or nonstick skillet over medium heat until hot. Brush lightly with vegetable oil. Remove the pan from the heat and ladle in just enough batter to lightly coat the bottom. Quickly tilt the pan to cover the bottom. (Pour off any excess and correct the amount the next time.)
- Return to the heat and cook 1 to 2 minutes or until there is no more wet batter.
- Turn and cook for 15 to 30 seconds on the second side.
- Repeat the procedure until all of the crepes are cooked.
- Spoon the filling into the crepes. Fold in ends and roll. Place, seam side down, in a lightly greased shallow baking pan.
- Drizzle with remaining sauce and sprinkle with remaining cheese. Place in a preheated 375-degree oven for about 15 minutes or until hot and bubbly.
- Makes 16 to 20 crepes (depending on size). Serves 8-10.

Make crepes ahead and store them in the freezer. Stack them in a thin stack of no more than a dozen on a large sheet of heavy-duty foil. Fold the foil, pressing out the air, and seal securely on the ends. Place in the freezer (for as long as 3 months). Remove to the countertop to thaw. When ready to fill, place the foil package in a preheated 350-degree oven for about 15 minutes or just until the crepes are warm enough to separate easily.

Filling

6 poblano chile peppers
1 tbsp. olive oil
1 tsp. ground cumin
1 cup chopped onion
3 cloves garlic, finely chopped
1 cup chopped Roma tomatoes
¼ cup chopped cilantro
4 tbsp. butter
4 tbsp. flour
1 cup chicken stock, heated
1 cup light cream
½ tsp. salt
½ tsp. hot pepper sauce
2 cups fresh corn kernels (about 4 ears)
1 tsp. dried oregano leaves
2 cups shredded Jack cheese (8 oz.)

- Place the chiles on the oven rack of a preheated 450-degree oven with a baking sheet underneath. Roast for 15 minutes or until skin is darkened and bubbly. (Or hold over a gas burner until blackened.)
- Remove to a plastic bag, seal, and allow to cool. Peel, stem, and seed. Cut into small strips and set aside.
- Heat the oil in a skillet. Add the cumin and cook over medium heat, stirring, for 30 seconds.
- Add the onion and garlic and sauté until the onion is tender, about 5 minutes.
- Stir in the tomatoes and cook for 5 minutes.
- Remove from heat and add the cilantro and chiles.
- Melt the butter in a heavy saucepan. Stir in the flour and cook over medium heat for 2 minutes without browning. Whisk in the stock and stir until thickened.
- Whisk in the cream and cook for 1 minute.
- Season with salt and hot pepper sauce. Add half of the sauce to the tomato mixture. Reserve the other half to go on top of the crepes later.
- Stir in the corn and oregano and simmer on low for 5 minutes, stirring.
- Stir in 1 cup of the cheese and stir over gentle heat until cheese melts. Reserve the other cup cheese to go on top of the crepes later.

Parmesan Mashed Potatoes

This is one of America's favorite dishes with the addition of Italy's favorite cheese, which introduces extra flavor without a lot more fat. Make this people pleaser often to go with everything from beef roast to grilled salmon. If you don't have a food mill, mash the drained hot potatoes with a potato masher or use an electric mixer. Never mash potatoes in the food processor.

2½ lb. potatoes, red skinned or Yukon gold,
    peeled and cut into quarters
3 tbsp. butter
½ cup freshly shredded Parmigiano-Reggiano
¾ cups milk, heated
1½ tsp. salt, or to taste
Freshly ground black pepper, to taste

- Boil the potatoes in a pot with salted water to cover, until very tender, 25 to 30 minutes. Do not overcook.

- When the potatoes are done, drain, and put them through a food mill. Return them to the pot over very low heat and stir in the butter and cheese. Gradually add the milk, beating with a wooden spoon until smooth and creamy. Season with salt and pepper. Serve immediately or keep warm.

- Serves 10-12.

Potatoes that are best for mashed potatoes include Yukon gold, large red-skinned, and cream-colored all-purpose potatoes. They all make lighter and fluffier mashed potatoes than russets, which are best for baking.

Always heat the milk or cream before adding it to mashed potatoes so the potatoes don't get cold.

If you need to make mashed potatoes ahead, put in a little more milk than usual so they stay moist. Keep them warm in a crock pot set on the lowest setting. You can hold them for 3 to 4 hours.

Buttered Parsley New Potatoes

Cutting one strip of peel around the center of little new potatoes allows the butter and salt flavors to go into the potato while the peel that remains adds flavor and texture. My husband refers to these as "belted potatoes."

> 2 lb. tiny red new potatoes
> 3 tbsp. melted butter
> 1 tsp. coarse sea salt
> ¼ tsp. freshly ground black pepper
> ¼ cup finely chopped parsley

- Scrub the potatoes. With a small paring knife, peel a thin strip of peel right around the center of the potatoes. Cover potatoes with salted water.

- Bring to a rolling boil, reduce to low, and simmer for 20 minutes or until fork tender. Drain. Return to the pan. Toss with butter, salt, pepper, and parsley.

- Serves 6.

Vegetables that grow below the ground start cooking in cold water. All those that grow above the ground start in boiling water.

Spicy Sweet Potato Casserole

Here is a yummy casserole that's perfect for a cold-weather dinner. It often finds its way onto my Thanksgiving menu. I like to serve it with ham, too. Use the shredding disc on your food processor to get this dish together quickly. Use whole or 2 percent milk.

> 4 large eggs, slightly beaten
> 2 cups milk
> 1 cup heavy cream
> ½ cup dark brown sugar
> 1 tsp. allspice
> ½ tsp. cloves
> 1 tbsp. grated gingerroot
> 1½ tsp. salt
> ½ tsp. cayenne pepper, or to taste
> 6 cups shredded raw sweet potatoes
> 2 tbsp. butter, cut into small pieces

Always buy whole spices, such as nutmeg, coriander, cumin, cinnamon, cloves, etc. They maintain their flavor much longer than ground spices. Nutmeg is quickly grated with a small grater. The other spices can be easily ground as needed in an electric coffee grinder that you use only for grinding spices.

- Whisk together the eggs, milk, and cream. Stir in the sugar, allspice, cloves, ginger, salt, and pepper. Stir until well mixed. Fold in the potatoes.
- Butter a 9" x 13" shallow baking dish. Pour in the mixture. Dot with the butter. Bake in the center of a preheated 350-degree oven for about 1 hour or until puffed and golden brown.
- Serves 8-10.

Roasted Root Vegetables

This is a favorite standby during the fall and winter in my kitchen and in my classes. Cut the vegetables an hour or so ahead and toss with the oil and seasonings so they are ready to go into the hot oven. This is a great side dish for any meat or poultry. Be sure to use fresh rosemary in this recipe.

> **6 to 8 small new potatoes**
> **6 medium carrots**
> **4 parsnips**
> **2 medium sweet potatoes**
> **Extravirgin olive oil**
> **Coarse sea salt**
> **1 tbsp. finely chopped fresh rosemary leaves**
> **Freshly ground black pepper**
> **½ cup chopped flat-leaf parsley**

- Scrub the new potatoes and cut into quarters. Place on a heavy sheet pan.
- Peel the carrots and parsnips and cut on the diagonal into 2" to 3" lengths. Add to pan.
- Peel the sweet potatoes. Cut in half lengthwise, then cut on the diagonal into thick slices. Add to the pan.
- Drizzle oil over the vegetables, using just enough to lightly coat. Sprinkle with salt. Sprinkle over the rosemary and pepper and lightly toss with fingertips to coat the vegetables.
- Place in a preheated 400-degree oven for 25 to 30 minutes or until the vegetables are just fork tender. Remove from the oven and toss lightly with the parsley. Serve hot.
- Serves 6.

Spicy Spinach Casserole

This flavorful dish will change the minds of those folks who claim to hate spinach. Though I always prefer fresh, you can use frozen chopped spinach in this dish. Simply thaw and cook in the microwave, cool, and proceed. Substitute three 10-oz. pkg. frozen chopped spinach. This is good for a vegetarian meal, or serve with sautéed fish or chicken breasts.

2½ lb. fresh spinach
½ stick butter
¼ cup chopped green onions
2 tbsp. flour
½ cup light cream, heated
½ cup spinach liquid
½ tsp. hot pepper sauce, or to taste
2 tbsp. finely chopped jalapeño peppers
1 clove garlic, finely chopped
1 tsp. salt
1 tsp. Worcestershire sauce
2 cups shredded Jack cheese
½ cup fresh breadcrumbs
2 tbsp. butter

- Wash the spinach and cook over high heat, covered, in a heavy pot with only the water that adheres to leaves, until just wilted. Cool, drain, and squeeze out liquid, reserving ½ cup, and chop coarsely. Set aside.

- Melt the butter in a heavy saucepan. Sauté the onions on high until softened, about 5 minutes, and stir in the flour. Reduce heat to medium and cook, stirring, for 2 minutes, without browning.

- Whisk in the cream and reserved spinach liquid and cook until thickened, whisking. Remove from heat and stir in hot pepper sauce, peppers, garlic, salt, Worcestershire sauce, and cheese. Stir until the cheese is melted.

- Fold in the spinach. Pour into a greased 1½-qt. casserole. Top with breadcrumbs and dot with butter. Bake in a preheated 350-degree oven for 30 minutes.

- Serves 6-8.

Stuffed Yellow Squash

Serve a tossed salad and some crusty bread with this pretty stuffed squash for a tasty, complete light meal. Elegant substitutes for the ham are shrimp or crabmeat, but this is a good way to use up that leftover ham. To make it a vegetarian dish omit the ham and add a small red bell pepper that is chopped and sautéed with the onions.

8 medium yellow squash
3 tbsp. butter
1 clove garlic, finely chopped
2 medium yellow onions, chopped
1 cup chopped cooked ham
¼ cup chopped parsley
2 cups fresh breadcrumbs
2 eggs, beaten
1½ tsp. salt
¼ tsp. cayenne pepper, or to taste
Paprika
2 to 3 tbsp. melted butter

A melon baller is the ideal gadget for scooping pulp out of squash, eggplant, or other vegetables.

- Cut the squash in half lengthwise. Scoop out the inside and chop coarsely. Reserve.
- Bring a large pot of water to a boil. Season with salt and blanch the squash shells for 2 minutes. Refresh in ice water and place, upside down, on paper towels to drain.
- Melt the butter in a skillet and sauté the garlic and onions for 5 minutes, stirring. Stir in the squash pulp and sauté 5 minutes longer.
- Stir in the ham, parsley, ¾ of the breadcrumbs, and the eggs. Season with salt and pepper and spoon the filling into the shells. Top with the remaining breadcrumbs and sprinkle with paprika. Drizzle with the melted butter. Place in a well-greased shallow baking dish and bake in a preheated 375-degree oven for 15 to 20 minutes.
- Serves 8.

Summer Squash Casserole

I've shared this squash dish from my Southern roots many times with my students; it is a great way to use up any surplus squash when it is in season. Serve it with any main course from the grill. Assemble the casserole ahead and bake it while the rest of the meal is cooked on the grill. If you want a spicier dish substitute Jack cheese with jalapeño or habanero chiles in it.

6 tbsp. unsalted butter
1 cup finely chopped onion
5 to 6 small yellow summer squash, washed,
    trimmed, and sliced
1 tbsp. fresh lemon juice
1 cup shredded Jack cheese
2 eggs, beaten
1 cup sour cream
1 tsp. salt
1 tsp. sugar
¼ tsp. cayenne pepper
1 cup fresh breadcrumbs
3 tbsp. chopped flat-leaf parsley

- Heat 4 tbsp. butter in a large skillet and sauté the onion for 5 minutes.

- Add the squash and sauté over high heat, stirring, until squash is tender and liquid has evaporated, about 10 minutes. Stir in the lemon juice the last couple of minutes of cooking time. Purée the mixture in the food processor and transfer to a bowl.

- Stir in the cheese, eggs, sour cream, salt, sugar, and pepper.

- Heat the remaining 2 tbsp. butter in a small skillet and toss in the breadcrumbs to coat with the butter. Stir in the parsley.

- Pour the squash mixture into a buttered 2-qt. baking dish. Top with the crumb mixture. Bake in a preheated 350-degree oven for 30 to 35 minutes.

- Serves 8.

Tomato-Olive Tart

If you are a nervous pastry baker, this is for you. This freeform tart from one of my phyllo classes is easily assembled and it doesn't require any of the skills or precise techniques that are necessary for working with fresh dough. You don't even need a special pan to make this flavorful treat, just a baking sheet. Serve it at cocktail hour or as an entrée for lunch or supper.

8 to 10 large fresh Roma tomatoes
5 tbsp. extravirgin olive oil
2 cups thinly sliced onions
2 cloves garlic, finely chopped
1 tsp. brown sugar
1 tsp. good balsamic vinegar
2 tbsp. shredded fresh basil
½ tsp. freshly ground black pepper
1 tsp. fine sea salt, or to taste
8 sheets phyllo
Extra olive oil, to brush on phyllo
¾ cup pitted kalamata olives, halved
1 cup shredded mozzarella cheese
½ cup grated Parmigiano-Reggiano

- Peel, core, and slice the tomatoes, crosswise, into ¼″ slices. Set aside.

- In a heavy skillet, heat 3 tbsp. of the oil. Add the onions and garlic and cook over medium heat until the onions are lightly browned, about 20 minutes, stirring.

- Stir in the sugar and vinegar and cook 5 minutes longer, until onions are glazed and golden.

- Stir in the basil, pepper, and half of the salt.

- Grease a heavy sheet pan. Stack the phyllo leaves in the center of the pan, brushing each with a light coating of olive oil. Roll each edge slightly toward the inside to form a rim around the rectangular tart shell.

- Spoon the onion mixture onto the pastry and distribute evenly. Arrange the olives on top. Top with the tomato slices and sprinkle with the remaining ½ tsp. salt.

- Brush the tomatoes and the edges of the tart with the remaining 2 tbsp. olive oil. Sprinkle over the cheeses. Bake in the bottom

For maximum flavor, store tomatoes at room temperature.

When working with phyllo dough keep the extra sheets covered with plastic wrap and a slightly damp dishtowel to prevent drying.

An easy alternative to brushing oil on phyllo sheets is to spray lightly with an olive-oil spray.

third of a preheated 375-degree oven for 20 to 25 minutes or until the edges are golden brown and crisp. Cool slightly before cutting into squares.

• Serves 12 as an appetizer, 6 as a main course.

Zucchini Pancakes

You can use any size zucchini for this recipe as long as they are not huge and tough. If the zucchini is mature enough to have large seeds, cut it in half lengthwise and scrape out the seeds before shredding. Serve these little pancakes with grilled fish or chicken instead of a starch such as potatoes. They may be topped with a dollop of crème fraiche or sour cream and then sprinkled with some basil or parsley.

> 2½ lb. zucchini
> 2 eggs
> ⅓ cup flour
> ½ cup finely chopped onion
> ½ cup freshly grated Parmigiano-Reggiano
> ½ tsp. finely chopped lemon zest
> 2 tsp. fine sea salt
> ½ tsp. freshly ground black pepper
> ¼ cup finely shredded fresh basil (or chopped
>   flat-leaf parsley)
> Extravirgin olive oil, for frying

• Shred the zucchini with a hand shredder or use the shredding disc of a food processor.

• Whisk together the eggs and flour until smooth. Stir in the onion, cheese, and lemon zest. Fold the egg mixture into the zucchini. Season with salt and pepper. Stir in the basil.

• Pour about 1" oil into a heavy nonstick skillet. Heat over medium high until hot but not smoking (about 260 degrees). Spoon batter by tablespoons into the hot oil and flatten with the back of a spatula. Cook on first side for 2 to 3 minutes until golden, turn, and repeat on second side. Remove to a paper-towel-lined dish and pat gently with a paper towel. Serve immediately or keep warm on a metal baking sheet for an hour or so in a 250- to 275-degree oven.

• Makes about 1 dozen.

Cooking Terms:

Blanch: to submerge in rapidly boiling water for a short period of time—from a few seconds to a few minutes, depending upon the food.

Parboil: to cook partially in a simmering liquid.

Refresh: to submerge in ice water or under cold running water to stop the cooking action—usually for blanched vegetables.

Steam: to cook by direct contact with steam.

Sweets

Sour Cream Coffeecake

Red-Wine Poached Pears
with Raspberries

Frozen Strawberry Mousse

Lemon-Lime Mousse

Apple-Blackberry Crisp

Chocolate Tulip Cups

Chocolate Flan

Cappuccino Brownies

**Marge's Fruitcake
Brownies**

Pumpkin Cake Roll

Basil Lemon Pound Cake

Pecan Tassies

Neapolitan Tea Cakes

**Fowla's Quick 'n Easy
Lemon Pie**

**Southwestern Bread
Pudding**
with Margarita Sauce

Brie en Croûte
with Apricot-Grand
Marnier Stuffing

And now the finale. You can see that a number of these recipes come from friends who practice their well-honed baking skills, some professionally and others just for the joy of creating these delectable treats. I admit I usually enjoy cooking over baking and savory over sweet, but that doesn't mean you have to be deprived of a perfect ending to a perfect meal. I present these recipes to you proudly with the hope that you will find time to make them all.

Sour Cream Coffeecake

Here is a sweet to go with your morning or afternoon coffee from my dear friend Alice Kasman Fixx. I met Alice when she hosted a food trip to Italy and we've been great pals since. Alice is an accomplished baker known for her perfect cookies and other goodies. A baked treat from her delicious collection was the obvious contribution for this book. Even in Alice's native New York City filled with fabulous bakeries you won't find a coffeecake this delicious. It is easily whipped up in your electric mixer to serve any time of the day.

> 2 cups less 2 tsp. sugar
> 1 cup butter (2 sticks)
> 2 large eggs
> 1 cup sour cream (no substitutes)
> ½ tsp. vanilla
> 2 cups flour
> 1 tsp. baking powder
> ¼ tsp. salt
> 1 cup chopped pecans
> 1 tsp. cinnamon

- Take out 4 tsp. of the sugar and set aside.

- Cream the butter and add the remaining sugar. Beat on low speed until light and fluffy. Beat in the eggs one at a time, beating well after each addition.

- Fold in the sour cream and vanilla. Sift the flour with the baking powder and salt and fold into the butter mixture.

- Combine the reserved sugar with the pecans and cinnamon.

- Grease and flour a Bundt pan or 9" tube pan. Spoon about ⅓ of the batter into the pan. Sprinkle with ¾ of the pecan mixture and spoon in the remaining batter. Sprinkle with remaining pecan mixture.

- Place in the center of a preheated 350-degree oven for 1 hour or until done through. Remove to a rack and cool to room temperature before taking out of the pan.

- Serves 8-10.

Red-Wine Poached Pears
with Raspberries

I think the perfect example of an easy, elegant dessert is a poached pear. You can poach these pears hours before dinner and leave them at room temperature until ready to serve. Buy eating varieties of pears: Anjou, Comice, Bosc, etc. For poaching, they should be firm. The red wine in the poaching liquid adds flavor and a lovely color. I usually use Pinot Noir for this recipe, but most any red wine will do.

> **6 ripe but firm pears (Anjou, Comice, or Bosc)**
> **2 cups Pinot Noir**
> **1 cup water**
> **³⁄₄ cup sugar**
> **2″ cinnamon stick**
> **1 lemon**
> **¹⁄₂ pt. raspberries, washed and sweetened, if**
> **desired**

- Peel the pears and, using a potato peeler or small sharp knife, core them from the bottom, leaving the stems intact. Cut a slice from the bottom so they stand upright.

- In a nonreactive saucepan, boil the wine, water, sugar, and cinnamon. Squeeze in the lemon and add the peel to the pan. Add the pears and simmer on low until the pears are tender, but firm—15 to 25 minutes, depending on the ripeness of the pears.

- Remove the pears to a side dish. Strain the poaching liquid, return to pan, and boil, uncovered, to reduce to ¹⁄₃ cup. Cool the pears and the sauce. At serving time drizzle the sauce over the upright pears and surround with a ring of raspberries.

- Serves 6.

Note: to add an elegant touch, pipe some whipping cream with a pastry bag and star tip around the raspberries at the base of each pear. Add a mint leaf to one side of each stem.

Frozen Strawberry Mousse

I like looking to the back of the room at the Cooks' Wares Cooking School to spot the bright smile of my good pal Faye Volkman. An important member of the staff there, she's observed many a class and always makes me feel good with her compliments. Faye, a great cook in her own right, recommends making this when strawberries are in season and full of flavor.

2 cups ripe strawberries
1 cup sugar
Pinch salt
1 tsp. fresh lemon juice
1 cup whipping cream
2 egg whites

- Hull and slice berries. Put into a saucepan with the sugar. Heat over high heat until sugar dissolves.

- Remove from the heat and mash the strawberries. Cool.

- Stir in the salt and lemon juice.

- Whip the cream to soft peaks.

- Beat the egg whites until stiff, but still shiny. Fold the whipped cream and beaten egg whites into the berry mixture and pour into a stainless-steel bowl. Place in the freezer. Freeze for 1 hour, remove, and stir. Return to the freezer for 3 to 4 hours, stir again, and freeze until ready to serve.

- Serves 6-8.

After separating eggs, return the yolks to the refrigerator. To prevent the yolks from forming a dry film over the top, hold the bowl under a gentle stream of water, allowing it to run down the inside of the bowl (not directly onto the yolks) until they are covered by about 1" water. Cover the bowl tightly with plastic wrap and chill. When ready to use, uncover and tilt the bowl over the sink, supporting the yolks with your fingers so the water runs out, but the yolks remain in the bowl.

For best results, allow egg whites to become room temperature before beating. Beat egg whites in a warm dry bowl. Be sure it is clean because the smallest amount of greasy residue will prevent the eggs from becoming light and fluffy.

Lemon-Lime Mousse

This light and fresh dessert is a frequent choice for spring menus at my house. I've taught it at a number of spring and Easter dinner classes too. Bring out your most elegant crystal dessert dishes for serving this lovely sweet-tart dessert or spoon it into some tall goblets or wineglasses.

5 large eggs
1 cup sugar
1 stick unsalted butter, melted and cooled
½ cup fresh lemon juice
½ cup fresh lime juice
2 cups heavy cream
1 tsp. each lemon and lime zest
Extra whipped cream, lemon or lime slices, and
    fresh mint leaves, for garnish

- Put eggs and sugar in a large mixing bowl (or electric mixer bowl). Beat with an electric mixer until thick and pale yellow—6 to 8 minutes.

- Beat in the melted butter by pouring it in gradually in a thin stream. Stir in the juices. Pour into top of a double boiler and cook over medium heat, whisking constantly, for about 15 minutes or until mixture thickens. Do not overcook.

- Transfer to a bowl and chill, covered, for 1 hour. Stir a couple of times.

- Beat the 2 cups cream until soft peaks form. Fold into the chilled mixture along with the zests. Spoon into stemmed glassed and top each with rosettes of whipped cream, a thin slice of lemon or lime, and a sprig of mint.

- Serves 8.

Zest is the grated peel of citrus fruits—lemons, limes, oranges, and grapefruit—and lends a fresh flavor because it contains citrus oil. Grate off the colored peel only, with a light touch so as not to remove the white pith that lies underneath, which has no flavor and can be bitter. (Look for the rasplike zester in the gadget section of a kitchen store.) Always wash the fruit with warm water and dry well before zesting.

A pastry bag is a great tool to add easy whipped-cream garnishes to many desserts. Nylon ones are best because they are easily washed and dry quickly. Buy a large bag (14" to 16") and a large star tip for whipped cream (8mm). To fill the bag, drop the pastry tip into the bottom and position securely. Twist the bottom and tuck it back up into the tip so the cream won't come out the end. Fold 4" or 5" of the top down into a cuff. Either hold with one hand, with cuff folded over the hand, while you spoon the cream in with a rubber spatula with the other hand, or place over a tall glass and spoon in the cream.

Apple-Blackberry Crisp

Take advantage of blackberry season because it doesn't last very long. The first seasonal apples start arriving just as the blackberries are at their peak and that's how a trip to a farmer's market inspired this fresh-tasting dessert. If you're not a pie baker, this is the fruit dessert for you. Serve plain or top with vanilla ice cream or sweetened freshly whipped cream. If you can't find fresh blackberries, you may use frozen ones in this dessert.

10 firm, tart cooking or all-purpose apples
½ cup brown sugar
½ cup sugar
1 tsp. cinnamon
½ tsp. nutmeg
½ tsp. ground ginger
2 cups fresh blackberries
Topping (see below)
Vanilla ice cream

- Peel and core the apples and slice thinly. Toss the apple slices with the sugars and spices. Gently fold in the blackberries.

- Pour mixture into a buttered 9" x 13" x 2" baking dish. Crumble the topping over the top, rubbing it between your palms to distribute evenly. Cover with foil and bake for 10 minutes in a pre-heated 375-degree oven. Uncover and bake 25 minutes longer. Serve warm topped with the ice cream.

- Serves 10-12.

Topping
2 cups all-purpose flour
½ tsp. salt
1 tsp. nutmeg
1 tsp. ground ginger
½ cup dark brown sugar
1½ sticks cold unsalted butter, cut into pieces

- Place all ingredients in the food processor with steel blade. Process until mixture resembles coarse crumbs. Chill until ready to top the berry mixture.

Wash fresh berries in wine instead of water. The flavor is not diluted and they are better preserved than when washed with water. This is a good way to use leftover red or white wine that is no longer drinkable.

Superfine granulated sugar is more easily dissolved in whipping cream and meringue than regular granulated sugar.

Chocolate Tulip Cups

This fun recipe is much easier to make than the finished product looks and you can create instant festive desserts with it. Your guests will think you are a professional like its contributor, pastry chef Glenn Rinsky. Glenn emphasizes the importance of purchasing good-quality coating chocolate for this recipe, because it keeps its shape and glossy color at room temperature. You'll find it at specialty stores that sell candy-making and baking supplies. "Do not use regular chocolate chips," he cautions.

1 lb. good-quality bittersweet coating chocolate
**6 to 8 latex balloons, blown up to size of single-
serving bowl (do not use helium filled)**
Softened butter, for greasing balloons

- Chop the chocolate into ¼" pieces. Place the chocolate pieces in a microwave-safe bowl. (Use a bowl large and deep enough to dip the balloons so that the chocolate will come far up on the sides when you dip them.)

- Place in the microwave oven and heat, uncovered, on the defrost setting (or half-power) for 1 minute. Remove and stir once (will not be melted yet). Continue to microwave at 30-second intervals until all of the chocolate is soft enough to stir into a smooth glossy liquid.

- Take care not to overheat the chocolate. It is good to check it with your instant thermometer. Don't let it go above 120 degrees.

- Lightly grease the top half of a balloon with the softened butter. Dip the balloon in the chocolate and roll around to coat evenly. Place the balloon into a cup, chocolate side up, and place in the refrigerator or freezer until the chocolate hardens. Repeat with remaining balloons.

- When the chocolate hardens, remove the balloons from cups. Hold the balloons by the chocolate tops and pop the balloons with a pin. Remove the deflated balloons and return the chocolate cups to the refrigerator or freezer until ready to use. Serve filled with ice cream, mousse, pudding, or fresh fruit.

- Makes 6-8 chocolate cups.

Your chocolate baked goods and candies will always look and taste better if you buy the best-quality chocolate possible. "Bittersweet" chocolate is normally better than "semisweet" because it has a higher percentage of cocoa butter and less solids.

Always melt chocolate with gentle heat and watch it carefully. It is ready as soon as it is soft when touched with the tip of a knife. Overheating ruins the texture and appearance of chocolate by causing the cocoa butter to separate from the solids. Bottom line: you have to throw it out and start over with some new chocolate.

Chocolate Flan

A velvety-smooth baked custard with Spanish roots, flan is a favorite dessert after a meal of Mexican food. I've baked many of them in various flavors for my students. This chocolate one stands out above the rest. There is no real secret here or difficult technique, but you will need a very heavy pan to caramelize the sugar successfully. I always use cast iron and prefer a porcelain-clad cast-iron skillet. As soon as the sugar is melted to a golden liquid, remove it from the range. Be careful when pouring it because sugar melts at a high temperature and one drop can cause a painful burn.

> ¾ **cup sugar**
> 3 oz. **good bittersweet chocolate**
> ¼ **cup water**
> 2 cups **half and half (light cream), scalded**
> 6 large **eggs**
> 2 **egg yolks**
> 1 tbsp. **vanilla**
> 1 cup **sugar**

- In an iron skillet over medium heat, caramelize the ¾ cup sugar to a golden color. Gently tilt the pan to heat it evenly. Stir occasionally if needed, but not constantly. Carefully pour into a 9" round layer-cake pan, coating the bottom. Set aside.

- Melt the chocolate with the water in the microwave or in a small heavy saucepan, whisking to make a smooth, shiny chocolate mixture. Whisk the chocolate into the warm cream. Whisk in the eggs and yolks, then the vanilla and sugar. Strain and pour into the coated pan.

- Place in a hot water bath with the water coming about halfway up the sides of the pan. Bake in a preheated 350-degree oven for 35 to 40 minutes or until puffed and golden brown on top. Remove to a rack to cool. Cover and chill overnight or for several hours.

- To unmold, carefully run a small flexible spatula around the edge. Invert onto a plate deep enough to hold the caramel, which will be liquid. Cut into 8 to 10 wedges and serve cold.

- Serves 8-10.

For the water bath ("bain-marie"), heat several cups water to boiling in a kettle. Place a baking pan large enough to hold the flan pan, with several inches on all sides, on a pulled-out oven rack. Place the uncooked flan in the center of the pan. Carefully pour the hot water into one corner of the large pan (without getting any in the flan) until the water comes halfway up the sides of the flan pan. Slowly push in the oven rack.

Cappuccino Brownies

I always look forward to my classes at the beautiful Dorothy Lane Market Cooking School in Dayton, Ohio. The friendly staff, headed by director Deb Lackey, and all of the marvelous students I've met make it such a pleasure to teach there. Deb submitted one of the school's favorite recipes, which comes from her predecessor and talented teacher, Kitty Sachs. These bite-sized brownies are the richest of the rich! I recommend always having some in your freezer, especially during the holidays.

> **4 oz. good-quality bittersweet chocolate, chopped**
> **6 tbsp. unsalted butter, cut into pieces**
> **1 tbsp. instant espresso powder dissolved in ¹/₂ tbsp. boiling water**
> **³/₄ cup sugar**
> **1 tsp. vanilla**
> **2 large eggs**
> **¹/₂ cup all-purpose flour**
> **¹/₄ tsp. salt**
> **¹/₂ cup chopped walnuts**
> **Cream-Cheese Topping (see below)**
> **Glaze (see below)**

- In a heavy saucepan, melt the chocolate and butter with the espresso mixture over low heat, stirring until smooth. Remove the pan from the heat. Cool mixture to lukewarm, and whisk in the sugar and vanilla.

- Beat in the eggs, one at a time, whisking well until mixture is glossy and smooth. Stir in the flour, salt, and walnuts. Spread the batter evenly in a buttered and floured pan, and bake in middle of a preheated 350-degree oven for 22 to 25 minutes or until a tester comes out with crumbs adhering to it. Cool completely in pan on a rack.

- Spread Cream-Cheese Topping evenly over the cooked and cooled brownie layer. Chill for 1 hour or until firm.

- Spread glaze over the chilled brownies. Chill, covered, for 3 hours or until cold. Cut into 24 squares while still cold and

To butter and flour a pan for baking cakes or brownies, generously butter with softened butter so there is a light, but visible layer of butter (or shortening). Sprinkle with flour, tilting the pan to cover sides as well as bottom. Turn upside down over the sink and tap the bottom and sides to shake out the excess flour.

serve cold, at room temperature, or frozen. Store in the refrigerator or freezer.

- Makes 24.

Cream-Cheese Topping

4 oz. cream cheese, softened
3 tbsp. unsalted butter, softened
¼ cup confectioners' sugar, sifted
½ tsp. vanilla
½ tsp. cinnamon

- With an electric mixer, beat the cream cheese and butter until light and fluffy. Beat in the confectioners' sugar, vanilla, and cinnamon, beating until well mixed.

Glaze

3 oz. good-quality bittersweet chocolate,
  chopped
1 tbsp. unsalted butter
¼ cup heavy cream
2¼ tsp. espresso powder, dissolved in 1 tbsp.
  boiling water

- In a double boiler or a bowl set over barely simmering water, melt the chocolate and butter with cream and espresso mixture, stirring until smooth. Remove from heat, and cool to room temperature.

Marge's Fruitcake Brownies

Richard Perry knows as much about food as anyone I've encountered. I am proud to call him my friend and have enjoyed many fun and enlightening conversations with him, some while we cooked together. He often served as substitute host on "Cooking with Marilyn." On a holiday show a few years ago he shared this recipe with my listeners. They still ask for it. Thanks to Richard and his friend Marge, who gave it to him.

1 cup raisins
1 cup chopped dried dates
1 cup chopped dried apricots
1 cup chopped mixed candied fruit
¼ cup brandy
1 cup flour
¼ tsp. salt
1 tsp. cinnamon
1 tsp. ground ginger
¼ tsp. ground cloves
2 cups walnuts
1 cup dark brown sugar
Zest of 1 lemon
4 eggs
1 tsp. vanilla

- Combine raisins, dates, apricots, and candied fruit. Pour over the brandy and let sit for 12 hours.

- Sift the flour, salt, cinnamon, ginger, and cloves together. Stir in the walnuts, brown sugar, and lemon zest. Stir in the eggs and vanilla.

- Fold in the fruit. Pour the mixture into a greased jelly-roll pan. Bake in a preheated 325-degree oven for 25 to 30 minutes or until done through. Slightly cool on a rack and cut into squares.

- Makes 24.

Pumpkin Cake Roll

Cindy Young and I have spent a lot of fun hours together in the kitchen. A talented colleague and true friend, Cindy is an accomplished baker with a tasty repertoire of goodies. She has made this recipe, inherited from her mother-in-law, a holiday tradition in her own home.

3 large eggs
1 cup sugar
²/₃ cup canned pumpkin purée
1 tsp. lemon juice
³/₄ cup all-purpose flour
2 tsp. cinnamon
1 tsp. ground ginger
¹/₂ tsp. nutmeg
1 tsp. baking powder
¹/₂ tsp. salt
1 cup chopped walnuts
Confectioners' sugar
Filling (see below)

- Beat the eggs in the electric mixer on high speed for 5 minutes.
- Gradually beat in the sugar. Add the pumpkin and lemon juice and beat until well blended. Combine the flour, spices, baking powder, and salt in a separate bowl, then fold into the pumpkin mixture.
- Spread evenly into a greased and floured 10" x 15" x 1" pan. Sprinkle the walnuts over the batter. Bake in the center of a 375-degree oven for 15 minutes.
- Turn out onto a lint-free dishtowel that is sprinkled with confectioners' sugar. Very carefully roll, beginning with long side, rolling towel and cake together. Cool completely.
- Unroll cake. Spread the filling evenly over the cake. Reroll and place, seam side down, on a tray. Refrigerate until ready to serve.
- Serves 8-10.

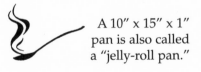
A 10" x 15" x 1" pan is also called a "jelly-roll pan."

Filling

1 cup sifted confectioners' sugar
2 3-oz. pkg. cream cheese
4 tbsp. butter (½ stick), softened
½ tsp. vanilla

- Combine ingredients in a medium electric-mixer bowl. Beat until smooth.

Basil Lemon Pound Cake

Pastry chef Glenn Rinsky provided me with his recipe for a plain but luscious cake with an interesting flavor combination. For a perfect cake, Glenn advises to pay close attention to his instructions, allowing the full time to incorporate the sugar into the butter and to mix it with the egg mixture. This technique is important for a moist cake with a proper texture or "crumb." "There is no substitute for real butter in this cake recipe," Glenn added. By the way, his favorite tool for folding in the flour is his hand.

6 eggs, room temperature
6 egg yolks, room temperature
¼ cup lemon juice
1 tbsp. lemon zest
1 lb. butter, softened
2½ cups sugar
1 tsp. salt
3¾ cups cake flour
1½ tbsp. chopped fresh basil
3 cups confectioners' sugar
5 tbsp. lemon juice
5 lemon slices

- Combine eggs, egg yolks, ¼ cup lemon juice, and lemon zest in a bowl. Beat just to combine.
- Place softened butter in a mixing bowl, and beat for a full 2 minutes. (If you have a mixer with a paddle attachment, use it.)
- Gradually add the sugar and continue beating for 5 minutes.
- Slowly add the egg mixture, beating an additional 5 minutes.

The cake-baking rule for baking in the center of the oven means the top of the pan should be centered. With a deep tube or Bundt pan the rack will be much lower than the center.

To freeze frosted cakes or cookies (while keeping the frosting intact), place on a tray and freeze for an hour or two (only) or until frozen. Remove and quickly wrap in freezer wrap or place in a freezer bag. Seal, pressing out the air. Immediately return to the freezer. When ready to serve, unwrap and thaw.

Cookie sheets and cake pans should be shiny to reflect the heat. Bread, pie, and tart pans should be dark to absorb the heat. Glass pans are a good alternative for baking pies and bread.

Bake cookies in upper one-third of the oven, cakes and breads in the center, and pies and tarts in the lower one-third. (Convection ovens are an exception to this rule because the forced air surrounds the food in all parts of the oven.)

- Add the salt. Sift the flour and fold it in, $1/3$ at a time. Be sure flour is well incorporated.
- Stir in the chopped basil. Pour into a generously greased 10" tube pan. Bake in a preheated 350-degree oven for 1 hour to 1 hour and 15 minutes. Cool completely on a cooling rack. Remove from the pan.
- In a separate bowl combine confectioners' sugar and 5 tbsp. lemon juice. Drizzle over the cake. Decorate with lemon slices.
- Serves 12.

  Note: this cake freezes well.

To make a quick pan liner for a round cake or tart pan, tear off a piece of parchment paper large enough to extend several inches on all sides beyond the pan. Fold into quarters; then continue to fold over to make a thin triangle. Turn the pan upside down. Place the point of the triangle in the center of the pan. Crease the paper where it comes to the edge and tear off that much margin. Open to a circle that fits inside the pan.

Pecan Tassies

Cooking teacher and school director Nancy Pigg works her food-processor magic to make some fancy little tarts that require no pastry-making talents whatsoever. You won't believe how easy they are! Make a bunch of them for a big party or the holidays and store in the freezer.

> 3 oz. cream cheese
> 1 cup plus 2 tbsp. flour
> 1 stick butter, cut into pieces
> 1 tbsp. sugar
> 1 cup brown sugar
> 2 eggs
> 1 tbsp. water
> 2 tbsp. melted butter
> 1 tsp. vanilla
> $3/4$ cup pecans

- In food processor with metal blade, process the cream cheese, flour, butter, and sugar just until mixed. Refrigerate this filling for 30 minutes.

- In clean food processor with metal blade, place the brown sugar, eggs, water, melted butter, and vanilla. Process to blend well. Divide this pastry dough into 24 pieces and press into miniature muffin pans, with pastry making a cup up the sides.

- Sprinkle the pecans evenly into each cup and pour in filling. Bake in a preheated 350-degree oven for 30 minutes. Cool slightly before removing from the pan to finish cooling on a rack.

- Makes 24.

Neapolitan Tea Cakes

Lisa Papa is one of those brilliant women with a demanding job who still finds time for her family and friends. When she married Will, who comes from a long line of expert Italian cooks and bakers, her Scandinavian background hadn't prepared her to cook any of his favorite foods. Now she is happy to share a Papa family favorite, one of many she has mastered and enjoys making for her family and friends. This is really a fun recipe, one you can bake on a lazy Sunday and store for weeks in the freezer.

8-oz. can almond paste
1 cup butter, softened
1 cup sugar
4 egg yolks
2 cups sifted flour
4 egg whites, room temperature
Red and green food coloring
¼ cup seedless red raspberry jam
¼ cup apricot jam
6 oz. semisweet chocolate pieces
1 tbsp. vegetable oil

- In a large mixing bowl, break the almond paste into small pieces with a fork. Add the butter, sugar, and egg yolks and beat with an electric mixer at medium speed until light and fluffy. With a wooden spoon, beat in the flour until well combined.

- In a medium bowl (with clean beaters), beat the egg whites on high speed until soft peaks form. Stir the egg whites into the almond-butter mixture, stirring until thoroughly blended.

- With nonstick spray, grease the bottoms of 3 baking pans or 2 rectangular baking pans (8" x 12" x 1"). Line the pans with waxed paper (or parchment paper) and grease the paper.

- Remove ⅓ of the cake batter to a medium bowl and stir in enough red food coloring to dye it a soft red.

- Add ⅓ of batter to another bowl and dye with green food coloring.

- Spread each of the 3 batters into one of the prepared pans, spreading evenly in the pan. Bake in a preheated 350-degree oven for 10-12 minutes. Cool slightly, then invert on racks to remove from the pans.

- To assemble, place the green layer, top side up, on a waxed-paper-lined tray. Spread evenly with the red raspberry jam, then top with the white layer. Spread the apricot filling over the white layer and top with the red layer. Cover well with plastic wrap and place a heavy cutting board on top. Place in the freezer.

- When the cake is cold, melt the chocolate and oil over gentle heat just until smooth and glossy. Spread half of it on the top of the cake. (Reserve remainder of the chocolate.) Return the cake to the freezer.

- Several hours later, remove and flip the cake over. Melt the remaining chocolate, frost that side, and put it back into the freezer until about 1 hour before serving.

- To serve, cut into 1" rows and then into little bite-size cakes (roughly ¼" thick—almost like a small cookie).

- Makes about 8 dozen.

Fowla's Quick 'n Easy Lemon Pie

One of my radio pals, the talented Wirt Cain, left his own show one day and crashed mine, armed with his mother's favorite pie recipe. My listeners loved it! I think half of them made it. We talked about it for weeks and I promised to put it into this book. It couldn't be simpler and if you like lemon you should give it a try.

> **1 medium lemon**
> **4 eggs**
> **1½ cups sugar**
> **6 tbsp. melted butter**
> **1 unbaked 9" pie shell**

- Wash lemon, slice, and cube (with rind intact). Remove seeds. Place the lemon pieces, eggs, sugar, and butter in the food processor or blender.
- Process, using high speed, until lemon is very finely chopped. Pour into the pie shell. Place on a cookie sheet and bake in a preheated 425-degree oven for 40 minutes.
- Serves 8.

Southwestern Bread Pudding with Margarita Sauce

This is a popular dessert from one of my many Southwestern cooking classes. I took one of my traditional New Orleans bread-pudding recipes and gave it the Southwestern flavor.

> **2 tbsp. butter, softened**
> **1-lb. loaf day-old French bread**
> **1 qt. milk**
> **4 large eggs**
> **1½ cups sugar**
> **½ cup dark brown sugar**
> **1 stick butter**
> **½ cup pine nuts**
> **1 cup golden raisins**
> **2 tbsp. fresh orange juice**
> **1 tbsp. orange zest**
> **2 tsp. vanilla**
> **Margarita Sauce (see below)**

Cut leftover French bread into cubes, toss into a freezer bag, and freeze. When you have collected enough cubes, remove from the freezer, thaw on the countertop, and make bread pudding (or croutons).

- Butter a 9" x 13" baking dish with the 2 tbsp. softened butter.
- Tear the bread into bite-sized pieces. Place in a large bowl and pour over the milk. Allow to sit about 1 hour or until the milk is absorbed by the bread.
- With a mixer, beat the eggs with both of the sugars until the mixture is thick and lemon colored.
- Melt the butter over medium heat in a heavy saucepan and lightly toast the pine nuts in the butter. Stir the butter mixture, raisins, orange juice and zest, and vanilla into the eggs. Pour the egg mixture over the bread and stir just to mix well.
- Pour into the prepared dish. Place the pan in a hot water bath and bake in a preheated 350-degree oven for about 1 hour or until a knife blade inserted in the center comes out clean. Serve warm with the warm sauce spooned over.
- Serves 8-10.

Margarita Sauce

1 stick butter
1 cup confectioners' sugar
¼ cup good tequila
2 tbsp. Grand Marnier
1 tbsp. fresh lime juice
1 tsp. lime zest

- Melt the butter over low heat. Stir in the confectioners' sugar. Heat, stirring, until sugar dissolves. Stir in the tequila, Grand Marnier, lime juice, and zest.

Brie en Croûte with Apricot-Grand Marnier Stuffing

This is not a true "sweet" but this cheese torte can serve as both cheese course and dessert. It's a good use of frozen puff pastry to make something that looks complicated very simple. Make it all ahead ready to pop into the oven before serving. Buy very fresh, firm Brie for this recipe and slice it in half when it is just out of the refrigerator. Be sure to bake it on parchment paper (or a silicone pad). Serve it with some mixed dried and/or glazed fruits (apricots, figs, dates, etc.) on the side, if desired, and a small glass of dessert wine such as port.

> **1 pkg. frozen puff pastry**
> **8 oz. dried apricots**
> **½ cup Grand Marnier**
> **2-lb. wheel Brie cheese, firm and chilled**
> **1 egg**
> **1 tbsp. milk**

- Thaw the puff pastry overnight or for several hours in the refrigerator.

- Snip the apricots into small strips into a small saucepan. Pour over the Grand Marnier, bring to a boil, reduce to low, and simmer for 15 minutes. Remove from heat and allow to sit until completely cool. (Most of the liquid should be absorbed into the apricots.)

- Cut the wheel of cheese horizontally through the center to form two equal "layers." Gently press the apricots into the bottom layer. Add the top and press around the edges.

- Place the sheets of chilled pastry side by side on a lightly floured pastry board, overlapping each other by about 2". Roll lightly with a floured rolling pin, sealing the two together to form one large sheet.

- Place the cheese in the middle of the pastry and fold the pastry around it, encasing the pastry and mitering the corners. Cut away extra pastry from the corners and reserve. Cover Brie and chill until ready to bake.

- Cut out some small decorative designs from the scrap pastry, using small cutters or a small knife. Place on a parchment-covered small dish, cover, and chill.

Instead of greasing, line cookie sheets with parchment paper or one of the silicone pan liners. It will prevent cookies from sticking, make cleanup easier, and preserve the shiny finish on the pan. Parchment and silicone liners are available at specialty kitchen stores.

- At baking time, preheat the oven to 400 degrees.
- Beat together the egg and milk to make an egg wash. Brush a light layer over the top and sides of the pastry-covered Brie. Add the decorations and brush with the wash.
- Line a flat baking sheet with parchment paper or use a silicone liner on the pan. Place the cheese in the center and bake for 15 minutes or until the pastry is golden and puffed. Allow to sit for 10 minutes before cutting into small wedges.
- Serves 12.

Index

Appetizers for Easy Entertaining, 17
Almond-Stuffed Spiced Olives, 19
Apple-Cheddar Quesadillas, 39
Avocado-Corn Salsa, 37
Baked Cheese Dip, 33
Bay Harbor Whitefish Bread Spread, 21
Brie Wafers, 32
Cured Salmon, 28
Dill and Lemon Dressing, 30
Dill Sauce, 28
Easy Caviar Spread, 22
Gravlax, 28
Green Olive Spread, 27
Herbed Pita Triangles, 26
Herbed Tartar Sauce, 29
Homemade Herb Cheese, 20
Hot Beef Dip, 36
Hot Lobster Puffs, 40
Lentil Salad, 30
May's Hummus, 25
Onion Cream, 30
Oven-Roasted Caponata, 23
Pork Satay, 35
Shrimp and Brie Quesadillas, 37
Skewered Raspberry Chicken, 34
Smoked Salmon Roulade, 30
Spicy Mixed Nuts, 19
Spicy Peanut Butter Sauce, 35

Cooking Chicken and Turkey, 145
Apricot-Rice-Stuffed Chicken Breasts, 149
Apricot Sauce, 149
Chicken Mexicana, 155
Chicken Rosemary, 153
Cream Gravy, 153
Creamy Curried Chicken, 150
Creole Chicken Supreme, 154
Great Guacamole, 160
Old-Fashioned Oven-Fried Chicken, 157
Parsley Rice Pilaf, 151

Porcini Mushroom Sauce, 156
Quick and Easy Chicken Burritos, 158
Soft Chicken Tacos with Great Guacamole, 159
Southern Cornbread-Pecan Stuffing, 166
Spicy Fried Boneless Chicken Breasts, 152
Supreme of Chicken, 156
Three-Onion Bread Stuffing, 165
Turkey Stock, 164
White Wine Turkey Gravy, 164

Elegant but Easy Seafood, 127
Almond Rice Pilaf, 135
Baked Fish with Garlic Breadcrumbs, 136
Baked Orange Roughy, 140
Boiled Shrimp, 142
Broiled Fish Fillets with Mustard Butter, 135
Cherry Tomato Salsa, 133
Chipotle Remoulade Sauce, 131
Cornmeal Fried Oysters, 141
Easy Grilled Swordfish, 137
Easy Pan-Fried Fish, 129
Fish Tacos, 132
Herb Vinaigrette, 139
Lemon Parsley Sauce, 140
Mediterranean Tuna, 134
Poached Salmon with Herb Vinaigrette, 138
Quick Crab Cakes, 140
Remoulade Sauce, 142
Salmon Cakes, 130
Sassy Scallops, 143
Southwestern Marinated Fish, 137

Great Grilling, 181
Barbecued Pork Tenderloin, 199
Béarnaise Mayonnaise, 202
Bourbon Barbecue Sauce, 197
Bourbon Marinade, 187
Flank Steak in Spicy Southwest Marinade, 202
Ginger-Pepper Steak Marinade, 185
Gourmet Burgers, 201

Great Grilled Salmon, 191
Grilled Asparagus, 207
Grilled Butterflied Leg of Lamb, 204
Grilled Chicken Salad, 197
Grilled Corn on Cob with Chili Lime Butter, 208
Grilled Fennel, 206
Grilled Fish and Vegetable Kebabs, 192
Grilled Lamb Chops with Shallot-Parsley Butter, 203
Grilled New Potatoes, 206
Grilled Orange Pork, 200
Grilled Vegetable Dip, 190
Herbed Mustard Marinade, 187
Honey-Lime Marinade, 185
Infused Chile Oil, 194
Lemon-Dill Marinade, 188
Lime-Marinated Chicken Kebabs, 193
Quick Southern Barbecued Chicken, 196
Ratatouille in a Package, 205
Red Wine Marinade, 186
Roasted Corn Salsa, 193
Rosemary-Lemon Pork Chops, 198
Russ's Grilled Chicken, 194
Santa Fe Dry Rub, 189
Savory Seafood Dry Rub, 189
Spicy Baked Pinto Beans, 209
Zesty Dry Rub for Pork and Beef, 188

Mainly Meats, 167
Apple Pear Chutney, 172
Barbecued Brisket, 174
Brown Sauce, 169
Cincinnati Chili Chops, 177
Cincinnati Chili Rub, 178
Cincinnati Chili Sauce, 178
Garlic Roasted Leg of Lamb, 179
Ginger-Lime Beef Tenderloin, 172
Marilyn's Zesty Meatloaf, 173
Pork Medallions with Apple and Cabbage, 176
Roasted Citrus Pork Tenderloin, 175
Roasted Rib Roast, 170
Roux, 170
Sauce Madeira, 171
Yorkshire Pudding, 171

Pasta and Risotto, 99
Béchamel Sauce, 105

Cheese Cannelloni, 104
Elegant but Easy Tomato Sauce, 111
Fettuccine with Leeks, Carrots, and Prosciutto, 109
Fettuccine with Porcini and Prosciutto Sauce, 108
Fettuccine with Spring Onions and Asparagus, 110
Grilled Eggplant Lasagna, 120
Homemade Pasta, 103
Homemade Spinach-Ricotta Ravioli, 106
Linguini in Herb Sauce, 119
Pappardelle, 111
Penne with Veal Sauce, 114
Pink Sauce, 104
Rigatoni with Roasted Garlic and Toasted Walnut Sauce, 113
Rigatoni with Roasted Vegetables, 112
Risotto with Roasted Radicchio and Toasted Pine Nuts, 124
Simple Tomato Sauce, 105
Spaghetti and Meatballs, 117
Spaghetti Puttanesca, 115
Spaghetti with Shrimp and Green Olives, 116
Three Mushroom Risotto, 123
Tomato-Basil Risotto, 122
Tomato-Beef Sauce, 121

Salads and Their Dressings, 69
Balsamic Vinaigrette, 73
Belgian Endive with Sliced Crisp Apples, Toasted Walnuts, and Bleu Cheese, 79
Berry Green Salad, 77
Black Bean and Corn Salad with Peppers, 80
Bleu Cheese Dressing, 96
Celery Seed Dressing, 94
Classic Vinaigrette, 92
Corn Salad, 74
Curried Chicken-Fruit Salad, 85
Duck Pastrami with Frisée Salad and Huckleberry Vinaigrette, 90
Frisée Salad, 91
Garlic-Herb Croutons, 92
Green Goddess Dressing, 97
Grilled Pork Tenderloin Salad with Mango and Avocado, 89
Guacamole Dressing, 97
Huckleberry Vinaigrette, 91

Italian Vinaigrette, 93
Luscious Lentil Salad, 80
Mango-Ginger Cream Dressing, 95
Marilyn's Chicken Salad, 86
Mushroom, Fennel, and Parmesan Salad, 73
My Best Green Bean Salad, 75
Piquant Egg Salad, 84
Potato Salad Deluxe, 82
Refrigerator Crock Slaw, 78
Roasted Vegetable Salad, 72
Shallot and Herb Dressing, 94
Steak and Potato Salad, 88
Summer Couscous, 83
Tangy French Dressing, 95
Tomato, Avocado, and Onion Salad, 71
Tomatoes Stuffed with Southern Shrimp Salad, 84
Tropical Dressing, 90
Walnut Oil Vinaigrette, 79
Winter Salad, 76

Stocks, Soups, and Stews, 41
Aromatic White Wine Stock, 46
Baked Bean Soup, 54
Beef Stock, 43
Black Bean Chili, 58
Bordelaise Beef Stew, 66
Cajun Seasoning, 54
California Consommé, 46
Carbonades of Pork, 61
Chicken Stock, 44
Cream of Leek Soup with Tomatoes, 50
Easy Cajun Chicken Gumbo, 53
Fish Stew, 63
Fish Stock, 45
Frankfurt Herb Soup, 49
Goulash Soup, 64
Herbed Rice, 63
Jalapeño Cornbread, 59
Kentucky Burgoo, 65
Lentil Soup, 57
Quick Chili, 60
Red and Yellow Pepper Soup, 51
Southwest Chile-Tomato Soup, 52
Spaetzle, 62
Spicy Chilled Tomato Soup, 48
Summer Beet Soup, 47
Zesty White Bean Soup, 55

Sweets, 233
Apple-Blackberry Crisp, 239
Basil Lemon Pound Cake, 246
Brie en Croûte with Apricot-Grand Marnier Stuffing, 252
Cappuccino Brownies, 242
Chocolate Flan, 241
Chocolate Tulip Cups, 240
Fowla's Quick 'n Easy Lemon Pie, 250
Frozen Strawberry Mousse, 237
Lemon-Lime Mousse, 238
Marge's Fruitcake Brownies, 244
Neapolitan Tea Cakes, 248
Pecan Tassies, 247
Pumpkin Cake Roll, 245
Red-Wine Poached Pears with Raspberries, 236
Sour Cream Coffeecake, 235
Southwestern Bread Pudding with Margarita Sauce, 250

Versatile Vegetables, 211
Brie-Stuffed Mushroom Caps, 222
Brussels Sprouts with Toasted Walnuts in Mustard Sauce, 216
Buttered Parsley New Potatoes, 226
Creamy Poblano Crepes, 223
Eggplant Sandwiches with Fresh Tomato Sauce, 219
Fresh Green Beans with Herbed Egg Sauce, 215
Fresh Tomato Sauce, 220
Lemon Asparagus, 213
Marilyn's Greens, 221
Parmesan Mashed Potatoes, 225
Roasted Root Vegetables, 227
Sautéed Corn with Tomatoes and Cilantro, 218
Sautéed Green Beans, 214
Scalloped Celery and Onions, 217
Southern Corn Pudding, 219
Spicy Spinach Casserole, 228
Spicy Sweet Potato Casserole, 226
Stuffed Yellow Squash, 229
Summer Squash Casserole, 230
Tomato-Olive Tart, 231
White Asparagus, 213
Zucchini Pancakes, 232